高等学校英语专业系列教材

Research Methods and Thesis Writing in Applied Linguistics

应用语言学研究方法与论文写作（第二版）

文秋芳　著

外语教学与研究出版社
FOREIGN LANGUAGE TEACHING AND RESEARCH PRESS
北京 BEIJING

图书在版编目（CIP）数据

应用语言学研究方法与论文写作 = Research Methods and Thesis Writing in Applied Linguistics ／ 文秋芳著. -- 2版. -- 北京：外语教学与研究出版社，2022.12

新经典高等学校英语专业系列教材

ISBN 978-7-5213-4209-3

Ⅰ. ①应… Ⅱ. ①文… Ⅲ. ①英语－应用语言学－研究方法－高等学校－教材 ②英语－论文－写作－高等学校－教材 Ⅳ. ①H319.3②H315

中国版本图书馆 CIP 数据核字 (2022) 第 256593 号

出 版 人	王　芳
项目负责	王　茜
责任编辑	王　茜
责任校对	刘小萌
封面设计	彩奇风
版式设计	锋尚设计
出版发行	外语教学与研究出版社
社　　址	北京市西三环北路 19 号（100089）
网　　址	https://www.fltrp.com
印　　刷	北京市鑫霸印务有限公司
开　　本	787×1092　1/16
印　　张	21
版　　次	2023 年 5 月第 2 版　2023 年 5 月第 1 次印刷
书　　号	ISBN 978-7-5213-4209-3
定　　价	69.90 元

如有图书采购需求，图书内容或印刷装订等问题，侵权、盗版书籍等线索，请拨打以下电话或关注官方服务号：
客服电话：400 898 7008
官方服务号：微信搜索并关注公众号"外研社官方服务号"
外研社购书网址：https://fltrp.tmall.com

物料号：342090001

记载人类文明
沟通世界文化
外研社
www.fltrp.com

"Give a man a fish and he eats for a day. Teach him how to fish and he eats for a lifetime."

Doing research is a mystery to many graduate students and second language teachers in China. This book aims to demystify the process of carrying out research in the field of applied linguistics, particularly in the area of second language acquisition and teaching. This book is written for those who have no previous research experience at all or those who have done some research without formal training. It is particularly useful for graduate students of applied linguistics, second language teachers, and teacher trainers.

Challenges faced by student researchers

This book is concerned with both how to conduct research and how to write a thesis/dissertation. Graduate students, I have found, face difficulties not only in actual research but also in writing up their theses/dissertations. This book addresses questions that have actually been encountered by myself and my students. For example: How can I select a suitable topic? Which research design should I employ? What is the best time for me to collect data and in which way? Should I analyze the data quantitatively or qualitatively? What is the difference between reporting a result and discussing a result? What should be covered by a literature review?

Structure of the book and target readers

In response to these challenges, this book provides readers with solutions, and with suggestions if there is no definite answer. The whole book consists of three parts. Part I serves as a general introduction in which some basic concepts are explained. Part II focuses on the research process and covers different phases of a single study. Part III describes the overall structure of a thesis/dissertation and what is expected to be included or not included in different chapters.

Altogether the book includes 14 chapters. It could be used as a textbook for a one-term course for postgraduate students. It also targets novice researchers who would like to study it by themselves. It can also be used as a reference book by all researchers whenever they feel uncertain about the research process or writing a particular section of a paper or a thesis/dissertation.

Salient features

This book is written in an accessible style and interactive manner so that readers can follow the text without too much difficulty. The book has cited various examples from theses and papers written by Chinese scholars and graduate students in order to facilitate the understanding of abstract terms and the research process. Moreover, unlike books on research methodology published in the Western context, this book has particularly focused on Chinese graduate students' difficulties and problems in their research and thesis writing. Therefore, this book can be used as a textbook for a course on research methods as part of the graduate program as well as a reference book for completing a master's thesis or a doctoral dissertation.

New to the second edition

The second edition of the book retains the overall structure. Meanwhile, the strengths of the book are kept unchanged, such as its accessible style and interactive manner, the explanation of a concept with illustrative examples, its clear focus on the difficulties Chinese students often encounter, etc. The major changes involve the following points.

1. What kind of researchers we should cultivate, how, and for whom—these are the fundamental issues that our postgraduate program on applied linguistics must address. Therefore, the qualities (i.e. academic honesty and professional ethics) of a researcher are particularly added and explained, such as qualities of a good researcher in Chapter 1, ethical issues in Chapter 13, and avoiding plagiarism in Chapter 14. I hope all student researchers will learn how to strictly abide by ethical principles and academic codes and become upright professionals.

2. The layout of the book is redesigned from the beginning to the end to make it look more attractive and user-friendly.

3. The boxes of question(s) and of Focus highlight are added to the text. The question(s) box is to make readers think more actively before and after reading. The Focus highlight box sometimes serves as a summary of the essential points of what has just been read and sometimes it provides additional ideas to push readers to think in a more sophisticated way.

4. Some examples and references are replaced by more recent ones.

5. Additional online resources are available on the FLTRP website. The resources

include appendices, the suggested answers to the questions at the end of each chapter, writing samples, and supplementary reading materials.

Other changes are related to the content which is revised or clarified in response to the suggestions and comments from the teachers and students who have used or read the book in different universities.

Acknowledgements

A book such as this cannot be produced without the assistance of many people. First of all, I would like to extend my thanks to the students in Nanjing University who have taken the course in which early versions of this text were used. Their responses to the text helped me identify which part was well written and which part needed clarification and elaboration.

I would also like to give my special thanks to Keith Johnson, Joanna Radwanska-Williams, Nancy Pine, and Kate Parry. They took great pains to proofread different parts of the manuscripts and provided insightful comments as well as suggestions before the first edition was published. Their kind and timely help made the book better than it would have been otherwise.

I am also very grateful to Wang Ling who helped me check the references and produce some figures; to Chen Qi, Qin Zhihong, Mao Qihong, Zhu Yeqiu, and Liu Qin who helped proofread earlier versions of the text. Particular thanks would go to the copy editors Zhao Rong and Liu Xiaomeng who carefully proofread the whole book.

Wen Qiufang

National Research Centre for Foreign Language Education, BFSU

Nov. 28, 2021

Contents

PART I
Introduction

Part I is an introduction consisting of two chapters. Chapter 1 addresses such questions as "What is research?" "How are different types of research classified?" and "What are the qualities of a good researcher?". Chapter 2 introduces the fundamental concepts involved in research.

Overall objectives

By studying this part, you will be able to

- ☐ describe the basic criteria for good research
- ☐ depict a general picture of the research process
- ☐ differentiate different types of research
- ☐ illustrate the qualities of a good researcher
- ☐ explain the fundamental concepts involved in research

Explaining what research is

This chapter will start with an interesting story which will illustrate the importance of knowing what research is. This is followed by a discussion of what research is and how to visualize research in terms of different components. Furthermore, classifications of research will be introduced to you. Finally, two essential qualities of a good researcher are explained, i.e. integrity and ethical acceptability.

?
- Can you use one example to illustrate your understanding of research?
- Why do we need to have a clear understanding of research?

If someone asks you to make a cake, you should know what kind of cake he/she wants. To look for a key, you must know what a key looks like. Without a good understanding of the outcome you intend to obtain, you will experience a lot of frustrations and even failures. The extreme case is that you might have spent your lifelong time and efforts doing a piece of work but the eventual results you obtained are not what you have desired at all. Similarly, once you make up your mind to make a commitment to research, the first legitimate question you should ask is: "What is research?" The importance of such a question is well illustrated in the following parable.

A Man Looking for Fruit

There was once a man who lived in a country that had no fruit trees. This man was a scholar and spent a great deal of time reading. In his readings he often came across references to fruit. The descriptions of fruit were so enticing that he decided to undertake a journey to experience fruit for himself.

He went to the market and asked everyone he met if they knew where he could find fruit. After much searching he located a man who knew the directions to the place where he could find fruit. The man drew out elaborate directions for the scholar to follow.

With his map in hand, the scholar carefully followed all of the directions. He was very careful to make all of the right turns and to check out all of the landmarks that he was supposed to observe. Finally, he came to the end of the directions and found himself at the entrance to a large apple orchard. It was springtime and the apple trees were in blossom.

The scholar entered the orchard and proceeded immediately to take one of the blossoms and taste it. He liked neither the texture of the flower nor the taste. He went to another tree and sampled another blossom, and then another blossom, and another. Each blossom, though quite beautiful, was distasteful to him. He left the orchard and returned to his home country, reporting to his fellow villagers that fruit was a kind of much overrated food.

Being unable to recognize the difference between the spring blossom and the summer fruit, the scholar never realized that he had not experienced what he was looking for.

—From Halcom's *Evaluation Parables*

The scholar mistook the blossom for the fruit simply because he did not know in the beginning what fruit looks like. We hope you can bear this parable in mind as you learn about the nature of research.

?
- **Why couldn't the man find out the right fruit? What insight can you draw from the parable you have just read?**

DEFINITION OF RESEARCH

In *Collins Cobuild English Language Dictionary*, "research" is defined as "a detailed study of a subject or an aspect of a subject. If you do research, you collect data and analyze facts and information and try to gain new knowledge or new understanding" (p. 1231). Although this is not a technical explanation, it gives readers a general picture about what research is. By this definition, you may know that research activities include data collection and data analysis, and their purpose is to obtain a better understanding of something. Now let's look at a technical definition offered by Hatch and Farhady (1982): Research is "a systematic approach to finding answers to questions" (p. 1). This definition is shorter than the one provided by the dictionary, yet it touches the nature of research. It implicitly tells us three essential elements of research: questions, a systematic approach, and answers. You may use "PPP" to stand for Purpose (questions), Process (a systematic approach), and Product (answers) (See Figure 1.1).

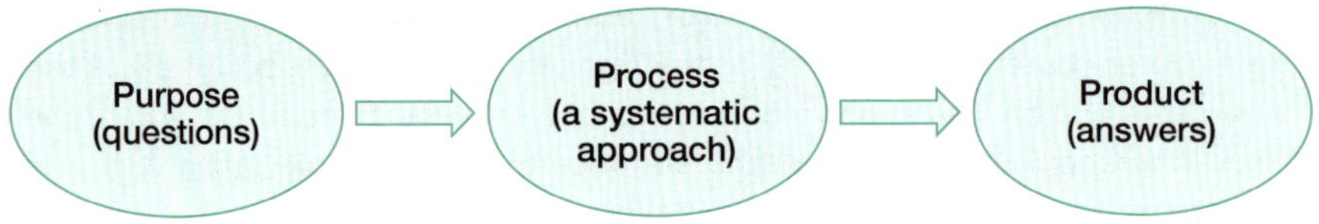

```
┌─────────────┐      ┌─────────────┐      ┌─────────────┐
│  Purpose    │ ──▶  │  Process    │ ──▶  │  Product    │
│ (questions) │      │(a systematic│      │  (answers)  │
│             │      │ approach)   │      │             │
└─────────────┘      └─────────────┘      └─────────────┘
```

Figure 1.1: A simplified model of research

The above three elements are interrelated with one another. All research starts with questions. Without questions in the first place, there will be no research. Does a good question guarantee a systematic approach used in the research? No way. The selection and construction of an approach need another set of skills which are different from those required by developing good questions. Without them, the methods chosen are most likely inappropriate, and valid answers can never be found. Even if researchers have good research questions and follow the procedures without errors, valid answers may not be natural results since the interpretation of the findings could be illogical or untenable. Therefore, each of the three elements in the definition should be paid equal attention to. If there is any flaw in one element, the whole piece of research will be ruined. The following parts will describe each of the three elements.

Having good questions

Before we discuss the qualifying features of good research questions, we must understand what a research question is. A research question must be a question to which the answer is not readily available and the researcher wants to find it out with concerted efforts (Bryman, 2016). In a thesis/dissertation, the research questions normally have a question mark at the end of it. They help explicitly illustrate what to be investigated by the researcher. Good questions ensure that the research goes in the right direction, delimit the research boundary, and keep you focused on what you intend to do. To have questions may not be that difficult, but to have good questions is not easy at all. What kind of questions can be qualified as good questions? The qualifying features can be illustrated by three adjectives: significant, original, and answerable.

A significant question must be of practical and/or theoretical value. Consider, for example, this question: "Do proficient writers make fewer grammatical mistakes in L2 compositions than less proficient writers?" Surely proficient writers should make fewer grammatical mistakes than less proficient ones. Otherwise they cannot be called proficient writers. Therefore, the question is trivial since the answer is self-evident and the findings can neither help improve teaching and learning nor contribute to theory-building. However, if you change the question into: "How do proficient writers differ from less proficient writers in grammatical accuracy?" The answer will be of importance. From the practical point of view, the findings might help readers understand specific differences between proficient and less proficient writers and thus they can help both less proficient and proficient writers improve their grammatical accuracy more effectively. For theory-builders, the findings might provide evidence to construct a model for L2 interlanguage development in support of or against the existing model.

A research question is regarded as original when it is different from questions which have been asked by other researchers in one or more aspects, such as learning contexts, types of learners, or methods used in data collection and data analysis. In other words, an original question does not need to be totally new. In reality, originality is just a matter of degree.

An answerable question is one that can be tackled by the researcher with the time and resources available. This requirement may appear to be unnecessary or the easiest to follow. However, almost all beginning student researchers fail to meet it because they tend to be overambitious and they lack the experience to anticipate difficulties.

To satisfy the above three criteria is invariably the most difficult part of research. Nevertheless, the importance of choosing appropriate questions is often underestimated and the difficulty in doing so is usually not fully recognized. Doing research is like taking a long journey. Asking an ill-formulated question is the same as traveling in the wrong direction and can result only in wasted time and effort. In this sense, "it is worth spending as much time as is necessary to get the question right" (Nunan, 1994, p. 211). How to develop a good research question will be further discussed in Chapter 3 "Developing research questions."

Focus highlight

Three criteria for good research questions: significant, original, and answerable.

- **A significant question must be of practical and/or theoretical value.**
- **An original question must be different from the questions proposed by other researchers in one or more aspects.**
- **An answerable question can be tackled by the researcher with the time and resources available.**

Employing a systematic approach

Using a systematic approach means that research should follow a set of procedures which are clearly described and can be fully justified. The research procedures in some cases are predetermined in the sense that they are decided before the data collection while in other cases they are developed during the research process. In either case, the procedures used for selecting subjects, data collection, and data analysis should be recorded and reported to other researchers. Furthermore, the reasons why certain procedures are adopted should be explained in terms of established principles in the discipline. Being transparent and justifiable, the procedures thus can be easily replicated by other researchers.

One thing is worth mentioning here: No approach is perfect, particularly when the research is to study human beings. Thus, a systematic approach should not be understood as an impeccable approach. Actually, it is common for researchers to admit that there are limitations in their studies.

Obtaining valid answers

The answer to a question, the last element in the definition of research but not the least important, must be of high validity. Validity is an essential yet difficult concept that cannot be explained in one or two sentences. You will understand it gradually through reading this book. At this initial stage, I will explain it in a very simple way. When an answer is said to be valid, it means that the claimed answer is the only answer we can obtain. If there is any alternative answer, the validity of the study will be called into question. For example, one study attempted to find out whether there was a relation between L2 learners' vocabulary size and their reading amount under the assumption that the more L2 learners read, the bigger vocabulary size they have. The findings from this study said that the amount of reading did affect the size of vocabulary as expected, which appeared to be reasonable and logical. However, an experienced researcher read the report very carefully and found that the vocabulary test was not scientifically designed. In this case, there are two competing explanations for the said relation. It is not sure the relation found was caused by the reading amount or due to the poorly designed test. Therefore, people have the reason to say that the answer is not valid. Another study aimed to find out whether there was any gender difference in L2 learning. The study revealed that female English majors outperformed male English majors in an English proficiency test and thus it was concluded that females were more talented than males in L2 learning. Obviously, we can find a dozen alternative answers to account for this fact, such as females spending more time learning than males, males being less serious about testing than females, and the most talented males usually going to the science stream rather than majoring in foreign languages. Since all these alternative explanations are plausible, the validity of the answer concluded is thus doubtful.

VISUALIZING THE RESEARCH PROCESS

Very often, people visualize the research process in various ways and from different perspectives. In this section, two alternative views are described. The first one is proposed by Rudestam and Newton (1992) who visualize the research process as a wheel. The second one is suggested by the author who depicts a research process as a flow chart in which a series of tasks are presented in a sequence.

The research wheel

According to Rudestam and Newton, we may use a wheel as a metaphor to describe the stages of the research process. The metaphor indicates that a series of steps are repeated recursively over time. To be simple, the research process consists of at least two cycles and each cycle contains four stages (See Figure 1.2). The sequential activities within the first cycle include: empirical observation, developing a proposition, constructing a theoretical framework, and generating research questions. Those within the second cycle are data collection, data analysis, referring back to the conceptual framework, and generating further questions.

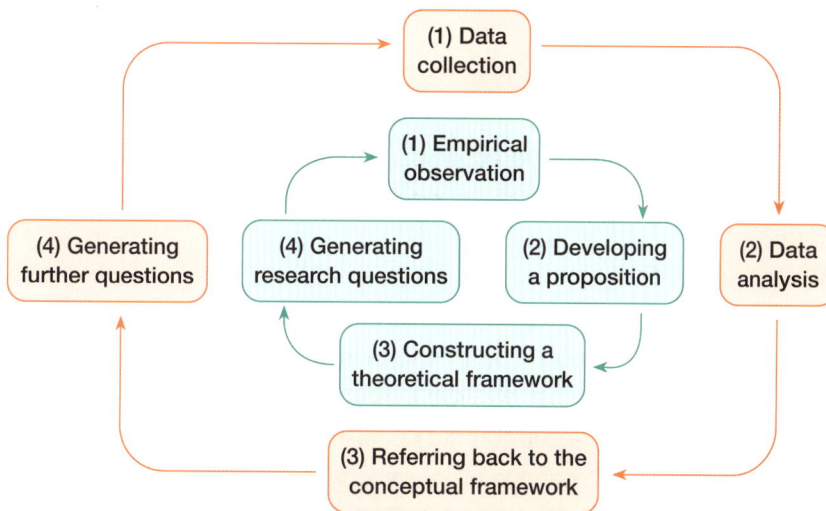

Figure 1.2: The research wheel

The first cycle

The first cycle starts with empirical observation through which the researcher chooses a topic. The next stage is to formulate a proposition, which describes an established relationship in the form of a statement (e.g. Learning purposes are related to the choice of learning strategies). At the third stage, the researcher should relate the proposition to a conceptual framework. In other words, the researcher at this stage needs to propose a theoretical framework, based on relevant theories and previous studies, in which the proposition can be placed. The novice researcher usually finds this task the most demanding and taxing of the research process. Moving forward along the wheel, the researcher is to generate specific research questions. Once the questions are specified and stated, the first cycle is finished.

The second cycle

The second cycle begins with collecting data which directly addresses the research questions. The data collection process can also be regarded as a form of empirical observation. Once the data are gathered, the researcher needs to analyze the data according to the research purposes. Results yielded from the analysis are generalizations made through induction. Then the generalizations are linked to the conceptual framework, and further research questions and implications for additional studies are recommended.

The wheel metaphor can successfully capture the dynamic aspect of research. However, it has been built up on only one type of research, which is quantitative in nature aiming at testing hypotheses. If a study is qualitative, the sequence is not the same as the one described here. This issue will be clarified later.

The flow chart

Compared with the research wheel, the flow chart (See Figure 1.3) is much simpler and less technical. It focuses on the activities a researcher must undertake rather than on how these activities interact in the process of research. It is particularly suitable for helping novice researchers understand what they are supposed to do in their research.

According to Figure 1.3, research involves six tasks: developing research questions, reading the literature, selecting research designs, collecting data, analyzing data, and writing up a thesis/dissertation.

The six tasks each have their own role to play in the research process and none of them can be overlooked. If one task is not completed adequately, the whole study will be put in jeopardy. Furthermore, the tasks are logically interrelated and the sequential order cannot be changed in many cases. For example, data collection cannot be

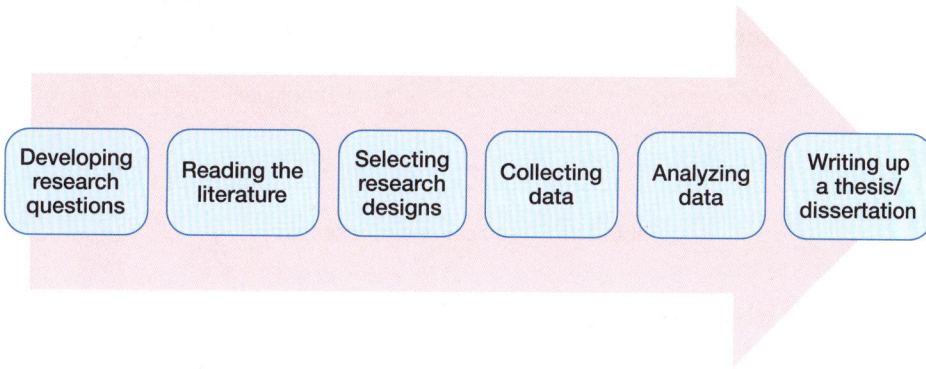

Figure 1.3: The flow chart for research

undertaken before the development of research questions. Similarly, a thesis cannot be written before the analysis of the data. However, the sequence is not always rigidly fixed. In some cases, there may be options. For example, developing research questions, reading the literature, and selecting research designs are not necessarily sequential in practice as presented in the flow chart. You may have a rough idea about your research interest and then go to read the relevant literature. Considering the existing literature, you specify your research topic and narrow down the scope. Then you go to read the relevant literature again to develop specific as well as general research questions. The selection of research designs is determined not only by research questions but also by the methods used in previous studies. Therefore, at the stage of constructing your research design, you also need to read the literature. The above explanation clearly shows that these three activities presented in the flow chart are not always happening in a linear fashion or in a fixed order.

As a would-be researcher, you are suggested to follow the sequence first. Once the cycle is on the track, you are encouraged to be flexible and move back and forth within the sequence. Remember that "real research is inevitably going to be a rather messy process" (Blaxter, Hughes & Tight, 1996, p. 7). In other words, these six tasks are recursive in nature. However, this recursiveness cannot be captured by this two-dimentional flow chart. One obvious advantage of the chart is its simplicity: It enables the reader to remember the tasks without much effort. Furthermore, the tasks described can be applied to both quantitative and qualitative studies.

CLASSIFICATIONS OF RESEARCH

When you read books on research methodology, you may come across various kinds of terms designating research. In this section, I will define some commonly used terms along with two classifying features: aims of research and sources of data (See Table 1.1).

Classifying features	Types of research
Aims of research	Theoretical/Practical
Sources of data	Primary/Secondary

Table 1.1: Classifications of research

Theoretical and practical

In terms of aims, two types of research can be identified: theoretical research and practical research. Theoretical research is primarily concerned with constructing theories or testing existing theories. Practical research is usually conducted to solve a genuine problem in real life by people directly involved in L2 teaching, such as L2 teachers, L2 textbook compilers, or L2 test writers. Its major aim is to seek a practical solution to a real problem. At the moment, it is assumed that researchers have a single aim, either theoretical or practical, when they carry out their research. In real life, the research aim is not clear-cut. The complexity of this issue will be discussed later.

Theoretical research

Theoretical research aims at developing or testing theories rather than at resolving practical issues. For example, the work undertaken by Krashen (1985) for constructing the Monitor theory can be regarded as theoretical research. His model consists of five hypotheses[1] as follows:

1. The Acquisition-Learning Hypothesis;
2. The Natural Order Hypothesis;
3. The Monitor Hypothesis;
4. The Input Hypothesis;
5. The Affective Filter Hypothesis.

The above theory was not invented by Krashen himself. For example, the Input Hypothesis was first proposed by MacNamara in 1972 (Krashen, 1985) and the Natural Order Hypothesis by Corder (1967). Krashen constructed the theory by studying, analyzing, and synthesizing the relevant literature coupled with his own empirical studies.

Examples of such research can be easily found in international journals such as *Language Learning* and *Applied Linguistics*, and domestic journals such as *Linguistics and Applied Linguistics* and *Foreign Language Teaching and Research*. Let's look at some examples.

---

[1] These five hypotheses will be discussed in detail in Chapter 2.

Example 1

The study intended to measure the effects of cultural background knowledge on L2 reading comprehension. The researcher chose two passages which were based on different cultures but with similar linguistic difficulty. One passage was about the Chinese Mid-Autumn Festival and the other was about the Thanksgiving Day in the United States. Sixty second-year non-English majors read these two passages each at a time. Once the reading was over, the students took a comprehension test. Eventually, the scores on the two comprehension tests were compared. The results showed that the students displayed a better comprehension in reading the passage about the Chinese Mid-Autumn Festival (Ye, 1994).

Example 2

The study aimed at finding out to what extent students' pragmatic knowledge was related to their language proficiency. Ninety second-year English majors were required to take a test on pragmatic competence. Then the students were divided into three groups according to their overall English proficiency: top, middle, and bottom. A statistical procedure was taken to compare these three groups' pragmatic competence. The results indicated that students' L2 proficiency was closely related to their pragmatic knowledge (Wu, 1998).

The two examples both attempted to test the existing hypotheses. It is generally agreed among researchers that cultural background knowledge is an important factor affecting the quality of reading comprehension. In Example 1, Ye tested this assumption in her study in which non-English majors were involved and the result confirmed the assumption. In Example 2, Wu examined the hypothesis that pragmatic knowledge and L2 proficiency are closely related to each other and her empirical data were in support of the hypothesis. Although the findings from the two studies have implications for L2 teaching and learning, they are not direct solutions to any practical problems.

For an M.A. or Ph.D. student, it is rare to write a thesis exclusively on theoretical research since this kind of research requires a profound understanding of the topic you are investigating.

Practical research

Practical research attempts to solve concrete problems in classroom teaching or learning or some other situations. The findings from such research usually can be directly tried out by practitioners. The following are some examples.

Example 1

The study tried to see to what extent a language laboratory could be used to teach spoken English (Wen & Wu, 1998) in order to find a practical answer to the question "How can we make 30 to 40 students active in a speaking class?" Twenty-nine second-year students who participated in this experiment were from the same class. They had their speaking class in a language laboratory for four months. At the end of the semester, the students were asked to answer a questionnaire anonymously to make an evaluation of the speaking class. The questionnaire items concerned four aspects: (1) the students' attitude toward the speaking class in a language laboratory; (2) the amount of their participation in the language laboratory in comparison with that in a classroom; (3) their degree of nervousness in the language laboratory in comparison with that in the speaking class before; (4) their rate of progress in spoken English this semester in comparison with that in their previous learning. Taking into account their responses to the questionnaire, we concluded that although the students noticed the limitations of the language laboratory setting, they made a positive evaluation of the speaking class in a laboratory.

Example 2

The study intended to see whether a spoken English test in a laboratory was feasible as a large-scale test format (Wen, 1999). The experiments were conducted consecutively in five years, in which several aspects were examined: (1) the content and the difficulty level of the test; (2) the administration of the test; (3) the evaluation of the tapes. The subjects involved in the experiments were 3,300 second-year English majors from 60 different universities within five years. After each experiment, the researchers made modifications based on the students' and the teachers' responses to the test. Finally, such a test format has been adopted in the CET-Spoken English Test Band 4 for English majors since May 1999.

The two exemplary studies mentioned above are primarily concerned with practical problems. In Example 1, the researchers wanted to find a method to teach a large class spoken English more effectively, and in Example 2, the researcher aimed at developing a large-scale spoken English test for English majors who were spread out in different parts of China. Although the results from the two studies all have a direct impact on actual teaching and learning, syllabus design, or testing, there is no sound theoretical basis for us to claim that teaching spoken English in a language laboratory or testing spoken English in a language laboratory is better than other forms. Actually, the solutions are selected only due to practical constraints.

Aims of research: Discrete categories or a continuum?

In the above discussion, I tried to give you various examples to illustrate the differences between theoretical and practical research according to their aims. You might get an impression that such a theoretical-practical distinction is clear-cut and easy to identify. Actually, it is not always true. In reality, such a divide is defined only in a relative sense. Theoretical research and practical research do not form discrete categories but a continuum. Moreover, in practice, one piece of research more often than not fulfills two or three purposes. It is not uncommon for theoretical research to have practical implications while practical research has theoretical value. The theoretical-practical distinction is sometimes blurred and theoretical research and practical research differ in degree rather than in kind. The distinction is made clear in the above discussion simply for the sake of convenience.

Primary and secondary

The distinction between primary research and secondary research depends upon the source of data. By saying primary research, I mean the data are collected directly from our past experiences. These data did not exist in any documents before. They are first-hand and original information. Secondary research is a kind of study which makes use of data in documents, books, and journals. These data have been collected by other people for their own purposes.

Secondary research

Secondary research is often called documentary or library research. Let's first consider the following example.

Suppose, as a requirement of the course, M.A. students are asked to write a term paper on the topic "Select two learner factors which you think are the most important in accounting for individual differences in L2 learning outcomes." To accomplish the task, the students use libraries to search for the written wisdom of other scholars. Suppose the students select "motivation" and "learning strategies." First of all, they may search for the books which include these two variables and then find out the papers which have reported empirical studies on them. They then synthesize diverse views from these secondary sources and various findings related to the issue. The resulting work, if not too bad, can provide some useful ideas about the topic at hand and the best papers can develop creative and productive insights into the given topic.

A review paper is a typical example of secondary research. The researcher reviews the recent work in a defined area and then summarizes, analyzes, evaluates, or synthesizes information that has already been published. Although the materials the researcher reviews are not new, the best review papers are insightful in the sense that they offer new syntheses, new ideas and theories. For example, a paper entitled "Research on language learning strategies: Methods, findings, and instructional issues" written by Oxford and Crookall (1989) is a review which intends to "survey research on language learning strategies (LLSs)." The authors describe and evaluate various primary research studies on LLSs according to the research methods used. Finally, they put forward some valuable suggestions for future research on the topic.

Primary research

Primary research is also called empirical research because its data are derived from the primary source (e.g. students who are learning a second language or teachers who are teaching a second language), in contrast to secondary research, which depends on secondary sources (e.g. books and papers about L2 learning and teaching). Primary research can be theory-oriented or practice-oriented. The following hypothetical studies can be classified as primary research.[1]

Example 1

In order to find out how good learners and poor learners differed in reading strategies, the researcher asked 60 second-year non-English majors to answer a questionnaire which contained 25 statements with a five-point scale ranging from "This statement is never or almost never true of me" to "This statement is always or almost always true of me." The responses were compared through statistical analysis.

Example 2

To specify in which way good learners and poor learners differ in reading, 12 students, divided evenly between good and poor learners, were asked to think aloud while reading one passage. The whole process was recorded individually and then transcribed. The students' reading strategies were thus identified and then categorized based on the verbal protocols. Finally, the categories of reading strategies employed by the good and the poor learners were compared.

Example 3

The researcher aimed at examining to what extent second-year English majors used L1 in the process of L2 writing. Fifty students were asked to answer a questionnaire that contained 15 items concerning whether L1 was used at different stages of L2 writing. Each item was responded to on

[1] Studies without references are hypothetical ones created by the author.

a three-point scale, i.e. never—sometimes—usually. The responses to the questionnaire were analyzed first by using statistical procedures. Then the 8 students who were reported to use L1 most frequently and least frequently were selected out respectively for interviewing. In the interview, they each were asked to describe their L2 writing process in detail, and explain how and why L1 was used in the process. The interview data were categorized and reported as supplements to the responses to the questionnaire.

Recently, due to the advancement of computer technology, quite a few linguistic corpora have been developed at home and abroad. These corpora can provide the researcher with recorded authentic speech or written texts. It is very convenient for a novice researcher to work with an existing set of data since it is extremely difficult for any individual researcher to carry out large-scale data collection given that time and funding are limited. Do we call this kind of research primary or secondary? The data in these corpora were collected by other people. However, the corpora contain raw data in the sense that they have not been analyzed. This kind of research is still primary by nature. The above discussion explains how primary research is different from secondary research. Actually, they each can hardly be conducted in isolation. Secondary research can only exist on the basis of primary research, while primary research must start with secondary research.

Requirements for graduate students

As graduate students in applied linguistics, you might ask: "What kind of research are we expected to do?" You are expected to learn to do the following: theoretical/practical research and primary/secondary research. For your theses, you have to carry out primary research that is supported by secondary research. In the case of writing a term paper, you usually do secondary research by searching the library, which may focus on findings from theoretical or practical research or both. One thing that has to be mentioned here is that a doctoral dissertation should report primary research which must have theoretical value.

QUALITIES OF A GOOD RESEARCHER

To be a good person is a basic requirement for a good researcher. However, this section will not take time discussing the qualities of a good person. Instead, I will focus only on the most essential qualities of a good researcher, i.e. academic integrity and ethical acceptability.

"Integrity" is defined in *Oxford Advanced Learner's Dictionary of Current English* (Hornby, 2010, p. 809) as "the quality of being honest and having strong moral principles." You should be honest in the whole process of research and writing. Particularly, you should avoid plagiarism at all costs (Read Chapter 14 for more details).

Ethical acceptability means that your behaviors in dealing with the participants involved in your research are able to be approved by the ethics committee. In general, you should respect their privacy and don't do any harm to their emotions and personal self-esteem (Read Chapter 13 for more information).

The above two qualities are minimum requirements for a good researcher. More qualities can be further listed. You may think for yourself and write down more. And then you can discuss with your classmates and your supervisors. Knowing is one thing and doing is another. I hope and also believe that all of you are determined to be good researchers.

▶≡ SUMMARY

Research is defined as "a systematic approach to finding answers to questions." For a piece of work to be qualified as research, it must meet three requirements: (1) having questions that are significant, original, and answerable; (2) having explicit and transparent research procedures that can be justified in terms of established principles in the discipline concerned; (3) having valid answers that address the questions being asked.

The process of research may be metaphorically described as a wheel or a flow chart. The metaphor of a wheel emphasizes the dynamic aspect of research while the image of a flow chart stresses six distinct activities that have to be carried out in a sequence. A novice researcher is recommended to first follow the sequence of these activities and later show flexibility.

Research can be classified in terms of its aims as theoretical or practical or in terms of its sources as primary or secondary. Postgraduate students are expected to learn to do various types of research. However, in their theses/dissertations for applied linguistic programs, primary research is usually the major component.

AFTER-READING ACTIVITIES

Reviewing

1 How does the definition of research in this book differ from your own definition, and from the definitions you have read in other books?

2 What is the relation among the three components of research: questions, a systematic approach, and answers?

3 What are the three criteria for good research questions?

4 What tasks does a researcher have to accomplish to conduct research effectively?

5 How are different types of research classified in this book?

Exploring

Find out one research paper in a recently published international journal and discuss the following questions with your classmates.

1 What are the research questions listed in the paper?

2 What are the procedures described in the paper?

3 What are the answers to the questions?

4 How does the author classify the research reported in the paper?

Chapter 2

Fundamental concepts

This chapter will introduce to you some fundamental concepts which will repeatedly occur in this book. A good understanding of these concepts will facilitate your comprehension of the ensuing chapters. The specific concepts to be discussed in this chapter are the following: hypothesis, theory, model, population, sample, variable, level of measurement, and operationalization.

HYPOTHESIS, THEORY, AND MODEL

No matter what kind of research you are engaged in, it is almost impossible for you to avoid the use of the concepts of hypothesis, theory, and model. They are so essential that a total absence of these terms may lead to doubts on the scientific nature of the work. However, mere use of terms does not make your work scientific.

Different types of hypotheses

As mentioned earlier, research aims at finding the answer to a question. Very often the investigator has already formed a tentative answer to the question before the research starts, and the function of the research is to check whether the conjectured answer can be confirmed or refuted by the evidence. Such a tentative answer is called a hypothesis. To be precise, a hypothesis in this case should be defined as a declarative statement that describes the hypothetical relationship between two or more variables. It is not a wild guess. Instead, it is made based on previous research findings or established theories.

Suppose the research question is: What is the relationship between the use of L1 by learners in learning English and their learning outcomes? Logically speaking, there are four possible hypotheses about the relationship between them.

1. H_0=null hypothesis: There is no relationship between the use of L1 and English learning outcomes.
2. H_1=positive, directional hypothesis: There is a positive relationship between the use of L1 and English learning outcomes.
3. H_2=negative, directional hypothesis: There is a negative relationship between the use of L1 and English learning outcomes.
4. H_3=non-directional hypothesis: There is a relationship but the direction of the relationship is not specified.

The hypotheses (H_1, H_2, H_3) that are in contrast with the null hypothesis (H_0) are termed alternative hypotheses. In other words, both directional and non-directional hypotheses are alternatives to the null one (See Figure 2.1).

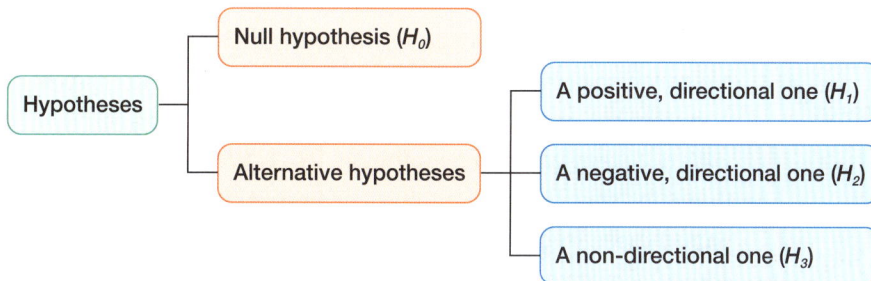

Figure 2.1: Different types of hypotheses

Given strong evidence from the previous research, you may feel that it is possible to predict whether the relationship is positive or negative. Such hypotheses are directional. However, it is often the case that there are inconsistencies or even contradictory findings among the previous studies. Thus, you may not feel sure which direction your hypothesis should follow. In this case, you may put forward a non-directional hypothesis: There is a relationship between the use of L1 and English learning outcomes. Or you do not even know whether there is any relationship at all. Consequently, you formulate a null hypothesis which predicts no relationship between the two variables. Nevertheless, no statistical procedures can directly confirm or reject a hypothesis, i.e. an alternative hypothesis. What they can do is to accept or reject the null hypothesis (See detailed explanations in Chapter 9). When the researcher does not explicitly state a null hypothesis, the logical reasoning behind the research is inevitably related to the null hypothesis.

Instead of forming hypotheses in advance and testing them in the designed research, some studies that are exploratory in nature do not have any hypothesis in the first place. The researcher keeps his/her mind open to all possibilities. The answer to the question gradually emerges in the process and becomes clear in the end. The eventual answer more often than not serves as a hypothesis for confirmation in future research. For example, in the study carried out by Wen and Guo (1998), the researchers did not know how L1 was used in the process of English picture composition when they started collecting data. The findings yielded from the study are hypotheses. Such hypotheses need to be tested by other studies. Furthermore, the hypotheses in this case may not be concerned with the relationship between two or more variables but with the variables themselves (See the hypotheses in a theory about L2 sentence-generating in the next section).

To sum up, formulation of hypotheses is essential for all research, although the hypotheses may be constructed at different stages of a study. The research may start with a hypothesis or end up with a hypothesis. In the former case, it is a process of confirming a hypothesis and in the latter, it is a process of generating one.

Focus highlight

- A hypothesis is a tentative answer to the question the researcher provides before the study. It takes the form of a statement or a sentence. A researcher must be familiar with different types of hypotheses (H_0, H_1, H_2, H_3).
- One thing that must be emphasized here is that in a published paper, there might not be any hypothesis. Instead, there are some research questions. This is not an uncommon practice. However, the hypotheses must underlie the research questions. As an experienced researcher, you should be able to transform research questions into hypotheses or the other way around.

Theory

A theory is broader than a hypothesis, because it is a complete account or worldview about the phenomena studied. A theory can usually generate new hypotheses within the general framework of understanding that it provides. Like hypotheses, a theory is testable and falsifiable. A typical example is the theory about second language acquisition proposed by Krashen[1] (1985), which consists of the following five hypotheses (pp. 1-3).

1. The Acquisition-Learning Hypothesis

Acquisition and learning are two independent ways of developing L2 ability. Acquisition is a subconscious process which is similar to the process of learning

---

[1] Some scholars have pointed out that his "theory" cannot be falsified and is therefore not a theory.

one's native language while learning is a conscious process in which the learner only obtains L2 linguistic knowledge.

2. The Natural Order Hypothesis

The order in which learners acquire the rules of language is predictable but it depends neither on the perceived formal complexities nor the sequence of teaching.

3. The Monitor Hypothesis

Conscious knowledge obtained through learning can only be used to serve as an editor under two conditions: The first condition is that the learner must be consciously concerned with accuracy and the second condition is that the learner must know the rule concerned.

4. The Input Hypothesis

L2 proficiency develops when the learner is exposed to sufficient comprehensible input which is a bit beyond the learner's current level of competence.

5. The Affective Filter Hypothesis

The affective filter is a hypothesized mental barrier which may be up or down. When the learner is poorly motivated and has a high level of anxiety, the filter is up, which will prevent the input from reaching the long-term memory.

Theories can provide you with a direction to or a focus on research by pointing to variables relevant to the study. Krashen's theory emphasizes the degree of consciousness of learning, acquisition order, monitoring, comprehensible input, and affective states. Your study may select any one of the above variables as the focus. Theories also specify the relationships between the variables. In the above theory, Krashen proposes that the less the confidence and the higher the level of anxiety the learner displays, the less input the learner can process. Such hypothetical relationships can serve as a basis on which you formulate hypotheses for your own study.

While others' theories can inspire you, your own study may also develop a theory which can stimulate others to conduct research. For example, in the study of Wen and Guo (1998) in which the process of L2 picture composition was examined with a focus on the use of L1, they proposed a theory based on the students' verbal protocols. The theory describes the active use of L1 in L2 sentence-generating when the learner is given a picture as a stimulus. The theory consists of the following hypotheses:

1. Once L2 writers receive a pictorial stimulus, they start sentence-generating by choosing one of the three paths: (a) Pictorial stimulus → L2; (b) Pictorial stimulus → L1, mediator for retrieving L2; (c) Pictorial stimulus → L1, mediator for generating ideas.

2. L1 serves as a mediator for generating ideas, retrieving L2, monitoring L2, confirming content, and controlling L2 writing procedures.

3. No matter which path L2 writers choose, none of them can totally avoid the

use of L1 in producing L2 sentences. Furthermore, they rely on the use of L1 for different purposes in different situations.

This theory was further examined by Wang (2000), who found that the functions of L1 use listed above were far from complete.

Model

Very often the terms "model" and "theory" are used interchangeably but they do show a difference sometimes. A model refers to the graphic representation of a theory while a theory refers to the verbal description alone. For example, Krashen's theory can be diagrammatically described as a model illustrated in Figure 2.2 (Krashen, 1985).

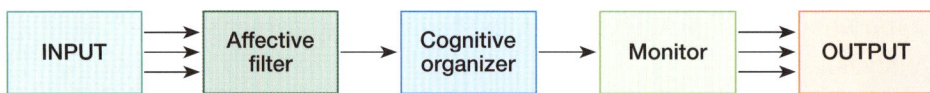

Figure 2.2: A model of second language acquisition

Obviously, a graphic form is more vivid and straightforward than a verbal account, but the graphic form alone is not sufficient for understanding. A verbal account describing the interrelations among the variables is more explicit and less ambiguous than a graphic form. Therefore, it is recommended that in thesis writing a graphic form and a verbal account be presented side by side so that readers can easily comprehend it.

POPULATION AND SAMPLE

Population

The researcher defines a population as whatever the researcher is studying. It can be a collection of persons, textbooks, or test papers. However, in most cases, it refers to people. For example, if a researcher intends to measure the secondary school students' English proficiency in Beijing, the population consists of the students in the whole city. A researcher might be interested in evaluating the difficulty level of the National Matriculation English Test (NMET) in the past 10 years. The population is then made up of 10 years' NMET papers.

Sample

A sample is a representative portion of the whole target population, which is typically obtained through random sampling. In random sampling, every unit of the population has an equal opportunity to be selected into the sample. The detailed description of random sampling techniques will be presented in Chapter 6.

Relation between population and sample

Since a sample is randomly selected, it is assumed to be a miniature of the population. By studying the sample, the researcher hopes in the end to make inferences about the whole target population from which the sample is drawn.

As shown in Figure 2.3, you first draw a sample from the population and then work at the sample. Once you have finished the work with the sample, you will get the results concerning the sample. However, you do not stop there. The next step is an attempt to generalize the results from the sample back to the population. How much generalizing power the results have depends on to what extent the sample can represent the population.

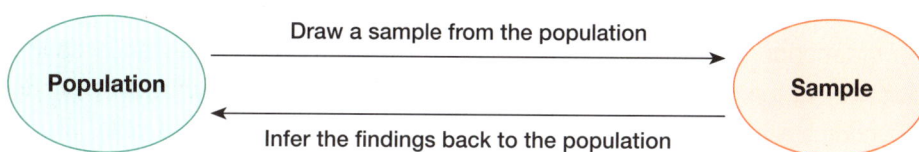

Population

Draw a sample from the population

Sample

Infer the findings back to the population

Figure 2.3: Population and sample (Punch, 1998, p. 106)

VARIABLES

Brown (1988) emphasizes the importance of understanding the concept of variable by saying "The variables are, after all, the focus and center of any study" (p. 9). In this section, I will first introduce to you the definition of the term "variable" and then discuss different types of variables in terms of their functions in research.

?
- Why does Brown say "The variables are, after all, the focus and center of any study"?
- Do you think it is worth researching something that does not vary in different contexts?

Definition of a variable

A variable, as its name suggests, is a feature that must vary from person to person or from object to object. Some variables have a very limited number of variations. For example, gender only has two, either male or female. Marital status has four variations: single, married, divorced, or widowed. Education level may have four or more variations depending on how education level is measured. The variations may include primary education, secondary education, tertiary education, and postgraduate education. However, some variables have a lot more variations. For example, the scores students get from an exam can vary from 0 to 100. People's height and weight have even more variations than test scores.

According to the functions of variables in a study, they can be classified into independent variables, dependent variables, moderator variables, control variables, and intervening variables. The following parts will describe each type of variables.

Independent and dependent variables

Independent and dependent variables are interrelated. They each cannot exist without the other. In other words, independent variables cannot exist without dependent variables, and vice versa. Therefore, these two kinds of variables always go together.

Independent or dependent variables can be used in two ways. In the first case, an independent variable is a stimulus variable or input which is manipulated by the researcher while the dependent variable is a response variable or output. Suppose the researcher studies the causal relationship between the two variables of X and Y. If their relationship can be explained as: "What will happen to Y, if X is made greater or smaller?" Then the researcher is thinking of X as an independent variable and Y as a dependent variable.

In the second case, an independent variable is the variable that is used to predict another variable while the dependent variable is the variable predicted by an independent variable. These two variables are correlated to each other but the relationship cannot be defined as a causal one on the basis of the evidence available. For example, one researcher carried out a correlation study to find out to what extent gender can predict one's L2 achievement. Then gender in this study is an independent variable (a predictor) and L2 achievement is a dependent variable (a predicted factor).

To sum up, in the first case, it is clear that the independent variable is a cause which produces changes in the dependent variable; whereas in the second case, the independent variable is a predictor which is used to predict the dependent variable.

A study may simply have a single independent variable and a single dependent variable. Or it may include a series of independent variables but only one dependent variable, or the other way around. Now, here are a number of hypotheses where independent and dependent variables have been identified.

Example 1

Hypothesis: L2 learners who have done six revisions of the same composition progressed faster than those who simply wrote six different compositions without revisions.
Independent variable: The methods of teaching L2 writing
- Method 1: multiple revisions
- Method 2: multiple compositions without revisions

Dependent variable: Improvement in L2 writing

In Example 1, the researcher assumes that the method of revising the same composition several times is more effective than writing several compositions without revisions in developing L2 writing abilities. In other words, the method of multiple revisions can produce more positive effects on the development of L2 writing abilities than the method of multiple compositions. Therefore, the method of teaching L2 writing is an independent variable while improvement in L2 writing is a dependent variable.

Example 2

Hypothesis: L2 learners who use more varieties of learning strategies and use them more frequently learn English better than those who use fewer varieties of learning strategies and use them less frequently.
Independent variable: Varieties and frequency of the strategy use
Dependent variable: English learning outcomes

In Example 2, the researcher hypothesizes that the use of learning strategies can determine L2 learners' English learning outcomes. The more varieties of learning strategies they use and the more frequently they use the learning strategies, the better the English learning outcomes they can obtain. That is to say, there is a causal relation between the strategy use and the English learning outcome. The strategy use is a cause, or an independent variable, while the English learning outcome is a result, or a dependent variable.

Example 3

Hypothesis: Students' perceptions of a "good" teacher are in part predicted by their attitudes toward education.
Independent variable: Students' attitude toward education
Dependent variable: Students' perceptions of a "good" teacher

In Example 3, the researcher hypothesizes that students' attitudes toward education can predict their perceptions of a "good" teacher. Therefore, the former is an independent variable, or a predictor, while the latter is a dependent variable, or a predicted variable.

> ## Example 4
>
> **Hypothesis:** Students' ways of learning English are determined by their beliefs about what can lead to success in learning.
> **Independent variable:** Students' beliefs about English learning
> **Dependent variable:** Students' way of learning

The hypothesis in Example 4 means that students' beliefs about English learning are closely related to their actual behaviors in learning English. In other words, students' beliefs can be used as the independent variable to predict the dependent variable, i.e. their actual English learning behaviors.

To sum up, Example 1 and Example 2 each claim a causal relationship between the two said variables where the cause is called an independent variable and the effect is called a dependent variable; Example 3 and Example 4 each hypothesize a correlation between the two said variables where the two variables cannot be regarded as the cause and the effect. The above distinction is extremely important for research.

Moderator variables

A moderator variable is measured to see whether it modifies the relationship between the independent variable and the dependent variable. It is sometimes called a secondary independent variable. The word "moderator" indicates the reason why this secondary independent variable has been singled out for study. If the researcher is interested in studying the effect of independent variable X on dependent variable Y but suspects that the nature of the relationship between X and Y is altered by a third factor Z, then Z is called a moderator variable. Let's examine the following two examples.

> ## Example 1
>
> The researcher wanted to compare the effect of a visual approach (using pictures) with that of an auditory approach (using audio tapes) for teaching an English lesson. First of all, she randomly assigned the students into two classes, one for the visual approach and the other one for the auditory approach. After three months' experiment, all the students were tested together for achievement, and the results of the two approaches appeared to be the same.

The researcher suspected that students' preferred learning styles might affect the results since some students had a propensity to receive the input through eyes or ears. Thus, she designed a questionnaire to measure students' preferred learning styles. Then she separated visual learners from auditory ones and the blurred picture became clear. The visual and auditory approaches were more effective if they matched with learners' preferred learning styles.

In Example 1, the hypothesis to be tested is that there is no relationship between the instructional approaches and the students' learning outcomes (H_0). The instructional approach is the independent variable and the effect of the instructional approach is the dependent variable. Why is it said so? You see, the researcher at the beginning of the study assumed that different instructional approaches (a visual approach vs. an auditory approach) could affect students' learning outcomes, but the initial results rejected the hypothesis since the students' test scores appeared to be the same. If the learners' learning styles are not considered, the researcher might draw a wrong conclusion that the visual and auditory approaches could produce similar learning outcomes.

Example 2

The researcher intended to study the relationship between the condition under which a test is taken (the independent variable) and the test performance (the dependent variable). All the students were randomly assigned to take the test under two conditions. Assume that the researcher varied test conditions between ego-orientation ("Write your name on the paper. We are measuring you.") and task-orientation ("Don't write your name on the paper. We are measuring the difficulty level of the task."). The test results showed that the two conditions did not lead to different results. Then, the test-takers' test anxiety level was analyzed as a moderator variable. The further analysis revealed that the persons with a high level of test anxiety did better under task-orientation and the persons with a low level of test anxiety performed better under ego-orientation. Then there is an interaction between the independent variable, moderator variable, and dependent variable.

In Example 2, the hypothesis to be tested is there is no relationship between the test condition and the students' performance (H_0). The independent variable is the test condition which has two variations (ego-orientation vs. task-orientation) and the dependent variable is the students' performance on the test. Without examining the students' level of test anxiety, the comparison of the results under two test conditions did not show any significant differences in the students' test performance. Thus, the hypothesis (H_0) would be confirmed. However, once the students' test anxiety level was measured, the relationship between the independent and dependent variables was changed, i.e. the students with a high level of anxiety performed better under task-orientation while the students with a low level of anxiety performed better under ego-orientation. That is why we called the students' test anxiety level a moderator variable.

The situations in second language teaching and learning are usually quite complex and therefore, the inclusion of at least one moderator variable in a study is highly recommended. Often the nature of the relationship between X and Y remains poorly understood because of the researcher's failure to single out and measure vital moderator variables—Z, W, and so on.

Control variables

It is impossible to study all of the variables in an environment at the same time; some must be neutralized to guarantee that they will not have a moderating effect on the relationship between the independent variable and the dependent variable. The variables whose effects are neutralized or kept constant are called control variables. The purpose of such control is to cancel out or neutralize any effects the variables might otherwise have on the observed phenomenon. For example, in a study on the effects of outside reading on the development of reading comprehension abilities, the researcher purposely selected all the students who had scores above 80 on CET-4. In this way, the subjects' overall English proficiency was selected as a control variable. In another study, the researcher intended to see to what extent testing strategy training might affect the test scores on the English test. The subjects chosen were all girls and thus gender was selected as a control variable in the study.

Certain variables appear repeatedly as control variables, although they occasionally serve as moderator variables. For example, sex, intelligence, and learners' previous performance are three variables that are commonly controlled. In constructing a study, the researcher always needs to decide which variables will be studied and which will be controlled.

Intervening variables

The term "intervening variable" or "extraneous variable" is an umbrella term that can refer to any variable that is not measured in a study but produces effects together with the independent and moderator variables on the dependent variables. There are two types of intervening variables. The first type includes the variables that are difficult, if not totally impossible, to measure even if the researcher wants to. The second type refers to the variables that can be measured but the researcher does not want to study due to limited time and resources or the researcher ignores due to insufficient research experience. Very often these two types of intervening variables exist simultaneously. For example, you plan to conduct a study aiming to find out the relationship between the amount of reading (the independent variable) and the size of L2 vocabulary (the dependent variable). Between these two variables, there might be a list of other variables functioning at the same time, such as the previous vocabulary size, motivation, the strategies used in memorizing words, the ability of memorizing, and the process of taking in, storing, and retrieving words. The first three variables can be measured if you decide to, while the last one, i.e. the process of taking in, storing, and retrieving words is not easily measured even if you are curious about it.

Suppose in another study, you intended to contrast presenting English MOOCs with face-to-face lectures. The independent variable in the study is the mode of presentation; the dependent variable is some measure of learning. Through three months' experiment, the final result was that students learned English better through face-to-face lectures than through MOOCs. Apparently, it was the mode of instruction that had the effect on learning outcomes. If you asked why one way of instruction was more effective than the other, the answer might be face-to-face lectures could provide students with a lot of opportunities to participate in class activities while MOOCs were one-way communication. In this case, the amount of students' participation was an intervening variable, which produced effects on students' learning outcomes. Actually, you can identify a list of intervening variables in this study such as the opportunity to replay the MOOCs, the students' unfamiliarity with the use of MOOCs, etc.

You, as a good researcher, must be able to identify the intervening variables in your study. Knowledge of intervening variables can help you explain why the independent variable causes changes in or predicts the dependent variable. Furthermore, a clear understanding of the intervening variables in your study leads to a cautious interpretation of your findings which, otherwise, tend to be overclaimed, or even wrong.

Relations among variables

How are the above five types of variables interrelated? The following diagram (Figure 2.4) adapted from Brown's (1988, p. 13) illustrates their relationships. The relationship between independent and dependent variables is either causal or correlated. Moderator variables are secondary independent variables, which can modify the relationship between independent and dependent variables. Control variables are the variables that are kept constant during the study in order to examine the robust effects of the independent variable on the dependent variable. Intervening variables are not observable or not measured and thus placed in a dotted arrow. The more intervening variables there are, the harder it is to claim a causal relation.

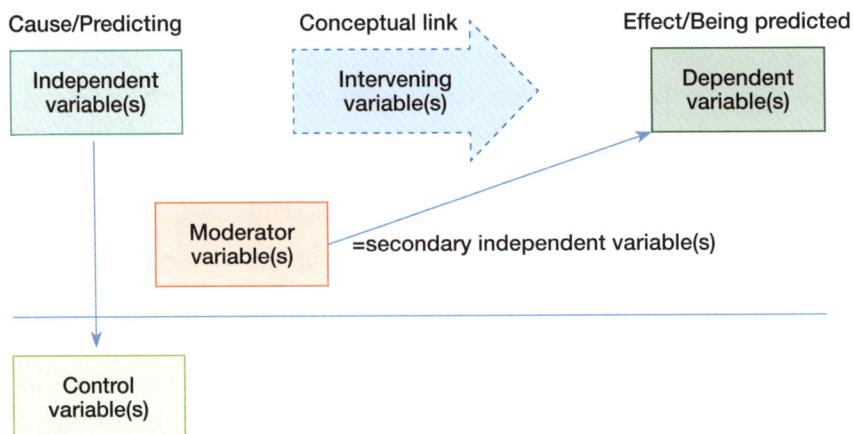

Figure 2.4: Relations among different types of variables

The function of a variable is not inherent in the variable itself. Thus, the conceptual status for any variable can change from study to study, or from part to part within the same study. A variable such as L2 motivation may be an independent variable in one study, a dependent variable in another, a moderator variable in a third, a control variable in a fourth, and an intervening variable in a fifth. The researcher, however, must clearly specify the conceptual status of each variable at each stage of the study.

> **Focus highlight**
>
> - In a quantitative study, the researcher must be able to specify the independent variable(s) and the dependent variable(s) to be investigated in the study in the very beginning. If you are not clear about them, I suggest you read the relevant part of this chapter again since this is very essential for your research.
> - Once you are able to differentiate the independent variable(s) from the dependent variable(s), you move further to comprehend what the moderator variable is and what the other types of variables are.

⧉ LEVEL OF MEASUREMENT

In addition to the functional differences, the variables also show differences in their levels of measurement, i.e. the ways in which they are measured. Generally speaking, there are three distinct levels of measurement[1] in the field of applied linguistics: nominal scale, ordinal scale, and interval scale. Accordingly, there are three kinds of variables: nominal variables, ordinal variables, and interval variables. The following parts will discuss these three scales one by one.

Nominal scale

A nominal scale, as its name indicates, is used to name objects or classify objects. It contains a list of categories, which are mutually exclusive. In other words, each category is unique. For example, you may classify individuals based on their first language, sex, or nationality. This type of measurement may seem rather simple, but many of the variables of greatest interest are nominal in nature. Among the more commonly studied nominal scales are sex, occupation, and mother tongue.

Nominal measurement is qualitative in nature. When you assign numbers to categories on a nominal scale, you must remember that numbers are only used as labels of categories and nothing else and you do it simply for the convenience of making some statistical analyses on qualitative data. For example, you assign the number "1" to males and the number "2" to females, or the other way around. Then you may easily find out the percentage of males and females in your study. Such practice does not

Example 1

Education level

1=primary education
2=secondary education
3=tertiary education
4=postgraduate education

Example 2

Marital status

1=single
2=married
3=divorced
4=widowed

Example 3

Mother tongue

1=Chinese
2=Russian
3=English
4=Japanese
5=Korean
6=Swedish

Example 4

Nationality

1=American
2=French
3=German
4=British
5=Australian
6=Canadian

---

[1] In many books under the topic of levels of measurement, the ratio level is regarded as a distinct level, which is separated from the interval level. In this book, I refer to ratio scales as interval ones because "it is common practice in the social sciences" (Bernard, 1994, p. 34).

make the variables quantitative because the number "2" here is not twice as big as the number "1" and they cannot be added, subtracted, multiplied, or divided. The numbers assigned are arbitrary since it makes no difference what number you assign to what category, so long as each category has a unique number. Nominal scales thus possess the property of distinctiveness. Examples 1-4 are nominal scales.

Ordinal scale

An ordinal scale provides information about the relative amount of some traits possessed by objects, in addition to naming it. For example, in an English speech contest, you might select the six best speakers and award them prizes. These selected speakers might be further ranked as the first prize winner, the second prize winner, the third prize winner, and so on. Such a rank order is an ordinal scale which can indicate who is better than who. However, the difference between the first prize winner and the second one or the difference between the second and the third prize winners cannot be measured precisely. In another case where students' compositions were evaluated, instead of giving them precise scores, you gave them five categories, namely A, B, C, D, and E. It is clear that the students who got A did better than the students who got B. But what is the exact difference between A and B or B and C? This kind of information is absent in an ordinal scale.

In the process of data coding, Arabic numbers are often used to represent the ordinal information. For example, you might use "5" to represent A and "4" to represent B. However, assigning numbers to the ordinal data still cannot quantify the exact distance between every two ranks. If you want to compare two ordinal variables, the direct way is 1<2<3 or 3>2>1. Or you may say: Zhang did better than Li in the English speaking test but less well than Zhu.

Interval scale

In contrast to nominal and ordinal scales, interval scales can provide information about the distance between two attributes. In other words, the interval measurement has the property of equal distances between every two consecutive points on the scale. For example, the difference between one minute and two minutes is the same as the difference between four minutes and five minutes. Similarly, the interval distance between two meters and three meters is the same as the distance between four meters and five meters. Therefore, the measurement of time and the measurement of length are interval scales.

In education, a 100-point marking system for a test usually involves an interval scale because the distance between every two successive points on the scale is the same, namely one point. If two subjects obtain scores 95 and 100 respectively, you say that one is better than the other to the extent of the value of the five points.

In other words, you assume that each of the five points has equal value. Assigning numbers to scores from 1 to 100 is based on the assumption that the intervals between 1 and 2, 5 and 6, and 99 and 100 are of equal value.

Nevertheless, it can be well argued that the above view is being overly simplistic here. Items on the test may vary considerably in difficulty. Therefore, the points earned by doing different items successfully are not of the same value. As a general practice, however, this difficulty is ignored in education, and the measurement is considered to be interval.

The difference between an ordinal scale and an interval scale is shown in Figure 2.5 which is adapted from Bachman's (1990, p. 28). For instance, the student who ranked first got 95 points and the one who ranked second got 93.5 points. The difference between them is only 1.5 points. But the person who ranked third got 90 which is 3.5 points lower than the second rank. Obviously, the distance between the first rank and the second one, and the distance between the second and the third are not equal at all. By contrast, the distance between any two consecutive points on an interval scale is one point.

Ideally, when you measure how much of a variable is present on an interval scale, you expect the intervals to be of equal value. In some cases, there can be little argument about the value of intervals, such as time and weight; in other cases you may not be so sure. For example, if age is the variable you are researching, you can assume that a year is a year. But the value of a year may differ along the scale for second language learning. Obviously the differences between each year in the 10- to 20-year range may be much smaller in value than the year intervals between 60 and 70.

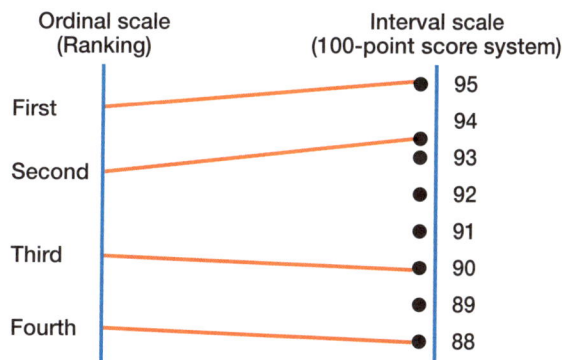

Figure 2.5: Comparison between ordinal and interval scales

Many researchers tend to treat some traditionally called ordinal scales as interval scales for the convenience of statistical analysis (Boyle, 1970; Labovitz, 1970). For example, there is no instrument that can give us precise and accurate measurement of people's interest in learning a foreign language. What you might do is to operationally define the variable in terms of three continuous categories:

not interested, interested, and very interested. Then you rank the subjects along this continuum. In the process of coding such data, you assign a number to each category. In this case, you code the answer "not interested" as "1," "interested" as "2" and "very interested" as "3." Then 1-2-3 is regarded as an interval scale and the means are calculated to be compared. Theoretically speaking, such an analysis is problematic since the distance between "not interested" and "interested," and between "interested" and "very interested" cannot be measured in the first place, nor can we speak of equal distances between every two consecutive points. However, in practice, many studies in social sciences do take such responses to questionnaire items as interval scales. It seems that such practice has already been widely accepted by the researchers of social sciences (Rudestam & Newton, 1992).

Relations among the scales

Nominal, ordinal, and interval scales form three levels of measurement in terms of precision. The nominal scale is at the lowest level, the least precise; the interval scale, at the highest level, the most precise; and the ordinal one is in between. Nominal scales only categorize the data. Ordinal scales not only categorize the data but also indicate the ordering of those categories. Interval scales, in addition to the information about categories and their ranking, indicate the distance between the points in the ordinal ranking. The three levels of scales along with their characteristics are summarized in Table 2.1 which is adapted from Brown's (1988, p. 23).

A scale at the higher level can be converted into a lower level of scale but not the other way around. Let's take students' proficiency level for example. You may easily change exact scores on a 100-point scale into five bands: A, B, C, D, and E. However, it is not possible for you to convert the rank order of the five bands into exact scores.

Levels of measurement		Category	Ordering	Distance
Highest level	Interval scale	+	+	+
	Ordinal scale	+	+	−
Lowest level	Nominal scale	+	−	−

Table 2.1: Levels of measurement and their features

Whether a variable is placed on a nominal, ordinal, or interval scale is usually decided by the researcher. The rule of thumb in research is "always measure things at the highest level of measurement possible. Don't measure things at the ordinal level if you can measure them intervally" (Bernard, 1994, p. 35).

▶ OPERATIONALIZATION

Whatever variables are to be involved in your study, they have to be defined so explicitly that you can measure them without difficulty. This process is called operationalization. In this section, I will discuss first the differences between conceptual and operational definitions and then how a variable is defined operationally.

Conceptual and operational definitions

A variable in a study must be defined conceptually and operationally. A conceptual definition is a theoretical explanation that helps clarify people's understanding of the variable investigated. It is also called a construct, which will be used as an equivalent to the conceptual definition of a variable in this book. The operational definition contains specified instructions which explicitly show how a variable is measured. The following examples illustrate how a conceptual definition is different from an operational one.

Let's first look at one example from our daily lives. You might have heard someone say, "Zhang's apartment is spacious." What does "spacious" mean? *Longman Dictionary of English Language and Culture* defines "spacious" as "having a lot of room" (1992, p. 1271). By this definition, it is difficult to decide whether someone's apartment is spacious or not because people have different conceptions of "spaciousness." In a study of people's housing problem, the researcher defines "spaciousness" as "the average living area of each person being more than 15 square meters." By the researcher's definition, it is easy for us to make a comparison between the areas of two apartments. In this case, the dictionary definition is conceptual while the definition given by the researcher is operational.

The second example is from the field of second language research. Gardner (1985) sees motivation as "the combination of effort plus desire to achieve the goal of learning the language plus favorable attitudes toward learning the language" (p. 10). That is to say, motivation includes three components: attitude, desire, and effort. Operationally, in his study, he regarded motivation as the responses to the questionnaire items concerning these three components.

Although a conceptual definition facilitates our understanding of the concept, it is of limited use because it does not allow us to measure anything. Without measurement we cannot make direct comparisons. An operational definition permits the researcher not only to measure the variable investigated but also to discuss it with another researcher and evaluate whether the measurement specified by the operational definition is appropriate or not.

In the field of applied linguistics and other social sciences, theoretical definitions often appear in the literature review and operational definitions in the description of methodology. In defining a variable conceptually, you have to notice that the conceptual definitions of the same term are not the same in the literature due to the researchers' different views or due to the development of theories. In this case, you have to take a position and select/adapt one of them with justifications. Take L2 proficiency as an example. L2 proficiency was once defined as knowledge about grammar, vocabulary, and phonology. In the 1950s and 1960s, it was defined as four skills: listening, speaking, reading, and writing (Lado, 1961). In the 1970s, it was regarded as communicative competence (Hymes, 1972). In the 1980s and 1990s, the concept of L2 proficiency was further expanded to include strategic competence (Ellis, 1994). If you want to investigate students' L2 proficiency, you face several choices. Which conceptual definition you choose will directly affect your operational definition. Suppose you view L2 proficiency in terms of the four skills. Your operational definition of L2 proficiency must accordingly be related to tests of the four skills. That is to say, the two kinds of definitions of the same term within a study must be compatible and logically related. Similarly, suppose you believe L2 proficiency consists of linguistic competence, pragmatic competence, and strategic competence and the test you select to measure students' L2 proficiency is TOEFL, your operational and conceptual definitions are then called into question since TOEFL does not aim at examining pragmatic and strategic competence.

However, compatibility does not mean that the operational definition must measure virtually everything described in the conceptual definition. Often, due to the weakness of instruments and limitations of time and resources, what is actually measured is less than what is conceptually defined. In other words, operational definitions are necessarily incomplete representations of conceptual definitions. For example, no single English test score could represent all aspects of the construct of L2 proficiency.

Furthermore, the operational definitions used in various studies may be different even if the conceptual definitions are essentially the same. For example, some researchers may define language aptitude operationally as the scores on the Modern Language Aptitude Test (MLAT) developed by Carroll and Sapon in the 1950s while the others, as the scores on the Language Aptitude Battery (LAB) constructed by Pimsleur in the 1960s. Although both tests claim to measure language aptitude, they actually do not measure exactly the same aspects. Skehan (1989) says, "Compared to the MLAT, the LAB emphasizes inductive language learning capacities and auditory ability...What the LAB does *not* have, in comparison with the MLAT, is a test of grammatical sensitivity, on the one hand, and any effective coverage of memory" (p. 29).

Logically speaking, you should start with a conceptual definition of a variable and then move on to its operational definition. In practice, the process more often than not is non-linear. For example, initially, you might like to follow the most comprehensive view of L2 proficiency and define it as a combination of linguistic competence, pragmatic competence, and strategic competence. Later you might realize that the authoritative test that can measure the three components simultaneously is not available at all. If you stick to the conceptual definition, you are not able to operationalize it. Therefore, you have to modify your conceptual definition.

Operational definitions

Operational definitions specify exactly what you have to do in order to measure something that has been defined conceptually. Such definitions are characterized by explicitness which makes possible not only measurement but also evaluation and replication. The following are operational definitions from my own study on the relationship between modifiable learner variables and learning outcomes.

1. L2 proficiency

   The scores on the Test for English Majors Grade Four (TEM4).

2. Effort

   The amount of time spent outside class in studying L2 within a week as reported by the students

3. Learning purpose

   The responses to the questionnaire items presented in the appendix, concerning learning reasons such as interest in the language and culture or longing for a better career in the future

4. Management strategy

   The responses to the questionnaire items presented in the appendix, concerning the strategies used in planning, goal-setting, and evaluation of the learning process and the learners' personal characteristics

If you stick to these definitions in constructing measurements, then you can compare the findings when the subjects are from different universities. For example, you can tell if the students in University A score higher than the students from University B on the TEM4; you can tell if the students in University A spend more hours outside class studying L2 within a week than the students in University B.

How is a variable operationalized? In the process of operationalization, you should first study the corresponding conceptual definition and make it clear what aspects you plan to measure in your empirical study. For example, in my study, the variable "effort" is conceptually defined as the quantity and quality of time spent in learning L2 in and outside class. In other words, the conceptual definition contains two components: the quantity and quality of time. It is obvious that both the quantity and quality of time are important for English learning outcomes. However, it is difficult to measure the quality aspect. Furthermore, the subjects involved in my study were second-year English majors who had a more or less similar number of English lessons every week. Therefore, the operational definition of the variable "effort" only focuses on the quantity of time spent outside class in learning English. Once I had chosen which aspect to be investigated, I had to think how to measure this selected aspect. Eventually, I decided to ask the students to report how many hours they spent outside class learning English within a week. Finally, "effort" is operationally defined as the amount of time spent on L2 learning outside class reported by the students. To sum up, you operationalize a variable by first selecting which aspect(s) in its conceptual definition to be examined and then by making the selected aspect(s) measurable.

The quality of operational definitions is essential for research. If an operational definition is unjustifiable, so are all the conclusions drawn from using it to measure something. For example, if you define L2 proficiency as scores on a test designed by a single teacher, it is obviously questionable in terms of validity and reliability. When a variable is defined operationally, the flaws in your measurement can be easily detected by your supervisor or other researchers and can be eradicated at the initial stage of the study.

Focus highlight

- **Defining a variable to be investigated conceptually and operationally is indispensable in any research. This is not only your first task to accomplish but also the spot that first attracts the readers' attention. Its importance never can be underestimated.**
- **A conceptual definition cannot be made without referring to the literature. For an M.A. student, you may simply choose an authoritative definition from the literature as your own conceptual definition. However, for a Ph.D. student, you cannot copy one's definition from the literature. What you need to do is to review several relevant definitions and make your own conceptual definition with explanations of in what way yours is different from or similar to the reviewed ones and why you define it in such a way.**
- **An operational definition must be clearly stated in the sense that it is readily comprehensible to readers. In other words, as readers, we can easily understand how to measure the variable.**

▶≡ SUMMARY

Fundamental research concepts discussed in this chapter include hypothesis, theory, model, population, sample, variable, level of measurement, and operationalization.

A hypothesis is a conjectured answer to the research question that is developed out of research findings or theories and is expressed in the form of a declarative statement. It may be tested in a new study, or generated from a study to be proved in future research. A null hypothesis explicitly or implicitly stated in a study is a statement in which no relation is assumed between two or more variables. Alternative hypotheses are either directional or non-directional.

A set of hypotheses with specified relations among the variables form a theory, which can be described verbally or graphically. In order to differentiate these two modes of representation, the verbal account is usually called a theory while the graphic description is called a model.

A population is the whole of whatever a researcher is investigating and a sample is a representative portion of the target population. The results from a sample are often used to infer information about the population.

Variables are attributes of a person or an object that have variations. With reference to their functions, variables are differentiated into independent variables, dependent variables, moderator variables, control variables, and intervening variables. In terms of the levels of measurement, variables are grouped into nominal variables, ordinal variables, and interval variables. All the variables involved in a study have to be defined both conceptually and operationally. A conceptual definition is a theoretical explanation that helps clarify people's understanding of the target variable while an operational definition contains a set of specified features of the target variable that make explicit measurement possible.

AFTER-READING ACTIVITIES

Reviewing

1 What are the different types of hypotheses? What is the difference between a theory and a model?

2 What is a population and what is a sample? What is the relationship between a population and its sample?

3 What are independent, dependent, moderator, control, and intervening variables?

4 How can a variable be measured differently in terms of levels?

5 What are the differences between conceptual and operational definitions?

Exploring

1 Select one suitable research paper from an international journal and read it carefully from the beginning to the end. Then list all fundamental concepts discussed in this chapter which are available in the paper and explain their meanings to your classmates such as:
- The hypothesis, theory, and model
- Different types of variables (independent, dependent, moderator, control, and intervening variables) and their measurement (nominal, ordinal, and interval)
- Definitions of the variables including their conceptual and operational ones

2 Do you find anything in the paper different from what is said in this chapter? Can you give any explanations?

PART II

Researching

Part II consists of nine chapters and deals with all the important issues occurring at different stages of research. It starts with the development of research questions and ends with the analysis of the data gathered. For each stage, the procedures are described and common problems are mentioned together with suggested solutions.

Overall objectives

By studying this part, you will be able to

- ❏ describe the basic procedures for research
- ❏ undertake the specified tasks at each stage
- ❏ use the strategies in coping with the frequently occurring problems or difficulties in the process of research

Chapter 3

Developing research questions

Developing research questions is not an instantaneous process, but one that takes place over time. During this period, you are likely to do a lot of background reading, discuss with other researchers, and think about the significance, originality, and feasibility of the questions. This chapter will describe general procedures for the development of research questions and discuss some common problems in formulating research questions.

▶☰ PROCEDURES

In developing research questions, you usually undertake the following tasks as shown in Figure 3.1:

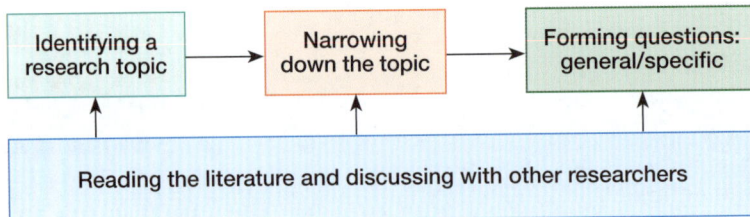

```
┌──────────────┐     ┌──────────────┐     ┌────────────────────┐
│ Identifying a │ ──▶ │  Narrowing   │ ──▶ │ Forming questions: │
│ research topic│     │down the topic│     │  general/specific  │
└──────────────┘     └──────────────┘     └────────────────────┘
        ▲                   ▲                       ▲
        │                   │                       │
┌─────────────────────────────────────────────────────────────┐
│ Reading the literature and discussing with other researchers │
└─────────────────────────────────────────────────────────────┘
```

Figure 3.1: Developing research questions

According to Figure 3.1, you start with identifying a general topic and then narrow down the topic to get a focus, after which you formulate general and specific questions. While you are researching a general topic to find the focus and form the questions, you need to read relevant literature extensively and discuss with your supervisors or classmates frequently. In this section, I will explain how to accomplish the above four tasks one by one.

- **Why do researchers need to read the literature and discuss with other people when developing their research questions? Can you give your explanations?**

Identifying a research topic

At an initial step, you engage in a literature search for a general research topic. You might decide that you are interested in the area of L2 teaching or L2 learning. These two areas are related but each has its own focus and different perspectives. If L2 learning is your starting point, then the topic is extremely general. Suppose your initial chosen area is L2 writing or more specifically, L2 expository writing. Then your topic is obviously less general than L2 learning. Evidently, the journey of developing research questions varies from person to person when the starting points are different. The more specific the topic you start with, the less heavy the workload for you at the second step, i.e. narrowing down the research topic.

What needs to be considered in topic selection? If you asked me for suggestions, I would say personal interest should be placed on the top of the list. The reasons are obvious. In the process of postgraduate study, there is more hardship than happiness. You might have to key in thousands of responses to questionnaire items; you might have to transcribe dozens of hours of recordings; you might find that you have searched in the library for several days without finding out the materials needed. Your personal interest in the topic is always the best driving force for you to reach the end of your arduous journey.

The second thing you need to consider is that you should not select topics which may evoke strong emotional reactions that can lead you astray. For example, some students show a high degree of anxiety and are very much afraid of speaking. Suppose one of them decides to study the relation between the degree of anxiety and oral English proficiency. He/she is likely to have a "position" on the subject that will interfere with his/her completing the research satisfactorily on a number of levels. The most important of these is the self-fulfilling prophecy phenomenon (Ambady & Rosenthal, 1992). If he/she is convinced that a high degree of anxiety will lead to failure in acquiring good speaking skills, the data collected can be biased. Furthermore, suggestions from supervisors or other people might be hard to accept when they are inconsistent with his/her personal understanding of the problem. However, according to the constructivists' view, all studies are somewhat biased. What is essential for the researcher is to reduce the degree of bias.

The third suggestion is that you should "avoid a topic which is overly ambitious and overly challenging" (Rudestam & Newton, 1992, p. 10). Many postgraduate students, before embarking on their journey of research, have made up their minds to do something unique so that they can make a remarkable contribution to the field they are investigating. These students, I should say, should be admired but their perceptions of the thesis are a bit unrealistic. Those apparently spectacular theses may end in two fates, either remaining unfinished or being completed with lower quality. Therefore, you have to temper your enthusiasm with practical concerns. Remember that even the best thesis is very often a result of compromises among our own ambition, the requirements of the supervisor, and practical constraints. What is being said here, however, does not mean that you are encouraged to choose a simple and easy topic and write a mediocre thesis.

In a word, I would suggest that you should select a small piece of an important topic or a small piece of an area that intrigues you.

Narrowing down the research topic

Narrowing down the topic usually causes researchers, particularly novices, the most trouble. There is no clear-cut rule specifying what is the right size of the topic that is sufficient for an M.A. thesis or a doctoral dissertation. Experienced supervisors can give their students help in this regard.

You can start with the questions beginning with "who," "what," and "how." Suppose you have selected the research topic "the acquisition of English vocabulary." Obviously, the topic is rather broad. Now you may first ask yourself: Who are the learners? Are they middle school students or university students? If they are university students, are they English majors or non-English majors? If they are English majors, are they freshmen, sophomores, juniors, or seniors? Let's decide to select sophomores. The second question is what kind of vocabulary you are interested in. Are you interested in receptive or productive vocabulary? If your interest is in productive vocabulary, then you have to decide whether you are interested in vocabulary in speaking or in writing. Let's say you are interested in speaking. The last question concerns how you will go about your research. Do you interview the students or ask them to answer a questionnaire, or observe their performance in class? Do you plan to measure the size of their productive vocabulary? Finally, how do you do it? Do you give them each a personal interview or an oral test in a laboratory? When you keep on asking yourself such questions, the topic will become narrower and narrower and better defined. When does this end? It depends on your research purpose.

Formulating general and specific questions

General questions serve as a blueprint that provides the direction for your research but they are not specific enough to be answered. Specific questions that are derived from the general questions are directly related to the details of research procedures such as subject selection, data collection, and data analysis.

The questions should not be finalized in a hurry since hasty decisions might overlook possibilities. You had better budget enough time to look for all the possibilities available before you reach closure on the specific questions. Often you may experience a stage where a small set of questions are expanded into a large set which you have to delimit again afterward. Such experiences are very common and you do not need to worry about them. In Punch's opinion (1998), the absence of such experiences may indicate insufficient time spent in generating possibilities in the first place.

Once the expansion of the initial set of questions is over, you must examine all the questions to weed out those unimportant ones. The general principle here is that it is better to answer fewer questions thoroughly than many questions superficially. In a study for M.A. or doctoral programs, you are unlikely to tackle five or more major questions. If you have more than five, you should probably be thinking of cutting them down in number and focusing on fewer.

Research questions should finally be grouped and ordered in a logical sequence. In other words, the hierarchical relationship among the questions should be self-evident. Such a relationship can be described diagrammatically in Figure 3.2.

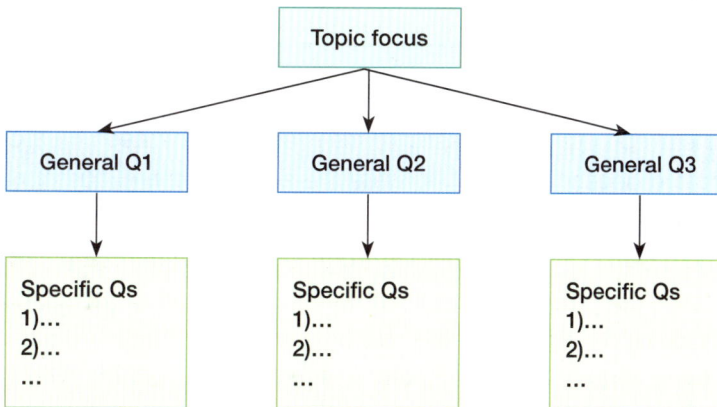

Figure 3.2: Relations between general and specific questions

Questions for quantitative research are often, if not always, constructed ahead of empirical work. They are sometimes stated as hypotheses. But for most people, straightforward questions are fine. Questions for qualitative research are usually general before data collection and specific questions only emerge as the research unfolds.

The following are research questions selected from some of our M.A. students' theses in 1998, quoted here in a slightly modified form.

In Example 1, the students' rhetorical knowledge is an independent variable, the discourse pattern, a dependent variable, and L2 proficiency, a moderator variable.

Example 1

Research topic: L2 argumentative writing

Topic focus: A study of university students' argumentative writing in English: rhetorical knowledge and discourse patterns

General and specific questions:

GQ1: What is the relationship between the students' rhetorical knowledge and discourse patterns?

SQ1: Do the students' perceptions of the rhetorical organization of English argumentative discourse vary from the expected English norms?

SQ2: Do the English argumentative essays written by the students demonstrate any deviations in rhetorical organization from the expected English norms?

SQ3: Are there any correlations between the students' rhetorical knowledge and the discourse patterns of their English argumentative texts?

GQ2: Does L2 proficiency moderate the relationship between rhetorical knowledge and the discourse patterns?

SQ1: Are the students of different linguistic proficiency levels different from one another in their perceptions of the rhetorical organization of English argumentative essay?

SQ2: Do the students show any differences in their performance in creating an English argumentative essay?

SQ3: What is the relationship between the students' rhetorical knowledge and their performance in writing if they are divided into groups according to their L2 proficiency?

(Wu, 1998, p. 3)

The first general question is to investigate the relationship between the independent variable and the dependent variable, while the second general question is to find out to what extent L2 proficiency as a moderator variable modifies the relationship between the students' rhetorical knowledge and the discourse patterns. Each general question contains three specific questions. Take the first general question as an example to see the internal logical relations among the three specific questions. The first general research question involves three specific aspects. The first one is related to the students' perceptions of rhetorical discourse organization; the second one concerns the students' actual performance in English argumentative writing; the third one is the relation between the students' perceptions of the rhetorical knowledge and their actual performance. One thing that must be emphasized here is that general questions should be constructed before specific questions since general questions help decide on the overall direction of the research. If they were not right, specific questions would not work at all.

In Example 2, the task variation and the length of planning time are two independent variables and L2 oral performance is a dependent variable which is operationalized as accuracy, complexity, and fluency of L2 oral performance. It is clear that this study intends to investigate more variables than the study in Example 1.

Example 2

> **Research topic:** L2 oral performance
> **Topic focus:** Influence of different tasks and lengths of planning time on second language oral performance
> **General research questions and specific hypotheses:**
> **GQ1:** What is the relationship between the familiarity of tasks and L2 oral performance?
> **Hypothesis 1:** The task with which students are most familiar would be performed with the highest degree of accuracy while with the most unfamiliar and difficult task, students might produce the lowest degree of accuracy.
> **Hypothesis 2:** The task which is most unfamiliar and difficult would generate language with the highest degree of complexity. In contrast, the task which is most familiar to students might be performed with the lowest degree of language complexity.
> **Hypothesis 3:** The task which is most familiar to students might be performed with the highest degree of fluency while the task that is least familiar to students might be performed with the lowest degree of fluency.
> **GQ2:** What is the relationship between lengths of planning time and L2 oral performance?
> **Hypothesis 1:** With more planning time, greater degrees of accuracy will be observed.
> **Hypothesis 2:** With more planning time, more complexities in language will be displayed.
> **Hypothesis 3:** With more planning time, more fluency will be achieved.
> (Zhu, 1998, pp. 11-12)

One more difference, if compared with Example 1, is that the specific questions are stated in the form of hypotheses. In fact, all the hypotheses can be easily transformed into questions. For example, the three specific hypotheses under the first general question can be changed into the following questions:

1. To what extent does the familiarity of tasks affect the accuracy of L2 oral performance?
2. To what extent does the familiarity of tasks affect the complexity of L2 oral performance?
3. To what extent does the familiarity of tasks affect the fluency of L2 oral performance?

Reading the literature and discussing with other researchers

In the process of research, the literature is reviewed from time to time, but for different purposes. As shown in Figure 3.1, you do a literature review in identifying a general research topic, deciding on the research focus, and developing general and specific research questions. If you have not found any interesting topics, reading others' research may give you some inspirations. You may pick up any recent issue of a well-established journal in the relevant field such as *Applied Linguistics*, *TESOL Quarterly*, or *Language Learning*, and read the papers which appeal to you. Usually, published papers include recommendations for further research in the last section. You may read the last section more carefully and see whether you can find any of the suggested topics attractive. It is also possible for you to be motivated by the findings of a reported study. For example, in Huang's study (1984), she concluded that functional practice (i.e. undertaking communicative activities) is a powerful predictor of Chinese learners' proficiency in oral English. You may be motivated to find out whether functional practice is also a good predictor of Chinese learners' proficiency in reading and writing.

If the research topic is initially motivated by your personal experience or observation, you have to read through the literature to examine whether the selected topic is worth investigating. You will go through major influential journals published in the past decade, searching for the papers relevant to your topic focus and reading the abstracts of each paper. If the reviewing of the literature reveals that your chosen focus has not been studied before or that yours differs from the previous ones in one or two aspects, you are assured that you can move on to undertake the next task, i.e. developing general questions into specific ones.

Once you reach the stage of developing general and specific research questions, you may also need to search through the literature in the relevant papers for the purpose of seeing the way the research questions are formed. You could follow the format in which the questions are stated if they are appropriate. Particularly, when you are not clear about the difference between the research question format of a quantitative study and that of a qualitative study, the short cut is to find suitable papers as models to see how the questions are presented in different types of studies.

While reviewing the literature, you need to discuss your research topic with other people, especially your supervisor. Such a discussion is very often stimulating and enlightening. It can facilitate your research topic identification and focus specification. One problem is that some students do not know how to make full use of human resources around them. They try to work on their own, seldom discussing their research with other people. As a result, they will miss opportunities to learn from others and gain help from others.

≔ PROBLEMS IN QUESTION FORMATION

As mentioned before, developing good questions is often the first difficulty novice student researchers encounter in preparing for their theses. According to my experience as a supervisor, the following are the common problems they come across.

Problem 1: no research idea

Some postgraduate students, by the time they have finished all their courses, have not yet developed any specific research interest. When it is time for them to write a proposal, they do not know what topic they are going to investigate. They expect their supervisors to choose a research topic for them.

This is obviously a wrong and unrealistic expectation because a supervisor, as the name suggests, is responsible for supervising your work rather than doing the work for you. Moreover, to learn to identify a research topic independently is part of postgraduate study. Once you have developed such an ability, you are capable of pursuing your research after graduation. Otherwise, the accomplishment of your theses would be the end of your research career.

Some supervisors who lack experience in supervision might provide their students with suggested topics out of goodwill. However, it has more disadvantages than advantages. Apart from not giving the students proper training in developing research questions, such practice has at least two additional drawbacks which may not be discerned by either the teachers or the students at the beginning. First of all, a thesis normally takes years to finish. Often there is a period of time when the students feel bored and/or begin to lose interest in the topic. If they do not select the topic themselves, such feelings will be much stronger than otherwise. Some of them will even feel regretful that they do not make their own choice of topic. Secondly, students usually expect their supervisors to find a solution to the problem since they think this is not their topic. Therefore, if the cycle of postgraduate training is to be complete, I strongly suggest that nobody should skip over this process of choosing a research topic.

How can you find an interesting topic? In addition to the existing literature, the following are two important sources from which you may find a topic that appeals to you.

Personal experience

One's personal experience of learning an L2 and being taught an L2 are usually primary and rich sources from which you can find research topics. However, without strong curiosity and high sensitivity, you are not able to get any inspiration from such valuable experience. But curiosity and sensitivity are not inborn qualities; they have to be fostered. Therefore, I suggest that whenever you have a question about language learning or teaching, you jot it down in a research ideas journal. These ideas are like sparks, which are transient. If you do not catch them, they will disappear quickly. Only when you get hold of them can they possibly develop into a full-fledged research project. For example, it is not uncommon for English learners in China to confuse "he" with "she" in spoken English. It is also not surprising to find their mistakes in the use of articles. One question you can ask is what are the most difficult forms in English for Chinese learners to master. Another question you can pose is what are the variations among Chinese learners in grasping these difficult forms. So long as you are curious enough about your L2 learning experience, you can find innumerable topics to investigate.

Here are two more genuine examples of finding the research topic for the undergraduate thesis from one's personal experience. One student found that in multiple-choice reading comprehension tests, she often chose the correct answer because of a wrong reason and selected the wrong answer when her comprehension was actually right. She thus had a strong doubt about the validity of such tests. She discussed her personal experience with me. Then I encouraged her to choose this topic for her study. She asked 10 students to do think-aloud[1] when they were doing multiple-choice reading test items selected from several TOEFL tests. She then analyzed the results to find out to what extent their so-called correct answers could reflect their reading comprehension ability.

Another student had a strong interest in finding out why some students read English texts much faster than other students even if they had similar English proficiency. I then pushed her to form an initial answer to the question. She guessed that the faster readers might focus their attention on the content words and ignore the functional words. The next task I asked her to undertake was to design an instrument to test her conjectured answer. By trying out various ways, she finally decided to ask 30 participants who had similar English proficiency to read a passage of 800 words as quickly as possible and underline the article "the" at the same time. After they finished reading, they were required to answer some reading comprehension questions to make sure they did reading seriously for comprehension. The reading task was undertaken individually so that the reading behavior was recorded and the reading time was measured. The eventual findings confirmed her hypothesis.

Attending conferences and talking with other researchers

The second source from which you can identify a research topic is attending conferences and talking with other researchers. Published papers usually report studies carried out two or three years ago. However, at a conference, presentations usually report recently finished studies or ongoing projects. By attending a conference, not only are you able to obtain the latest information about the studies in the field concerned, but also you can meet a group of distinguished scholars as well as active researchers themselves. The discussion section after each presentation is often the most stimulating. You can ask the presenters questions personally and get great help in a very convenient way. You should take every opportunity to attend academic conferences related to your research and try not to miss any guest speaker's lectures

---

[1] Think-aloud requires the participants to speak out their inner thoughts while they are doing a task such as writing or reading. This will be discussed in detail in Chapter 8.

in your own institution. Furthermore, you should try to have a conversation with them when they finish their presentations or public speeches and ask them what questions they think need further research in their areas of expertise.

Let me share with you my own experience. The research topic for my own doctoral dissertation was on learning strategies of Chinese English learners. This was a cutting-edge research area in 1989 when there were not many books and papers for references. In July 1989, I went to participate in a conference held by The Chinese University of Hong Kong where I met the American scholar Douglas Brown, who was a keynote speaker in the conference. In his talk, he showed the audience the newly-published book written by Oxford (1990) entitled *Language learning strategies: What every teacher should know*. It was the book I most wanted, which was, however, not available in the market in Hong Kong yet. I approached him and asked whether I could buy this book from him. He said that he could post it to me after he finished his talk in Taiwan. A few days later, I got this posted book, which gave me tremendous help in my research. First of all, I had a comprehensive list of references on language learning strategies which saved me a large amount of time in reference searching. Furthermore, I got a lot of inspirations from Oxford's strategy inventory for language learning when designing my own questionnaire. Imagine that without such an incidental meeting with Douglas Brown to get this book, it would be impossible for me to finish my dissertation as I planned.

Problem 2: the topic being too broad

Topics selected by researchers with limited experience tend to be broad and without a clear focus. This is not a problem at all if it occurs at the initial stage. It is a problem only when the researcher does not know how to deal with such a situation, or worse, when he/she does not know the topic needs further narrowing down. For example, one of our students said that he wanted to investigate to what extent affective factors influence non-English major graduate students' English learning. The question was apparently appealing in the sense that most of the previous studies focused on cognitive factors and only a few of them investigated the effects of one or two affective factors. In this sense, designing a study of the learners' affective factors is desirable. The problem he had was that he was not able to see why the topic was too broad.

From his point of view, he had already tried to narrow the topic down to some extent. In his view, he selected affective factors rather than all the factors related to learners, and he only intended to study non-English major graduate students rather than all the university students. But he did not think of the fact that there might be as many as a dozen affective factors and it would be difficult, if not impossible, to cover all of them in a single study. Nor did he realize that there were very few valid instruments available for measuring the affective aspects. Eventually, with the help of his supervisor, he was able to narrow down the topic and focused on one affective factor in his research, i.e. motivation.

According to my own research experience, the process of drawing a clear boundary of one's research area or specifying the research focus cannot be accomplished at one go. It normally takes a longer time than a researcher expects. Patience and caution are absolutely needed in the whole process. Furthermore, the supervisor is always the first person who can offer help in this regard. It is often the case that the research area is broader at the beginning than it needs to be for the final thesis. Gradually, the topic is being narrowed down along with the progress of your research. It is not rare that the research focus is finally specified when you have written up your thesis.

Problem 3: questions not worth investigating

Some questions raised by researchers may not be worth investigating if the questions are trivial and have neither practical nor theoretical value. You might wonder how this can happen. It is true that no researcher would like to invest time and effort in a meaningless way. However, an inexperienced researcher has difficulty in detecting triviality in the questions put forward. For example, one student tried to see how first-year English majors and third-year English majors differ in summary writing. The general question sounds interesting and seems not insignificant at all. Let's look at the specific questions: (1) Do these two groups of students show differences in their overall scores on summary writing? (2) Do these two groups of students show differences in the number of important points included in their summaries? (3) Do these two groups of students show differences in the total number of grammatical errors in summary writing? All these questions appear to be well constructed with a clear focus. My question is: Why did she want to find out the answers to these questions? Without the empirical data, I am sure, you can provide the answers without too much thinking because the third-year students should get higher scores, include more important points, and make fewer grammatical errors than the first-year students. Otherwise, there must be something wrong with our education system. Then what implications could we draw from such findings? Do these findings have any implications for improving our teaching or learning or do these findings have any contribution to theory building? Absolutely not. Therefore, the specific questions are trivial and are not worth investigating at all.

From the above example, you may notice that by saying questions are trivial, I mean that the answers to the questions do not have practical value or theoretical value even if the process of research is very complicated or labor intensive.

Problem 4: questions like a shopping list

It is very common for novice researchers to form a set of questions like a shopping list. The questions do not display a strong logical link and there is no distinction between general questions and specific ones. The occurrence of such a problem is mainly due to insufficient thinking on the part of the researcher. For these researchers, the process of question formation is somewhat like shooting bullets in the sense that questions are formed one after another without considering the internal link at all. Obviously, these questions are not matured enough to serve as the final set, which need further time and effort to work at.

If you are in this situation, what should you do? I suggest that you list general questions first and then establish a link among them based on your thorough understanding of your topic. Such a link is extremely important since it enables your study to be an organic whole. Once the general questions are internally connected, you move on to the stage of developing specific questions, which is comparatively easier than the previous one. Let's look at the following example which can well illustrate what kind of questions I refer to as a shopping list and what questions have a hierarchical structure. The first set of questions is the one which was formed at the initial stage of research. It does not display a strong logical link. The second set is the final one that resulted from a substantial revision.

The first set in the early draft of one student's thesis:

1. Is there any use of first language in the second language composing process of university students? If yes, how much L1 is used in the L2 writing process?
2. When does first language occur in the second language composing process?
3. What functions does first language have in the second language writing process?
4. Why do writers use their native language in the process of composing in second language?
5. Does L1 use in L2 writing vary with the types of writing tasks?
6. Is there any correlation between L1 use in the L2 composing process and the quality of the composition?

The second set which is the final version:

1. How is L1 used by tertiary level English majors in China in the L2 composing process?
(1) How much is L1 used in the L2 composing process?
(2) When is L1 used in the L2 composing process?
2. Does L1 use vary with such factors as the types of writing tasks and the development of L2 proficiency?
(1) Does L1 use in the L2 writing process vary with the types of writing tasks?
(2) Does L1 use in the L2 writing process vary with the writers' L2 proficiency?
3. What roles does L1 play in L2 writing?
(1) What functions does L1 have in the L2 writing process?
(2) Is there any relation between L1 use in the L2 composing process and the quality of the composition?

In the first set, the researcher addressed six different issues concerning the use of L1: how much, when, what functions, why, the effect of the types of writing tasks on L1 use, and the relation between L1 use and L2 writing quality. These six issues are arranged in such a way that it is difficult for the reader to figure out the internal link among them. By contrast, the second set of questions are reorganized into three general questions and each general question contains two specific questions. The first question is to obtain an overall picture of the use of L1 in L2 writing, the second question to find out to what extent the use of L1 is affected by other factors such as the types of writing tasks and L2 proficiency, the third question to identify specific functions of L1 in L2 writing and the relation between L1 use and L2 writing quality. The link among the three general questions has thus surfaced (See Figure 3.3).

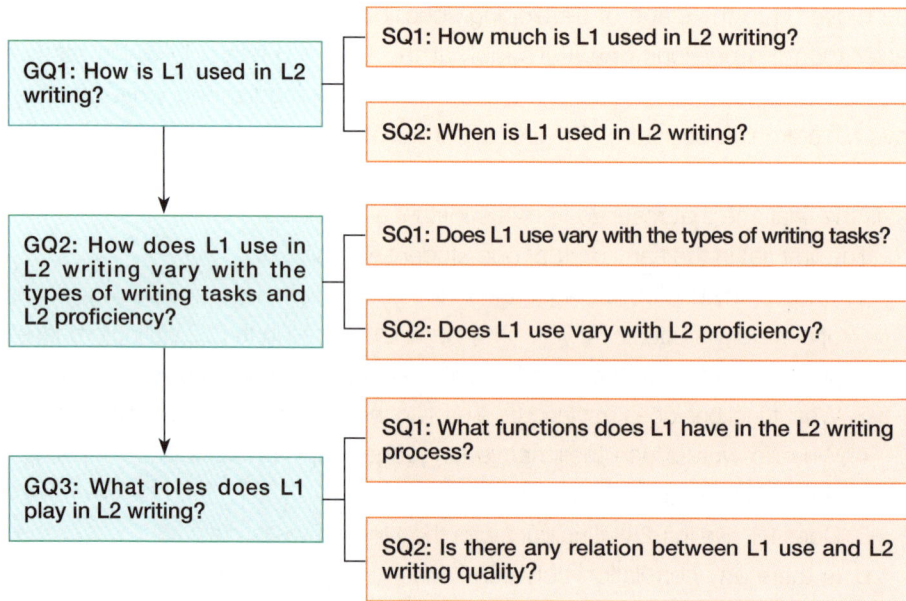

GQ1: How is L1 used in L2 writing?	SQ1: How much is L1 used in L2 writing?
	SQ2: When is L1 used in L2 writing?
GQ2: How does L1 use in L2 writing vary with the types of writing tasks and L2 proficiency?	SQ1: Does L1 use vary with the types of writing tasks?
	SQ2: Does L1 use vary with L2 proficiency?
GQ3: What roles does L1 play in L2 writing?	SQ1: What functions does L1 have in the L2 writing process?
	SQ2: Is there any relation between L1 use and L2 writing quality?

Figure 3.3: A graphic description of the second set of questions

Now let's work together to revise the following set of questions. The following study is to investigate the relationship between risk-taking beliefs and behaviors of English majors in China. Wang (1999) formed a set of questions at the beginning, which in my opinion is like a shopping list:

1. What do Chinese students think of risk-taking in English learning?
2. What risk-taking behaviors do Chinese students show in L2 learning?
3. To what extent are their risk-taking beliefs and risk-taking behaviors correlated to each other?
4. What do high, moderate, and low risk-takers think about risk-taking respectively?
5. What are the behaviors of high, moderate, and low risk-taking believers?
6. What is the correlation between the risk-taking beliefs and the risk-taking behaviors if the students are divided into high, moderate, and low risk-taking believers?

Suppose you were the supervisor of Wang, how would you help her revise the questions? I would like to share my experience with you when I was her supervisor. First of all, I asked her to list different types of variables. She explained that in her study, students' risk-taking beliefs are an independent variable and students' risk-taking behaviors are a dependent variable while differences in risk-taking beliefs are a moderator variable. Secondly, I asked her to form general questions first, which should cover the different types of variables she intended to investigate. She formed two questions: (1) To what extent do Chinese students' risk-taking beliefs affect their risk-taking behaviors? (2) To what extent do the differences in Chinese students' risk-taking beliefs modify the relationship between the risk-taking beliefs and the risk-taking behaviors? Once the two general questions were constructed, she moved to shape the specific questions which in fact reflected her research procedures for answering each general research question. In other words, she could not get answers to the general questions directly. What she could do was to dissect each general question into several sub-questions or specific questions. In general, once the researcher can well construct the general questions which are logically linked, it would be much easier for the researcher to shape the specific questions under each general question.

Figure 3.4 shows how to revise the questions which are not logically

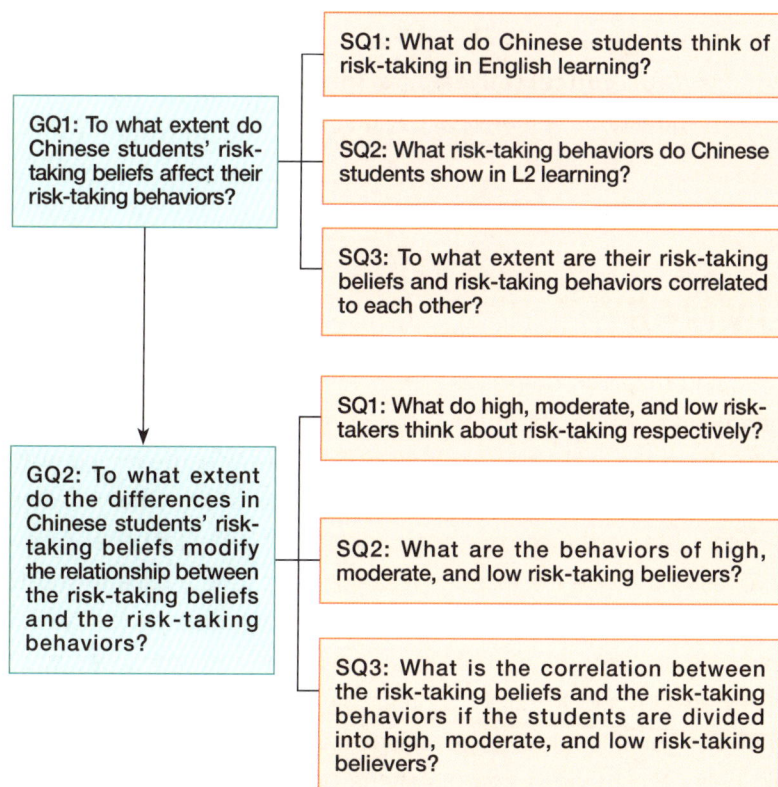

Figure 3.4: The revised version of Wang's research questions

connected. The basic procedure for such revision involves three steps. The first step is to specify the types of the variables (independent, dependent, or moderate); the second step is to form general research questions, which should involve all the variables; the third step is to construct specific questions to answer each general question. For the sake of discussion, I have described them in a sequence. However, the real practice could be recursive.

SUMMARY

Developing research questions starts with identifying a research topic that needs narrowing down to obtain the focus of research. The strategy that can help you narrow down the topic is to keep on asking questions beginning with "who," "what" and "how." Reading the literature and discussing with other researchers are necessary for obtaining a research topic, determining the focus, and developing research questions. Once the focus of research is specified, general questions are expected to be developed together with a subset of more specific ones. Would-be researchers are very often troubled by having no research ideas at the initial stage. They are advised to reflect on their own learning experience, and attend conferences or guest lectures to gain inspirations. They may also be troubled by the topic being too broad or the questions being trivial. The last problem they often encounter is that their questions are presented as a shopping list without a hierarchical structure.

AFTER-READING ACTIVITIES

Reviewing

1 What are the general procedures by which research questions are developed?

2 When you identify a research topic, what should you consider first?

3 What strategies can you use in narrowing down your topic to get a focus?

4 What kind of contribution can doing literature review make to the development of research questions?

5 Why do we need to formulate general as well as specific questions?

Exploring

1 Try to narrow down the following topics.
- The learning of English articles
- The mastery of modal verbs by Chinese learners
- The teaching of English tense system
- The teaching of L2 argumentative writing
- The relationship between the use of L1 and L2 learning

2 Classify the questions given to show the logical relationship between general and specific questions. (Note: These questions are from a student's thesis with some modifications).

A study of error correction in university EFL classrooms

(1) How do intensive reading teachers correct their students' errors?

(2) Is there any difference between English-major teachers and non-English major teachers in error correction?

(3) What are the students' attitudes toward error correction?

(4) Is there any difference between English majors and non-English majors in their attitudes and preferences?

(5) As far as error treatment is concerned, to what extent can the teachers' behaviors match the students' expectations?

(Hu, 1999)

Chapter 4

Reading the literature

Reading the literature is a task that should go hand in hand with the progress of your research. However, at different phases of research, the purposes of reading the literature are not the same. In the previous chapter, it was mentioned that reading the literature can help you draw inspirations and find an interesting topic, check whether your chosen topic is worth investigating, and learn how to present research questions. However, the way of doing a literature review is not demonstrated and explained. This chapter will give you a detailed account of how to do a literature review in order to develop research questions. To be specific, this chapter will focus on the first round of reviewing the literature while presenting some basic knowledge of doing a literature review in general.

SOURCES OF LITERATURE

At the most general level, materials for the literature review can be roughly divided into two groups: One is within the field of applied linguistics and the other is in related fields such as sociolinguistics, psycholinguistics, education, psychology, and sociology. In a thorough and extensive literature review, the sources of literature should not be confined to the field of applied linguistics since the research on second language teaching and learning often borrows ideas and research methods from related fields. The question as to how much you should review within your own field and other fields will also be discussed.

In each field, there are various kinds of sources for locating references, such as indexes, unpublished papers, journals, and books. I will introduce these different types of resources one by one.

Indexes

Indexes or bibliographies are published monthly, quarterly, biannually, or annually. They are good sources for activating your literature review. Table 4.1 lists some examples which are most commonly used by applied linguists.

Indexes offer readers a large number of references on a variety of topics, which are presented according to an author's name and subject. They provide various types of useful information such as the year of publication, the place of publication and the name of the publishing house, where and how it can be obtained, and the form in which it was published (paper, article, or report). Most indexes also contain abstracts or summaries of the material concerned.

Name of the index	How often it is published	Where it is published	Information provided
Language Teaching	Quarterly	Cambridge: Cambridge University Press	References to journal articles, books, and reports
Resources in Education	Monthly	Washington, DC: Government Printing Office	References to articles, abstracts of reports, conference papers, and other studies
Current Index to Journals in Education	Monthly	Phoenix, AZ: Oryx Press	References to articles related to education appearing in about 780 journals

Table 4.1: Examples of indexes

Unpublished papers

Unpublished papers[1] refer to conference papers or manuscripts circulated among colleagues for discussion. They can be valuable sources for finding out about ongoing or recently completed work. Very often in such papers, in addition to the titles of papers and abstracts, you will find the names of presenters and their mailing addresses as well as email addresses. Thus, you can easily contact the author if you want any additional help from him/her. Some unpublished materials can provide you with up-to-date references while some published materials are usually reports on projects finished one to three years ago.

Journals

A journal or periodical is a collection of papers, which is published regularly. Different journals target different readers. In second language acquisition, some journals are primarily

---

[1] Unpublished papers should be listed in your references just like published papers; you should specify "manuscript" and where and when it is circulated (e.g. course handout, which course; conference paper, which conference; M.A. thesis, which university). The same goes for papers published on the web; the website URL should be given. Otherwise you will be regarded as committing plagiarism.

for researchers; some more oriented toward practitioners; some for both types of readers.

The following list of journals covers major ones in the field of applied linguistics: *Applied Psycholinguistics*, *Applied Linguistics*, *Annual Review of Applied Linguistics*, *The Canadian Modern Language Review*, *ELT Journal*, *English Teaching Forum*, *Foreign Language Annals*, *Interlanguage Studies Bulletin*, *Language Testing*, *Language Acquisition*, *Language Learning*, *The Modern Language Journal*, *Second Language Research*, *Studies in Second Language Acquisition*, *System*, *TESOL Quarterly*, *English for Specific Purposes*, *TESOL Journal*, and *Asian Journal of English Language Teaching*.

Among the journals listed above, for example, *Applied Linguistics* and *Language Acquisition* are typically oriented toward researchers; *ELT Journal* and *English Teaching Forum*, primarily for practitioners; *System* and *TESOL Quarterly*, for both types of readers. Generally speaking, the journals oriented toward researchers are more valuable for your literature review than those targeting practitioners. However, if you read papers for practitioners with a critical eye, you can get a sense for the current problems in teaching methodology, which may be quite relevant to formulating research questions.

Books

There are four kinds of books that can be used for locating references: (1) textbooks; (2) encyclopedias and dictionaries of linguistics; (3) research monographs; (4) an edited collection of papers.

Textbooks provide good introductory surveys and explain concepts more systematically than research papers do. They provide an overview of a topic area which student researchers neglect and which is invariably taken for granted by writers in journals. Furthermore, papers in journals never have the space to give background knowledge.

Reference sources like encyclopedias and dictionaries of linguistics are particularly good for finding out the definitions of key concepts and the origins of the research into these concepts. Working with recent literature, you might get the most recent controversy or definition but not the original source. The most useful encyclopedias and dictionaries for you include David Crystal's *The Cambridge Encyclopedia of Language*, Tom McArthur's *Oxford Companion to the English Language,* and Jack Richards, John Platt, and Heidi Weber's *Longman Dictionary of Applied Linguistics*.

Research monographs give a single author's (or joint authors') theory or viewpoint about a topic, and can be quite important for the development of the field, e.g. *Language Two*.

An edited collection of papers arises out of a conference, or an invitation from the editor, or the need for collaborative research on an interdisciplinary topic. The papers pool together the expertise of many people to shed light on the central topic or topics. They have a clear focus and deal with topics from a particular perspective.

Compared with indexes, unpublished papers, and journals, books as a source for locating references may have their own weaknesses. For example, the references in a book are usually not recent ones since it takes much longer time to write a book than a paper. Remember that books give you the background while journals bring you what is new.

PROCEDURES FOR REVIEWING THE LITERATURE

Novice researchers often have the experience of feeling overwhelmed once they enter the library, because of the vast amount of materials surrounding them.

In this section, I will recommend to you a set of procedures which can help you get done the job of reviewing the literature effectively (See Figure 4.1). However, this is not the only possible approach.

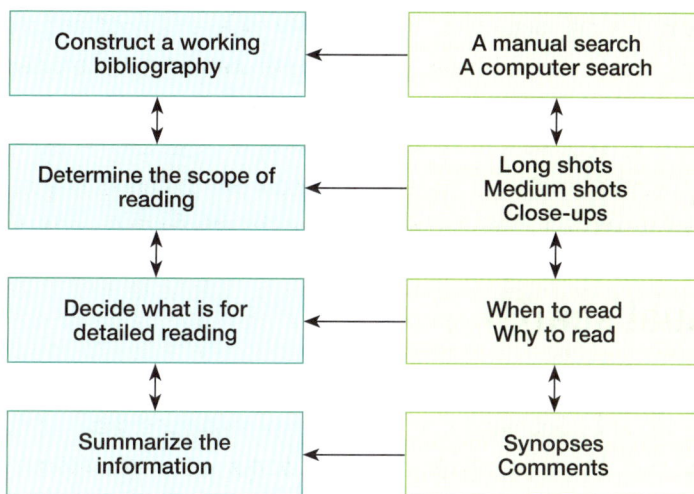

Figure 4.1: Procedures for reviewing the literature

CONSTRUCTING A WORKING BIBLIOGRAPHY

What is a working bibliography?

A working bibliography is a tentative list of references constructed by the researcher for the preparation of reviewing the literature. It may serve two purposes. Firstly, it can be used as a blueprint to guide your review of the literature. Secondly, it can be taken as a resource bank based on which you construct the section of references at the end of your thesis. Normally, you keep revising your thesis. As a result of revision, the materials you refer to are changing. You might refer to a paper today, cross it out tomorrow, and add it again the day after tomorrow. If you change the section of references after each revision, it will be very troublesome. The more economical way is to produce a reference list by selecting the cited works from your working bibliography once you finish all the revisions of the thesis.

The references in a working bibliography should be arranged alphabetically and each entry should contain the name(s) of the author(s), the title of the reference, facts about publication, page numbers, and so on. If the reference is to a journal article, it should include the name of the journal, the volume, and inclusive page numbers. If it is to a book, it should contain information about the publisher and the date of publication. Each entry should be double-checked to make sure all the information in the entry is accurate. Tolerating a mistake at this stage will lead to a huge trouble afterward. It might take you an enormous amount of time to retrieve the page number of a reference paper, or the correct spelling of the name of an author.

How do you locate the resources to construct such a list? Primarily, there are two kinds of searches through which you can locate them: (1) a manual search; and (2) a computer search. A computer search is obviously more advanced and more efficient than a manual one. However, libraries in some universities are not computerized, or the databases for applied linguistics and its related fields are not available. In this situation, you have to search for the sources manually without other choices. Even in those universities where a computerized system is available, a manual search cannot be totally avoided. Thus, in the following parts, these two kinds of searches will be introduced in turn.

A manual search

In a manual search, the researcher has to locate the materials physically without the help of computers. From my own experience and those of our graduate students, we feel that a snowballing method works rather effectively in this case: You start with a few references, each of which can generate a few more and after you repeat the process, your reference list grows. To be specific, you may begin with the references in one paper that you think is most closely related to the topic. By screening through the whole list of references, you weed out those that appear to be irrelevant. Through such a screening, if you are lucky enough, you may have 10 to 15 references left, among which you can find 5 to 10 in your library. At the second stage, you read the abstracts of these 5 to 10 papers to decide whether they are related to your topic or not. Suppose among them only five papers are valuable. As a result, these five are kept and the others are removed from the list. Then you repeat the procedures for the first stage to go through each of these five papers: screening through the reference list at the end of each paper to get rid of the irrelevant ones and searching for those apparently relevant references. Gradually, the number of references grows exponentially till the list can well form a working bibliography.

Remember, at this stage, you only need to read the abstract of each paper rather than the full paper. Reading the full papers will be too time-consuming and will get you bogged in details, whereas comparing the abstracts allows you to see a larger picture of the range of references which are relevant to your topic.

A computer search

In a computer search, we can easily and efficiently construct a working bibliography based on the information provided by electronic databases. We can use a search engine to obtain some relevant information. The popular engine we now often use is EBSCOhost which includes about 60 databases and among them 10 can provide full texts. If you key in EBSCO, you will see the following picture "Select Resource" (See Figure 4.2). Then you further click "one stop search" (一站式检索), you will see the search screen as in Figure 4.3. To obtain the relevant reference materials, you can search by topic or by author or by entering the appropriate keywords in the appropriate boxes.

Figure 4.2: The EBSCOhost screen

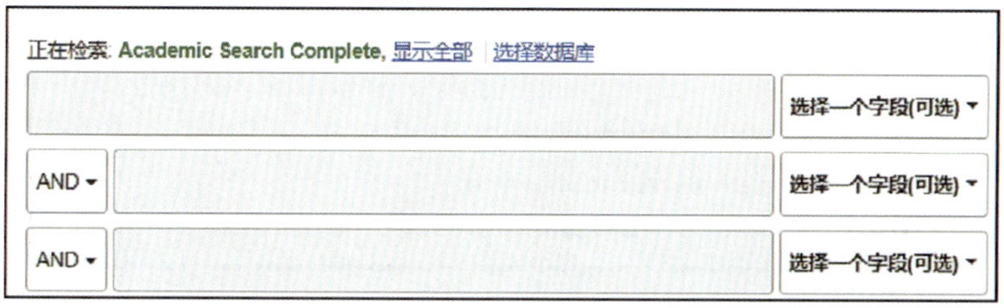

Figure 4.3: The search screen of EBSCOhost

Suppose you are interested in vocabulary teaching in the foreign language context. The keywords you enter are "vocabulary teaching" and "foreign language teaching" (See Figure 4.4).

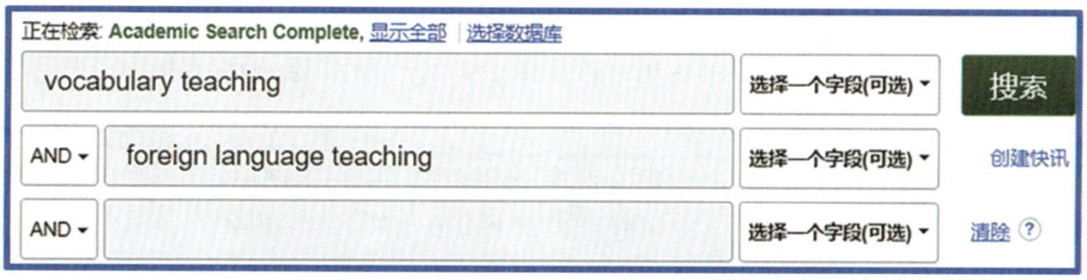

Figure 4.4: The screen with keywords entered

Clicking "search," you can get the following results as shown in Figure 4.5. It shows you that the total number of relevant papers (1,172), the papers' titles, and some detailed information concerning citations.

Figure 4.5: The results of entering the keywords "vocabulary teaching" and "foreign language teaching"

The most important database in second language acquisition is provided by ERIC (Education Resources Information Center) within the U.S. Department of Education. It contains over 700,000 references and abstracts; its indexes cover about 800 journals and 13,000 documents annually (including selected books).

A list of relevant references can be generated from the database once you input the keyword. Figure 4.6 is what is immediately shown on the screen from ERIC once you key in "interlanguage." It consists of two parts. The first part reports general information about the search, i.e. altogether there are 656 citations which are in "Titles Display" format and the first page only contains the first 10 citations. The second part is a list of citations, each of which provides information about the author, the title, and the accessing number in ERIC, etc. At the end of each citation there are two links, i.e.

"Abstract" and "Complete Reference," each of which can be accessed by clicking the mouse.

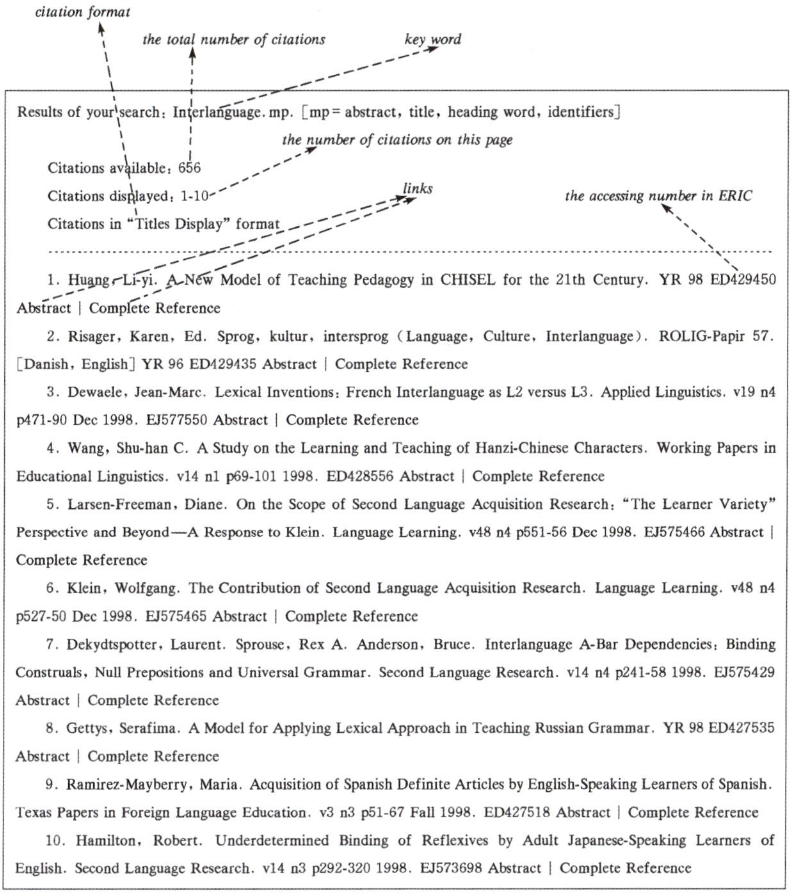

citation format

the total number of citations　　　*key word*

Results of your search: Interlanguage. mp. [mp = abstract, title, heading word, identifiers]

the number of citations on this page

Citations available: 656

Citations displayed: 1-10　　　　　　　　　*links*　　　　　　*the accessing number in ERIC*

Citations in "Titles Display" format

....

1. Huang, Li-yi. A New Model of Teaching Pedagogy in CHISEL for the 21th Century. YR 98 ED429450 Abstract | Complete Reference

2. Risager, Karen, Ed. Sprog, kultur, intersprog (Language, Culture, Interlanguage). ROLIG-Papir 57. [Danish, English] YR 96 ED429435 Abstract | Complete Reference

3. Dewaele, Jean-Marc. Lexical Inventions: French Interlanguage as L2 versus L3. Applied Linguistics. v19 n4 p471-90 Dec 1998. EJ577550 Abstract | Complete Reference

4. Wang, Shu-han C. A Study on the Learning and Teaching of Hanzi-Chinese Characters. Working Papers in Educational Linguistics. v14 n1 p69-101 1998. ED428556 Abstract | Complete Reference

5. Larsen-Freeman, Diane. On the Scope of Second Language Acquisition Research: "The Learner Variety" Perspective and Beyond—A Response to Klein. Language Learning. v48 n4 p551-56 Dec 1998. EJ575466 Abstract | Complete Reference

6. Klein, Wolfgang. The Contribution of Second Language Acquisition Research. Language Learning. v48 n4 p527-50 Dec 1998. EJ575465 Abstract | Complete Reference

7. Dekydtspotter, Laurent. Sprouse, Rex A. Anderson, Bruce. Interlanguage A-Bar Dependencies: Binding Construals, Null Prepositions and Universal Grammar. Second Language Research. v14 n4 p241-58 1998. EJ575429 Abstract | Complete Reference

8. Gettys, Serafima. A Model for Applying Lexical Approach in Teaching Russian Grammar. YR 98 ED427535 Abstract | Complete Reference

9. Ramirez-Mayberry, Maria. Acquisition of Spanish Definite Articles by English-Speaking Learners of Spanish. Texas Papers in Foreign Language Education. v3 n3 p51-67 Fall 1998. ED427518 Abstract | Complete Reference

10. Hamilton, Robert. Underdetermined Binding of Reflexives by Adult Japanese-Speaking Learners of English. Second Language Research. v14 n3 p292-320 1998. EJ573698 Abstract | Complete Reference

(Note: The italicized words are explanatory notes made by the author.)

Figure 4.6: Results generated by ERIC as an exemplar

Unlike a manual search, a computer search can generate a list of references in a few seconds which, however, is not what we call a working bibliography. Such an initial list of references has to be screened through at least three times to get rid of those irrelevant ones. In the first screening, you simply delete the citations which are obviously not useful. The second screening can be made after you read the abstract concerned by activating the link "Abstract." Finally, you have to search the computerized library system to see whether the materials are available or not. The references that survive the three times' screening can become part of your working bibliography.

A working bibliography can be produced simply by sitting in front of a computer and clicking the mouse. In this sense, the computer search can help save time and energy. Furthermore, the resources in the database are abundant and updated. Thus, a working bibliography built up through a computer search is more comprehensive than one yielded by a manual search. However, the problem with ERIC and other computer-based sources is that there is too much quantity but too little quality. You need to spend an enormous amount of time winnowing out the irrelevant literature.

≣ DECIDING ON THE SCOPE

Once a working bibliography has been constructed, you have to decide on the scope of reading, i.e. drawing a boundary for reviewing. If the scope of reviewing is too broad, you may be overwhelmed by too much reading and thus lose the right perspective on the research; if it is too narrow, you may overlook studies which contain relevant and important information. Therefore, the task of delimiting the scope of reviewing cannot be skipped over. In this section, I will provide you with some suggestions on how to set up such a tentative boundary.

Long shots, medium shots, and close-ups

To draw a boundary is to decide what should be included in the review and what should not. As we know, when drawing a picture of a landscape, instead of concentrating on the details in the beginning, the painter sketches a draft in which he/she decides what is placed as a foreground, what is set as a background, and what is in between. Similarly, for the delimiting of the boundary of a review, the researcher does not need to pinpoint the specific function of each reference or to give a detailed account on every paper or book. What is required instead is to decide which reference should be used in which type of review: a background review, a foreground review, or something between the two categories.

For the sake of having separate terms for each type of review, I would like to borrow from film-making the terms "long shots," "medium shots," and "close-ups" (Rudestam & Newton, 1992). These three kinds of shots in film production differ in the distance between the camera and the subject matter. Now their metaphorical difference in the literature review lies in their degree of detail.

A long shot or background review usually provides your project with a general framework or theoretical definitions of certain variables. This can demonstrate the justifications for your research from a theoretical perspective. A close-up or foreground review focuses on the details of some specific studies on which the design of your study is based. This is the place for you to identify the gaps in previous research. A medium shot gives a description of empirical studies on the topic in general. This part can serve as the bridge between the theory and your own study. Nevertheless, the differences among these three kinds of reviewing are relative. They can only be understood with reference to concrete cases. In other words, without the context, it is difficult to clarify what is a long shot, what is a close-up, and what is a medium shot.

> **?**
> • Do you think the literature review should include long shots, medium shots, and close-ups from the very beginning of your research? Please give an explanation of your answer.

The following are examples which can serve to illustrate the differences among the three types of reviewing.

Example 1

A study of the relationship between second-year English majors' risk-taking behaviors and L2 performance in the Chinese context:
Long shots: Materials in the field of education concerning the relationship between risk-taking behaviors and academic achievement in general
Medium shots: Materials in the field of second language acquisition that address the issue of the relationship between risk-taking behaviors and L2 performance both theoretically and empirically
Close-ups: Empirical studies on this issue in and outside the Chinese context pertinent to the proposed study

Example 2

A study of the effects of modifiable learner factors on L2 achievement of second-year English majors in the Chinese context:
Long shots: Theories in the field of education about factors affecting learning outcomes
Medium shots: Theoretical models on this issue in the field of second language acquisition; materials about English teaching and learning in the Chinese context
Close-ups: Empirical studies on this issue in and outside China

Example 3

How is L1 involved in the process of L2 composing?
Long shots: Theoretical claims on the use of L1 in L2 learning
Medium shots: Empirical studies on the same issue
Close-ups: Empirical studies confined to L2 writing with a focus on the use of L1

According to the three examples, it is clear that long shots are usually related to the materials that are theory-driven; close-ups are only concerned with empirical studies that are most relevant to your own design; medium shots can be theory-driven or data-driven.

Strategies

When you select the papers or books for reading, the initial difficulty might be the insufficiency of reading materials but later you may find there are too many papers for you to choose from. How do you deal with these two difficulties? The first difficulty is comparatively easy to overcome so long as you are familiar with the databases in your library. At the beginning, you might get frustrated and feel that your efforts are not rewarded. However, such feelings will be gone soon. Once you are patient enough to keep on searching, you might encounter the second difficulty which is more challenging to deal with. I would like to share with you three strategies to overcome it. The first strategy for you to select the reading materials is up-to-dateness, which means you should review journal articles published recently since the initial literature review is primarily for you to decide whether the topic is worth researching or not. Journal articles usually report the most recently completed studies which normally provide some suggestions for future research at the end of the articles. The second strategy for choosing the literature is the degree of authority. For example, the papers in the first-ranking international and local journals could be your first choice compared with those in other types of journals. The third strategy for winnowing out the papers from those shown in the databases is the degree of relevancy. As we discussed before, you might use EBSCOhost to retrieve the papers for the first round of the literature review. Don't download everything on the screen. Apart from considering a paper's up-to-dateness and authority, you should further read the abstract quickly to decide whether you would include it in your working bibliography. Otherwise, you will get drowned in a sea of papers later and it will take you a lot of time to sort them out.

≔ DECIDING WHAT IS FOR DETAILED READING

Before you embark on detailed reading of the selected materials, you should know clearly which aspect of the papers should be focused on in reviewing. The answer is not straightforward since the content for the reading depends on when to read and why to read as shown in Figure 4.1.

The literature review conducted at different stages of research serves different purposes. At the very beginning, you read the research papers to identify a research area, or to find out whether the topic is worth researching. In other words, this kind of literature reviewing is to define the topic and the need for it. Once you have identified the research topic, the review of the literature will help you form appropriate research questions and design your study effectively. Finally, you review the literature to discuss implications of the findings. As I pointed out above, literature reviewing occurs frequently throughout the process of research. Usually the researcher goes to the library at least once a month to read the newly published journals and update his/her working bibliography.

⬛ SUMMARIZING THE INFORMATION

When you have selected sufficient relevant materials, you will start reading them. I suggest that you read backward, beginning with the most recent one and moving back to the old ones. What should you do during and after your reading? You are supposed to synthesize the information from reading and record it in electronic cards. It is best to prepare three sets of cards: (1) cards for abstracts; (2) cards for critical comments; and (3) cards for comments concerning the potential use of the materials. Having separate cards for three kinds of information might appear to be a waste but such a filing system can facilitate retrieving afterward. Its advantage can be recognized when you are writing up your thesis. Finally, these three sets of electronic cards need to be cross-referred so that you can easily search for the information you want to retrieve.

Electronic cards for abstracts

An abstract should include the most important information in a paper. The cards are usually arranged in alphabetical order and/or according to different subheadings related to the research topic. Each abstract is entered on one card, and should contain the following information:

1. The reasons for the proposed study
2. The underlying assumptions of the study
3. The procedures used for collecting the data
4. The subjects and instruments involved in the study
5. The procedures for analyzing the data
6. The major findings of the research
7. The specific new contribution the study makes to the existing literature

In most cases, the papers themselves include abstracts, which, however, are not written to serve your purpose and thus need a lot of modifications. If a paper does not have an abstract, you have to write one. To save time, such an abstract does not need to be a coherent summary, but should be in note form.

In other words, it may contain incomplete sentences. The basic requirement for the notes is that the information recorded should be adequate for your subsequent literature review.

To write an abstract is not that difficult but it is time-consuming. Some graduate students tend to be conscientious at the beginning but grow impatient and lazy gradually since they feel their memories are good enough to remember the information and it is not worth spending so much time writing. However, they will soon realize their memories are not so reliable, and they have to go back to the piles of papers and read them again. In order to avoid such subsequent troubles, you had better form a good habit, i.e. writing an abstract as soon as you finish the reading of each paper.

Electronic cards for critical comments

Critical comments are formed through the evaluation of a study. You write down the strengths and weaknesses of the study, especially the flaws you have identified. You are advised not to wait to write them down until you finish the reading. Such comments may occur in your mind while you are reading, and are often instantaneous and transient. Note down the ideas before they disappear and organize them on a card once the reading is over.

To write evaluative comments is not as easy as writing a descriptive abstract since you have to examine the reading materials with a critical mind. You might find flaws in subject selection, or in instrument design, or in data collection, or in data analysis, or in the interpretation of the findings. A few flaws are self-evident but many more are covert. The flaws can be easily found by relating the study you are reading to other similar studies you are familiar with. Your appraising ability can be improved if you strive to be critical all the time. To be critical is not necessarily to be cynical. Apart from searching for weaknesses, you should also be sensitive to the studies' strengths and unique features which might be mentioned in your review.

Electronic cards for comments concerning the potential use of the materials

When you read a paper, you are interested in its important information, its strengths as well as its weaknesses. More important than this is that you are interested in to what extent the paper you read can be related to your own study. For this reason, we have a third kind of card, i.e. the card for comments concerning the potential use of the materials. These comments indicate to you how the material can be used at the stage of designing a study and at the stage of thesis writing. For example, you might write: This part can be referred to in developing instruments, or this point can be used in describing the conceptual framework.

Such comments do not necessarily form a coherent paragraph, or even a complete sentence. Notes can serve the purpose well so long as they make sense to you and are easy to be put in a file. According to my own experience, you need to read the most relevant papers at least twice. For the first reading, you produce those different cards mentioned. The second reading occurs when you are writing up your thesis.

Focus highlight

- As mentioned at the beginning of the chapter, reading the literature goes along with the whole process of your research. Most probably, as a researcher, you read the current issues of prestigious journals from time to time and produce different types of cards. However, you need a block of time concentrating on reading the literature at different stages of research. In this sense, you need to conduct at least three rounds of literature reviewing. The first round occurs at the beginning of your research which has already been discussed in this chapter.

- The second round of reviewing the literature takes place when you carry out your planned research. The third round is conducted when you write the "Literature review" chapter in your thesis/dissertation. How to read the literature in the second and third rounds will be discussed in later chapters.

⊟ SUMMARY

Reading the literature is a task frequently undertaken by a researcher through the whole process of research. There are various kinds of literature available in the field of applied linguistics and in related fields, such as indexes, unpublished papers, journals, and books. We may locate reading materials either by a manual search or a computer search. To begin your literature review, you construct a working bibliography, followed by delimiting the boundary of reading. The next task is to decide what to choose for detailed reading. Finally, you are expected to produce three sets of cards by synthesizing the information from reading: cards for abstracts, critical comments, and comments concerning the potential use of the materials.

AFTER-READING ACTIVITIES

Reviewing

1 What is a working bibliography?

2 Can you explain the procedures for literature reviewing?

3 What does it mean to use a snowballing method to search for the relevant reference materials?

Exploring

1 Make a list of journals that can be useful for your literature review according to the resources available in the databases of your library.

2 Use a snowballing method to produce a tentative working bibliography for a study on the risk-taking beliefs and behaviors of English majors in China.

3 Identify different types of reviewing (long shots, medium shots, and close-ups) in the following studies.

(1) Miss Wang intended to investigate how L1 is involved in the process of L2 composing. She reviewed a lot of papers. Some papers make claims on L1 use in L2 learning from a theoretical perspective; some papers are about the empirical studies on L1 use in L2 learning; and some papers are about the empirical studies on L1 use in L2 writing.

(2) Mr. Li aimed to find out the relationship between L2 learning strategies and learning outcomes of senior middle school students. He searched the EBSCOhost and selected 60 most relevant papers. Among them, 15 papers are about previous studies on the relationship between learning strategies and academic achievement; 10 papers focus on the studies on the relationship between L2 learning strategies and learning outcomes of middle school students; and the remaining ones concern university students.

4 Choose one paper from an influential journal to see what is reviewed as background, what as foreground, and what as something in between and then produce three types of cards mentioned in this chapter.

Chapter 5

Selecting research designs

Once you have formulated your research questions, you will move on to the next stage, i.e. selecting research designs. Generally speaking, there are two opposing camps in the fields of social sciences, i.e. quantitative and qualitative. In this chapter, I will first present to you a general picture of quantitative and qualitative designs, then discuss the link between research questions and research designs, and finally illustrate some important issues involved in research design selection.

QUANTITATIVE AND QUALITATIVE

> • What is your understanding of the differences between a quantitative design and a qualitative one? Why should the researcher differentiate between these two kinds of designs?

The general description in this section will start with definitions of quantitative and qualitative designs followed by their general differences, and then move on to the historical development of the two designs. The section will end with the advantages of using the two designs in combination.

Definitions

It is difficult to define quantitative research and qualitative research in one or two sentences since they do have a series of differences. To make the whole issue simpler at the beginning, let's first look at Punch's definitions (1998, p. 4).

- Quantitative research is empirical research where the data are in the form of numbers.
- Qualitative research is empirical research where the data are not in the form of numbers.

According to Punch's definitions, both quantitative and qualitative research are primary research but they differ in the form of data. Quantitative data are numeric while qualitative are not. Thus, the best and simplest way to differentiate these two kinds of research is to check whether the data collected are presented in the form of numbers or not. Other researchers such as Blaxter, Hughes, and Tight (1996) and Tashakkori and Teddlie (1998) also suggest the numeric-narrative[1] contrast to capture their essential difference although they admit that it is oversimplified to some extent.

Let's now look at some examples of numeric data.

Example 1

Suppose you wanted to find out your students' vocabulary size and thus you designed a test. The test consisted of 100 words randomly selected from the syllabus, and the students were asked to give a Chinese equivalent to each English word given. If an answer was correct, one point was obtained. Once the test paper was corrected, each student got a test score representing the vocabulary size. Here the test scores are numeric in nature and are thus quantitative data.

Example 2

Suppose you intended to find out the strategies used by students in increasing their vocabulary. You constructed a questionnaire that contained 20 statements about the strategies, such as "I pay attention to the new words used by my teachers and classmates" and "I try at every opportunity to use the words I have just learned." Each statement was followed by three choices from which the students were only allowed to choose one. These three choices form a three-point scale: Often—Sometimes—Rarely. Once the students' questionnaires were collected, you converted their responses into numbers: "1" standing for "Rarely," "2" for "Sometimes," and "3" for "Often." Eventually, all the selected responses were changed into numbers. Hence, in this case, the use of strategies is converted into quantitative data.

In contrast to quantitative data, qualitative data are narrative in most cases, if not in all. For example, to investigate vocabulary expansion strategies, instead

---

[1] "Narrative" means describing something in words.

of using a questionnaire, you may interview 20 students and ask them how they increase their vocabulary. They answer this open-ended question verbally and their answers are bound to be varied. Such diversified verbal answers are hence narrative data. Consider two more examples. In the first example, Researcher A intended to find out the difference between the less successful English learners and the successful English learners in their after-class listening activities. She interviewed 10 second-year students majoring in English who were evenly divided into two groups according to their English proficiency level. Wang Hong as the first one of the less successful learners was interviewed by Researcher A. In the second example, Researcher B aimed to find out English teachers' attitudes toward the production-oriented approach in Chinese universities. She interviewed three English teachers who have 10 more years' teaching experience. Zhang Fang was the first English teacher who was interviewed by Researcher B.

Example 1

Researcher A: When do you listen to English programs?
Wang Hong: Every night before I go to sleep, I like to listen to English programs. However, I fall into sleep gradually. I also like to do listening activities while washing my clothes or doing house chores.
Researcher A: Do you think your listening skill has been improved?
Wang Hong: I don't think I have made any noticeable progress in listening.
Researcher A: Have you ever thought of why you could not achieve marked improvement?
Wang Hong: I don't know why. You see if I know "why," I can easily solve the problem. I believe practice makes perfect. I just try to do more listening in my spare time. Although I cannot make fast progress, I will move forward bit by bit.

Example 2

Researcher B: Have you ever heard of the production-oriented approach to teaching English?
Zhang Fang: I have read the paper about the production-oriented approach. I think this is innovative in solving the problem of separation of input from output.
Researcher B: Do you think you would like to try it out in your English teaching?
Zhang Fang: I wish I could have a try but the problem is that I don't think I have a sound understanding of the theory of the production-oriented approach. Moreover, I lack the ability of putting theory into practice.
Researcher B: If you have an opportunity to attend a workshop on the production-oriented approach, would you like to participate in it?
Zhang Fang: Sure, I would like to.

In the two examples mentioned, the interview data are verbal accounts which are narrative in nature and cannot be transformed into figures.

Apart from the critical difference in the form of data, the two types of research designs have many more important differences which affect various phases of a research process. In the following part, these important differences will be described.

More differences

Table 5.1 adapted from Malhotra's (1993, p. 159) summarizes the differences between quantitative and qualitative designs in addition to the numeric-narrative contrast.

	Quantitative	Qualitative
Objectives	Examining variables identified Testing hypotheses	Identifying variables Generating hypotheses
Questions	Specified before data collection	Gradually specified in the process
Sample	A large sample	A small sample
Data collection	Structured	Less structured
Data analysis	Statistical	Non-statistical and statistical
Outcomes	Generalizable	Ungeneralizable

Table 5.1: Differences between quantitative and qualitative designs

According to Malhotra, quantitative and qualitative designs are used to achieve different objectives. For the former, its goal is to examine variables that have already been established in the literature and to see to what extent hypotheses regarding these variables can be confirmed or refuted; for the latter, the aim is to identify variables for further research and to formulate hypotheses for testing in the future. In other words, quantitative research is more powerful when the research is to validate the findings in previous studies; qualitative research is more useful when the research is exploratory in nature.

Questions for the quantitative design are prespecified in the sense that they are constructed ahead of the empirical study. The prespecified questions help decide on the procedures for subject selection, data collection, and data analysis in advance. The researcher thus has fewer uncertainties and ambiguities once the research starts. In contrast, questions for the qualitative design are rather general before data collection and become focused gradually along with the progress of the research. Consequently, it is quite common in qualitative research that the focus of data collection shifts and the way of data analysis changes over time.

Quantitative research often needs a large sample to satisfy statistical requirements when it tests hypotheses. By contrast, qualitative research usually involves a small sample because an in-depth study requires an enormous amount of time and energy. However, whether the sample size is large or small cannot be defined in an absolute sense. A sample involved in a quantitative study could vary from 30 to 3,000 while a sample for a qualitative one could range from 1 to 30 depending on the purpose.

As for data collection, quantitative data are usually collected through more structured procedures in the sense that the procedures are prespecified and standardized. By contrast, procedures for data collection in qualitative research are more flexible and dynamic. In other words, qualitative researchers cannot design a detailed plan with specific steps for data collection. What he/she can do is to construct an overall plan which can point out the general direction. For the small details, he/she needs to make decisions aligned with the progress of the research.

Quantitative data can only be analyzed statistically while qualitative data are normally analyzed non-statistically although statistical analysis could also be an alternative. That is to say, quantitative data analysis has only one option while qualitative one has two. However, the choice is selected to best serve the purpose.

Due to the exploratory nature of qualitative research that involves a few cases, the outcomes are less generalizable than the findings yielded by quantitative research. After all, qualitative research in the first place is not aimed at establishing universal laws that can be applied beyond the cases in question.

Historical development of the two designs

The debate on the quantitative-qualitative issue has been going on for years. Reviewing the history, we may roughly identify two stages: (1) the mono-design stage; and (2) the mixed design stage (Tashakkori & Teddlie, 1998).

The mono-design stage

From the 19th century to the mid-20th century, either the quantitative or qualitative design was employed in a single study although some researchers tried to collect data by different techniques within either the quantitative or qualitative design. Thus, we designate this period as the mono-design era.

Before the 1950s, the quantitative design was in a dominant position while the qualitative one was peripheral. The popularity of the quantitative design was primarily due to its remarkable success in natural sciences in the 20th century. Social sciences, in order to justify their status as scientific, followed natural sciences. They tried to quantify what they studied and establish the relation or pattern between two or more variables. Quantitative findings were believed to be more powerful and convincing than verbal accounts since it was widely assumed that without numbers, the scientific nature of a study would be called into question.

However, in the 1960s, quantitative designs started to be challenged and qualitative designs gradually moved into the mainstream of social science research. Many social scientists argued that social reality was different from natural reality and thus transplanting the quantitative design for natural sciences into social sciences was not appropriate. Obviously, human beings and the societies in which they live cannot be studied in the same way as natural objects such as rocks and trees. Furthermore, natural scientists can study physical objects in a detached way but social scientists who are part of a society cannot be totally separated from the society even if they want to. Starting in the 1960s, the debate on the quantitative-qualitative issue became more and more intense. Supporters of the two designs were often intolerant and unreconciled. Each side criticized the other harshly and strove to argue for its own superiority. Naturally, studies conducted by the researchers from the two different camps were either quantitative or qualitative.

The mixed design stage

Since the 1980s, many social scientists, having realized that such a debate on the superiority of designs is unproductive, have tried their best to make peace between the two opposing camps. They advocate that the world is so complex that both quantitative and qualitative designs are needed if the eventual purpose of research is to have a whole picture of the world. In their opinion, these two designs each have strengths as well as weaknesses. They are complementary to each other rather than in conflict. A quantitative design can be used in a large-scale study, which can provide a succinct and parsimonious pattern. The results are generalizable, but are often oversimplified and show poor ecological validity[1]. A qualitative design can produce a more realistic picture of reality and reveal more complexities, but it is time-consuming and the results are not generalizable (Cohen & Manion, 1989; Keeves & Sowden, 1992). Merton and Kendall who promoted the combination of these two designs said, "Social scientists have come to abandon the spurious choice between qualitative and quantitative data: They are concerned rather with that combination of both, which makes use of the most valuable features of each." (cited by Cohen & Manion, 1989, p. 42) Marton (1981) emphasizes that the results obtained by the two designs can present a better picture of the

---

[1] Ecological validity refers to the extent to which the findings can be applied to real life. Very often a quantitative study, in order to strictly control the factors not investigated in the study, is conducted in a laboratory. Therefore, the findings obtained from the laboratory can be hardly applied successfully to a real situation.

object investigated. They are more reliable and of higher validity in comparison with a single design approach. Markee (1994) maintains the same view by saying "Qualitative and quantitative studies are in reality complementary ways of creating new knowledge. Recently, more researchers, instead of relying on one design exclusively, use whatever design is appropriate for their studies." (e. g. Wang, 1999; C. X. Wu, 1998; Préfontaine & Kormos, 2015)

Advantages of using the two designs together

As said before, the use of the two designs together, compared with the use of a single design, can produce more powerful and more convincing results. The following is an example used by Patton (1990) to illustrate this point.

In the early 1970s, a new accountability system was implemented in some schools in Michigan. The new system was rather complicated, and included comprehensive and systematic procedures to evaluate the teachers, such as standardized achievement tests, criterion reference tests, teacher peer ratings, student ratings of teachers, parent ratings of teachers, principal ratings of teachers, and teachers' self-ratings. The school authorities made a very positive assessment of such an accountability system while the teachers' association and teachers themselves had rather different views about it. In the spring of 1976, the Kalamazoo Education Association, with assistance from the Michigan Education Association and the National Education Association, conducted a study to find out the teachers' evaluation of and their own attitude toward the accountability system. The teachers were asked to answer a questionnaire that included both multiple-choice questions and open-ended questions. The quantitative data from multiple-choice questions indicated that almost all the teachers felt the accountability system was ineffective and inadequate. Seventy percent of the teachers who responded to the questionnaire also answered one of the open-ended questions and their answers filled 101 pages.

In this case, the quantitative findings informed the school authorities of the overall evaluation given by the teachers about the accountability system. The disadvantage of numbers was being "detached" and "frozen" since they were not able to evoke readers' emotions. Furthermore, school board members could easily regard the quantitative findings as a predictable attempt of the union to discredit school officials. However, once the school officials read through a few pages of the teachers' own personal comments and the verbal descriptions of their anguish, fear, and frustration with the accountability system, they understood the problems and also thought about what they should do to deal with the problems.

The above example vividly shows the strengths of combining quantitative research with qualitative research. Quantitative research in this case involves a set of standardized statements which are difficult to design but can easily be answered by the teachers. Furthermore, the data analysis is simple and straightforward. However, the findings presented in the form of numbers usually cannot touch upon people's emotions. By contrast, the questions for qualitative research are simple in design but troublesome to answer.

The qualitative data are more detailed and more diversified in content, and thus the analysis of them is much more difficult. Yet, the open-ended responses enable the researcher to understand and capture the points of view of other people which otherwise are not available.

≡ LINKS BETWEEN QUESTIONS AND DESIGNS

In this section, I will try to answer an important question in design selection: What is the relation between questions and designs?

Questions first or designs first?

What is our starting point when we select a research design? Should we start with research questions or with a research design? Logically speaking, questions should always come first. In other words, questions dictate the design rather than the other way around (Punch, 1998; Tashakkori & Teddlie, 1998). In this sense, the formulation of research questions must be finished before the choice of the design. To put it simply, we should first think clearly what we are trying to research and then consider how we are going to conduct the research. If we are not sure what we aim at, then, there is no point in thinking of the design.

However, some researchers tend to put research designs before research questions. They may first decide what design they would like to use and then find the research questions that can fit into the design. In this way, their research questions would be guided by the design. Such a reversed sequence is very dangerous and can "lead to polarized thinking and intolerant and exclusionary attitudes" (Johnson, 1992, p. 228). That is to say, the researchers may perceive different designs as in conflict with each other which cannot be reconciled; or they may maintain that one type of design is superior to another without considering their strengths in addressing particular questions.

Actually, there are no good or bad designs as such. Each design is effective in answering certain types of questions but not others. Each design has its own strengths and weaknesses. What counts is whether the design fits a particular question.

- **Why should the researcher focus his/her primary attention on the development of research questions and then select a proper research design to answer the questions?**

How to match questions with designs?

Different questions need to be tackled by different designs. Generally speaking, all research questions can be put into two big groups. One group of questions must be answered by the quantitative design while the other must be answered by the qualitative design. The common practice in today's research is to include two groups of questions in a single project. Thus, matching questions with designs becomes more essential. Often the wording of a question has implications for the designs to be chosen. For example, words and phrases like "variables," "the correlation between X and Y," "factors affecting L2 achievement," etc. imply a quantitative design, while "how" and "why" might imply a qualitative design. However, novice student researchers often mismatch a question and a design. One of the reasons is their being unfamiliar with the implications of these words and phrases.

Let's look at some research questions and see how the wording of a question may offer us information about the research design. Suppose we are doing research on motivation. The first question might be: What is the relation between students' motivation and their L2 learning outcomes? (Or, to what extent can students' motivation predict their L2 learning outcomes?) The wording like "relation" and "predict" clearly implies that the questions are quantitative in nature and thus a quantitative design such as a survey can well serve the research purpose. A second question might be: Which approach (the Traditional Approach or the Communicative Approach) is more effective in motivating middle school students to learn the past tense in an L2 class? To make a comparison of the effectiveness of the two teaching approaches, a quantitative design such as an experiment is needed. A third question might be: Why are some students better motivated than others? Obviously, the reasons that can account for motivation might be various and difficult to quantify. Most likely, we would employ a qualitative design such as a case study to find out such reasons.

Although certain words and phrases may imply designs, in many cases the wording of questions does not give us any clues to which design should be used. For example, our question might be: What are the differences between well-motivated and poorly-motivated learners? This question can be tackled by both the quantitative design and the qualitative design depending on how much previous research has been done in this area and the focus of the study. If there are a lot of similar studies available and the area is rather well-researched, a quantitative design might be a better choice to confirm or dispute previous findings. If you are interested in detailed and vivid differences between these two kinds of learners rather than quantitative differences, a qualitative design certainly can do a better job.

A MONO-DESIGN AND A MIXED DESIGN

By using a mono-design, I mean only one design is employed, either quantitative or qualitative. Within the same design, the researcher may collect data from a single source or multiple sources. If a mixed design is employed, both quantitative and qualitative designs are adopted. They may be arranged in a different sequence. This section will discuss these two types of designs in turn.

A mono-design

A mono-design can be simple or complex. In a simple design, data are collected from one single source. Let's start with a simple quantitative design first. Suppose one researcher intended to find out the best ways to motivate students to learn an L2. The researcher asked students to answer a questionnaire in which various ways were listed and students were asked to rank order them. In this case, the data are from a single source, i.e. the students' responses to the questionnaire. The same study can adopt a complex design as well. For example, in addition to the questionnaire for students, the researcher might also ask L2 teachers in 10 different schools to answer a questionnaire in which they are asked to rank order the same set of motivating strategies. The study could become further complicated by adding an experiment in which different motivating strategies are compared in terms of their effectiveness.

Similarly, a qualitative design can range from simple to complex. Let's look at the same question: What are the best ways to motivate students to learn an L2? Suppose you interviewed 15 students who represented three levels of L2 proficiency in a class. The interviews were conducted individually and each student was asked to list the methods through which their teachers had tried to motivate them and then to make comments on these motivating strategies. If the study is limited to students' interviews, then it is a simple qualitative design. You may make the design complex by including interviews of teachers or by adding the component of observing the classes to see how students respond to teachers' motivating strategies, and what strategies teachers are actually using.

Let's look at two examples of simple designs.

Example 1

A simple quantitative design

The study intended to examine the relationship between learner factors and English learning outcomes. In March 1995, more than 1,700 non-English majors who were from three universities located in Heilongjiang, Shandong, and Jiangsu provinces responded to the Learner Factors Questionnaire and in June 1995, they took CET-4. The results yielded by multiple regression analysis indicate which learner factors have predicting power in relation to students' scores on CET. (Wen & Wang, 1996)

Example 2

A simple qualitative design

The study attempted to find out whether students with higher L2 proficiency used reading strategies differently from students with lower L2 proficiency. The subjects involved were four students who majored in Russian and Japanese, and studied English as their second foreign language. All of them were good students in their major study but in English learning, two of them were at the lower-intermediate level, and the other two at the upper-intermediate level. The researcher selected two reading passages to match their English proficiency respectively. Each student was asked to read the passage individually while speaking aloud what was going on in his/her mind. The whole process was recorded and transcribed subsequently. The strategies used by the students were categorized and then presented. A comparison was made between these two groups in terms of their use of reading strategies. (Lu, 1997)

In the above two examples, each study employed a simple design. In Example 1, the researchers used a questionnaire to obtain data about learner factors and the scores on CET-4 as the students' learning outcomes. It is clear that in a simple quantitative design, one instrument is employed for one variable. In Example 2, the researcher asked four good Russian and Japanese learners with different proficiency levels of English to read English passages which matched their English proficiency. The four participants were required to read the passage while doing think-aloud. Obviously, the participants only accomplished one reading task while thinking aloud for the purpose of collecting data about the use of reading strategies. To sum up, when the data about each variable in a study are from a single source, the design is called a simple design.

Now let's look at another two examples of complex designs.

Example 1

A complex quantitative design

The study aimed at examining the relationship between the use of English vocabulary learning strategies and vocabulary learning outcomes. Sixty second-year university students from two intact classes were invited to respond to a questionnaire on vocabulary learning strategies in general. Then they were asked to learn 10 new words while ranking order the specific strategies provided in relation to the learning of these words. Their vocabulary learning outcomes were measured by two tests. The first test was about their vocabulary sizes and the second was about the results of learning the 10 new words.

Example 2

A complex qualitative design

The study intended to find out the differences between higher-level and lower-level English learners in their habits of reading English. Ten first-year university students were invited to participate in the study. They were evenly divided into two groups in terms of their English proficiency. They were asked to accomplish two tasks. The first task was to write journals for one week recording their behaviors of reading English such as when, how long, and what to be read, etc. The second task was to perform a reading activity individually while a video camera was recording everyone's behavior.

In the first example listed above, the researcher collected the data about the participants' vocabulary learning strategies from two sources. The first is a questionnaire concerning vocabulary learning strategies in general and the second is the list of learning strategies given in relation to learning 10 specific new words. Furthermore, their vocabulary learning outcomes are measured by two instruments: One is a vocabulary-size test in general and the other is the test of the 10 new words. All the data in Example 1 are numeric in nature. In the second example mentioned above, the participants' habits of reading English were identified also from two sets of data which are, however, not figures: students' journals and video recordings. To sum up, a complex design, no matter whether it is quantitative or qualitative, involves data collected from more than one source.

A mixed design

A mixed design, as its name suggests, always involves both quantitative and qualitative designs. However, the ways the two designs are arranged may be various. In terms of the time, we may have sequential or parallel designs. In a sequential design, the quantitative design is used before the qualitative one, or the other way around. The sequential order of the two types of designs is logically decided by the research questions. The order cannot be changed unless the research questions are revised. In a parallel design, the quantitative design or the qualitative design is implemented independently. They can be operated simultaneously if sufficient human resources are available, or one after the other since they are not dependent on each other.

Using a mixed design, we may have three possibilities as shown in Figure 5.1. The first possibility as shown in Figure 5.1a is a parallel design in the sense that the quantitative and the qualitative designs are used independently. The second one and the third one differ in their sequence. For the second one displayed in Figure 5.1b, the quantitative design is implemented before the qualitative one while for the third one as shown in Figure 5.1c, the sequence is reversed.

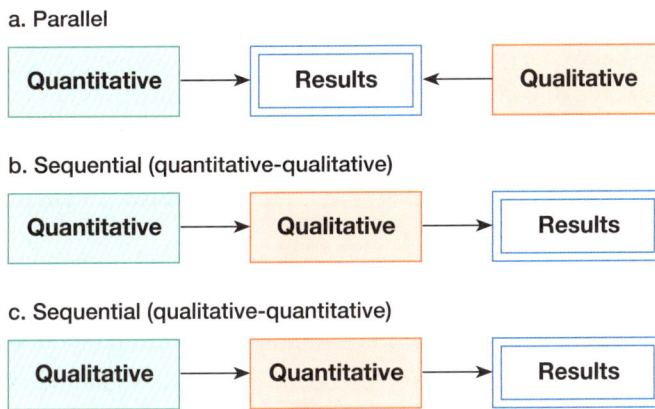

a. Parallel

Quantitative → Results ← Qualitative

b. Sequential (quantitative-qualitative)

Quantitative → Qualitative → Results

c. Sequential (qualitative-quantitative)

Qualitative → Quantitative → Results

Figure 5.1: Variations within a mixed design

Now let's look at three examples which show the three types of a mixed design respectively.

Example 1

Parallel

The study intended to seek an answer to the question: Should English learning start from Primary One in the Chinese context? The subjects involved in the study included students, parents, teachers, and administrators. The study consisted of two parallel components: quantitative and qualitative parts. In the quantitative part, Primary One students and their parents were asked to answer two different questionnaires respectively. In the qualitative part, primary school English teachers and the school/district administrators were interviewed individually. The two sets of data answered the same question from different perspectives.

In Example 1, the study involves two sets of data which answer the same research question. The quantitative set includes responses to the questionnaires by the students and the parents, and the second includes interview data elicited from the English teachers and the administrators. The order of collecting these two sets of data is not fixed, and they can be collected simultaneously if human resources are sufficient.

Example 2

Sequential (quantitative-qualitative)

The study attempted to address two questions: (1) to what extent L1 was involved in L2 writing; and (2) how L1 was used in L2 writing. First of all, 100 students responded to a questionnaire in which various kinds of questions concerning the use of L1 in L2 writing were asked. Based on the students' responses to the questionnaire, 15 students who reported using L1 most frequently were selected to join the qualitative part in which they were required to write an English composition while speaking out what was going on in their minds. The results from the quantitative part addressed the first question and the results from the qualitative part addressed the second question.

In Example 2, there are two research questions. The questionnaire responses could answer the first research question and the think-aloud data could answer the second one. However, the quantitative data must be collected before the qualitative data since the participants were selected based on the questionnaire responses. As a result, the order of collecting these two sets of data cannot be arbitrarily changed since such a sequence is arranged logically.

Example 3

Sequential (qualitative-quantitative)

In Gu's study (1997), he intended to find: (1) what strategies were used by non-English major undergraduates; and (2) to what extent their use of strategies was related to their vocabulary learning. To answer the first question, he employed a qualitative design in which a group of second-year undergraduates representing three levels of English proficiency were interviewed individually. Based on the findings from the interviews, he constructed a questionnaire which was subsequently used in the quantitative part to answer the second question.

In Example 3, Gu intended to answer two research questions. The interview data were used to answer the first question and the questionnaire data to answer the second one. Like Example 2, the order of collecting the interview data and the questionnaire responses cannot be reversed since the questionnaire items are constructed based on the interview data.

In a word, there are variations in a mixed design which can be used to deal with different types of studies illustrated in the three examples. I often encourage graduate students to use a mixed design in their research. However, in an individual case, such a combination may not always be necessary.

Focus highlight

- As a researcher, you might have a preference for a quantitative design or a qualitative one or a mixed one, or you might be more familiar with the techniques used in one type of design.
- There is nothing wrong with having preference for any particular type of design. But one thing you must remember is that your personal preference or strengths should not lead to bias or prejudice against any particular type of design.
- If you are a supervisor of postgraduate students, you'd better learn both mono-designs and mixed designs and introduce them to students without any bias.
- When you judge the quality of postgraduate students' theses, you should examine whether the research design can well answer the research questions rather than focus only on the use of one particular type of design.

COMPLEXITIES IN CLASSIFYING DESIGNS

In the views of Punch (1998), Blaxter et al. (1996), and Tashakkori and Teddlie (1998), there is a clear-cut division between quantitative and qualitative designs. Following their argument, we have to say a design is quantitative if the data are in the form of numbers. Otherwise, it is qualitative. However, in reality, the situation is much more complicated. In this section, I will use one example to illustrate the complexities and discuss possible solutions.

An illustration

The following is an example taken from a student's research.

Children's vocabulary learning strategies

In Chen's study (2000), she intended to address the following three questions:

1. How frequently do Chinese children adopt strategies in remembering the spelling of new English words?
2. Are there any differences in the use of vocabulary learning strategies by good and poor child learners?
3. How can learner factors (i.e. age and length of learning) affect the use of vocabulary learning strategies?

One hundred school children were involved in her study who were asked to remember 20 new words while speaking out what was going on in their minds. She first read the children's verbal accounts repeatedly to identify the strategies used by them in remembering the spelling of new words. Altogether she set up 10 categories, that is, "Rote learning," "Form association," "Familiar word," "Phonetic alphabet," "Syllable cutting," "Word building," "Pronunciation rule," "Visual frame," "Chinese sound," and "Arbitrary cutting." All these categories were not available in the existing literature and were thus not preconceived ahead of her research. These categories emerged only in the process of analyzing the data. By repeatedly checking, she made sure that the 10 categories were well grounded in the think-aloud data. She then counted the frequencies of each category occurring in their verbal accounts and then carried out Independent-samples t-test to examine whether there was any difference in the use of vocabulary learning strategies by good and poor child learners. Finally, she used correlation analyses to see the relationship between the use of strategies and the two learner factors. In the chapter of "Results and discussion," she answered each of the three questions one by one based on the quantitative results she got from the analysis of the data. Specifically speaking, the answer to the first research question was a table of frequencies, the answer to the second question was the results yielded by Independent-samples t-test, and the answer to the third question was a set of correlation coefficients.

Consider the above example. Did the research use a quantitative design or a qualitative design? Following the definitions given by Punch, we have to say the study was qualitative because the original think-aloud data were in the form of words rather than numbers. However, all the research questions were answered by figures rather than verbal accounts. Many researchers would intuitively feel it unacceptable if such a study is classified as a qualitative one. Let's closely examine the whole study step by step (See Figure 5.2).

There is no doubt that the original data collected in Step One were qualitative in nature and the initial analysis in Step Two was qualitatively made. However, the subsequent analyses were all statistically made. Above all, the answers to the research questions were presented in the form of numbers. Evidently, it is an oversimplification to say Chen's study is either qualitative or quantitative.

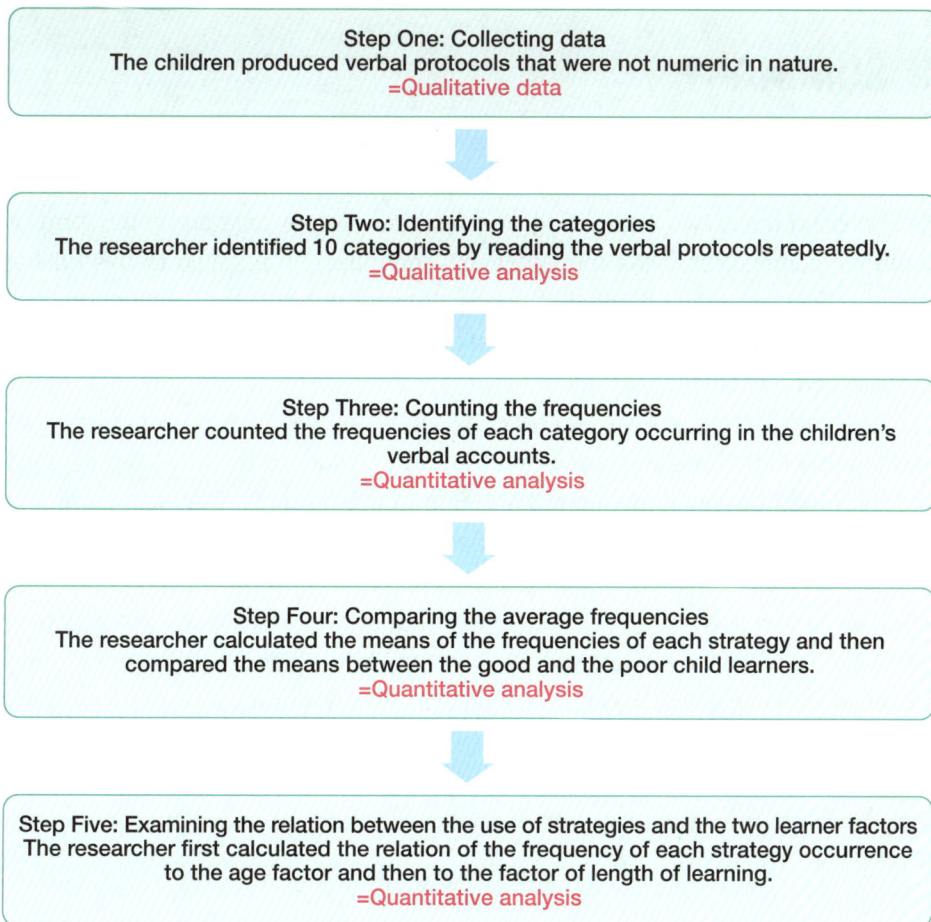

Figure 5.2: Analysis of Chen's study

Suggestions

In my opinion, it is not appropriate to decide whether a design is quantitative or qualitative simply by looking at the data form. We should also take data analysis into consideration. Instead of using "quantitative" or "qualitative" as a cover term to describe a research design, I suggest that we specify the data form and the way of data analysis separately. In this way, a study may have quantitative or qualitative data, or both, and the data may be analyzed quantitatively or qualitatively or both. Quantitative data are normally processed quantitatively while qualitative data have more choices. It is clear that complexities typically arise when the collected data are not in the form of numbers.

≡ SUMMARY

Research designs are classified into two opposing camps: quantitative and qualitative. Some researchers regard the data form as the most critical feature for differentiating these two contrasting designs, i.e. whether data are in the form of numbers (numeric) or in the form of words (narrative). In addition to this critical feature, there are many other differences between them. These differences are shown in the objectives, research questions, sample size, data collection, data analysis, and outcomes.

Generally, we can identify two historical stages of the development of research designs: the mono-design stage (from the 19th century to the mid-20th century) and the mixed design stage (from the 1980s to the present). The most prevailing view now is to make use of the advantages of the two designs.

The selection of research designs is primarily decided by research questions which very often give you some clues in wording for what kind of design to choose. Once a mixed design is determined, you may have a series of choices. With reference to the time, you may have sequential or parallel designs.

At the end of this chapter, the complexities in classifying designs are further analyzed. It is suggested that instead of using a cover term ("quantitative" vs. "qualitative") to describe a research design, it is better to specify a study along two dimensions: data form and data analysis.

AFTER-READING ACTIVITIES

Reviewing

1 What are the important differences between quantitative and qualitative designs?

2 What is a simple mono-design? What is a complex mono-design? Can you give examples to illustrate your understanding?

3 Use an example to illustrate the advantages of combining quantitative and qualitative designs.

4 What is the relationship between research questions and research designs?

5 What are the possible combinations of quantitative and qualitative designs?

Exploring

1 Read the following studies to identify variations within a mixed design and discuss their advantages.

Study One

The study investigated Chinese learners' motivation for English learning and their English teachers' motivation for English teaching by respective questionnaires. With the responses given by the students and the teachers, the study further examined the relationship between the students' and the teachers' motivation. The study also intended to get a detailed picture of 10 less motivated learners' and 10 less motivated teachers' behaviors by interviews.

Study Two

The project studied the differences in risk-taking between high L2 achievers and low L2 achievers by a mixed design. The researcher first selected 16 students from second-year English majors based on their previous scores on English tests and then interviewed them individually. She found a lot of interesting differences among which she decided to single out four striking differences related to L2 production for a survey study to validate these four differences. Thus, a questionnaire was constructed and 100 students were asked to respond to the questionnaire.

Study Three

In 1990, I carried out a study on the relationship between modifiable learner variables and English achievement, which used a mixed design (Wen,

1993). In the first part of this study, the subjects were asked to answer a questionnaire on learner factors. The results presented an overall picture of the extent to which learners' English achievement was influenced by the modifiable learner factors. Such results helped me narrow down the focus of the second part of the study. Specifically speaking, the first part of the study indicated that the areas worth further researching for advanced level English language learners were "Vocabulary strategy," "Mother-tongue-avoidance strategy," "Tolerating-ambiguity strategy," "Management strategy," etc. However, the results obtained from the first part of the study were general and oversimplified because the results didn't show how successful learners differed from less successful learners. The second part of this study included interviews, observations, and diaries. The subjects involved in the second part were five high achievers and five low achievers. The data yielded uncovered a lot of information on the strategies used by successful and less successful learners, which formed a more complex and more realistic picture of the relation of the modifiable learner factors to English achievement. It is clear that without the general framework provided by the first part of the study, the focus of the second part of the study may not be easily narrowed down.

Chapter 6

A survey study

In Chapter 6, I will introduce to you how to carry out a survey study that primarily collects quantitative data. I will first give you a brief description of a survey study followed by detailed procedures for data collection in the survey. A paper that reports a survey study is presented as Appendix One.

▷≣ A BRIEF DESCRIPTION OF A SURVEY STUDY

A survey study usually involves a relatively large sample and is descriptive in nature. It either describes the features of a few variables or the relation between two or more variables. When your interest is confined to the relation between two variables only, the study is a correlation design. However, people nowadays have realized that understanding a phenomenon in terms of two variables is an oversimplification. A phenomenon is usually a result of interaction between a series of variables. Thus, a more common design is multivariate in which the relation between a set of independent variables and dependent variables is examined.

A survey study may be cross-sectional or longitudinal. A cross-sectional study collects data from different groups of people at one point of time while a longitudinal study collects data from the same group of people at different points over a period of time. The following are two examples.

Example 1

Cross-sectional

Wen (1993) conducted a study which investigated the changes in the use of learning strategies in English learning by the first-year, second-year, and third-year students. All the students were asked to respond to the questionnaire on learning strategies designed by Wen at the same time.

Example 2

Longitudinal

Wen and Zhang (2016) carried out a study which examined the changes in critical thinking disposition (CTD) of 163 foreign language majors in their three years of undergraduate study by conducting four surveys at the beginning of the first year, and the end of the first, second, and third years respectively.

?
- Can you explain what is the difference between a cross-sectional study and a longitudinal one?
- What are the advantages and disadvantages of these two types of study?

The first example shows how a cross-sectional study collects data. Specifically speaking, though the students studied in the university for different numbers of years, the data were gathered at one point of time. In the second example, the researchers followed the same group of students for three years and collected the data at the four points of time.

Talking about the advantages and disadvantages of these two types of study, in fact, we can easily identify them. The cross-sectional one in Example 1 can save the researchers' time and they do not need to wait for three years to complete the task of data collection, as in Example 2. However, the first-year, second-year, and third-year students belong to different groups and the changes shown in these three groups could also be caused by the differences existing when they entered the university. The longitudinal one in Example 2 traces the changes in the same group of students so that the changes cannot be attributed to the initial differences displayed in different groups. Although a longitudinal study is ideal for researchers to detect the changes in one or more variables along a temporal dimension, M.A. or Ph.D. students very often cannot afford three or four years to finish the task of data collection. The cross-sectional study could be an alternative to the longitudinal one but researchers must be aware of its limitations and admit them in their theses/ dissertations.

To collect data in a survey study, you are expected to undertake several tasks: (1) constructing an instrument for data collection; (2) selecting subjects for the study; and (3) collecting data either personally or through correspondence. For the first two tasks, it does not matter which one is carried out first. For your convenience, I will describe these three tasks one by one in the following sections.

≔ INSTRUMENT DESIGNING: QUESTIONNAIRE

?
- Were you ever asked to respond to a questionnaire? What does a questionnaire look like?
- Do you think it is easy to construct a questionnaire?

The questionnaire[1] is one of the most widely used techniques for collecting quantitative data. Compared with interviews and observations, it requires less time and less effort. A questionnaire consists of a series of questions which a participant is required to answer. The great weakness of questionnaire design is lack of theory in the sense that there are no scientific principles that guarantee an optimal or ideal questionnaire. Questionnaire design is a skill acquired through experience, and is an art rather than a science. What I can do here is to give you some guidelines. Although these rules can help you avoid major mistakes, the fine tuning of a questionnaire comes only from your creative and rich practice.

Qin (2009) wrote a book *A Questionnaire for Foreign Language Teaching Research*, which presents all the details of designing a questionnaire. In this section, I will only give you a brief introduction which includes the criteria for preparing a sound questionnaire and the process of constructing a questionnaire. I strongly suggest that you read Qin's book carefully if you want to use a questionnaire for a survey study.

Criteria for a good questionnaire

Any good questionnaire should at least meet the following two criteria: (1) having high internal validity; and (2) having a professional look.

Having high internal validity

By saying a questionnaire should have high internal validity, I mean that items in the questionnaire must measure the variables you really want to investigate. You might say this criterion is unnecessary since no researcher would be so stupid as to fail to do so. It is true that no researcher would like to violate this requirement intentionally. However, they might fail to meet the criterion because of lack of skills or experience. Actually, having lower internal validity is a common flaw of a

---

[1] The questionnaire can also be used to collect qualitative data if the questions are open-ended. This chapter will only focus on structured questions that are used to collect quantitative data.

questionnaire constructed by a novice researcher. Let's look at some examples taken from the initial drafts of some B.A./M.A. students under my supervision. The study in the first example intended to investigate whether senior middle school students used L1 in the process of L2 reading. Besides many other items, the questionnaire included the following ones.

Example 1

L1 use in L2 reading

1. I often read reference materials in Chinese in order to help me understand the context in which an English story took place.
2. I read English novels, newspapers, journals, etc. in my spare time.
3. I only have English-Chinese bilingual dictionaries.

Suppose some of the students responded to the first item by choosing "This statement is always or almost always true of me." Did this response imply that they used L1 in the process of L2 reading? It is not clear at all since it only tells us that they would like to get the relevant contextual information in Chinese before they read the English story. So far as the second item is concerned, frequent reading in English cannot guarantee the avoidance of the use of L1 in L2 reading. The third item might not be working at all since almost all the senior middle school students would give the same response. Furthermore, even if there were variations in the responses, the responses could not give us any information directly concerning the use of L1 in L2 reading.

The study in the second example was conducted by one of my M.A. students who wanted to investigate students' degree of anxiety in L2 speaking. The following three items were included in her draft of the questionnaire.

Example 2

Anxiety in L2 speaking

1. I try to avoid answering questions in class.
2. I try to sit in the corner of the classroom so that I will not be asked questions frequently by the teacher.
3. I do not like to speak in public.

What do you think of the above items? If a student did admit that the above three statements were true of him/her, could you say that this student showed a high degree of anxiety in L2 speaking? Obviously not. The avoidance of answering questions in class may be due to a variety of reasons, such as the student's poor preparation for the lesson, the student's lower L2 speaking ability, and the student's introverted personality, in addition to the student's anxiety in L2 speaking. Therefore, the three statements would measure many other factors mixed with the student's degree of anxiety in L2 speaking.

From the two examples, you might have a better understanding of the internal validity of the questionnaire items. To make a self-evaluation, you may ask yourself from time to time these questions: What does the student's response to a particular item mean? Does it have one or multiple interpretations? If there is only one interpretation which is directly linked with the variable you are examining, then the item concerned is of high validity. Otherwise, you have to revise it or delete it.

> **?**
>
> • Can you revise the items in Example 1 and Example 2 to make sure they could measure the variables the researchers intended to measure?

Having a professional look

How a questionnaire looks can affect the attitudes of respondents which in turn influence the quality of their responses. For instance, if a questionnaire is printed on poor-quality paper or looks shabby in appearance, the respondents will think the research project is not important and, as a result, they will not take it seriously. A good questionnaire with a professional outlook should not contain the following problems.

First of all, if a questionnaire contains more than five pages you should avoid clipping or stapling them together. In this case, it is better to take the form of booklets since booklets do not easily fall apart like clipped and stapled papers. Furthermore, booklets allow the use of a double-page format for questions, and look more professional. Secondly, one question or response categories should not be printed across two pages since split content may lead respondents to think that the question has ended at the end of the previous page. Thirdly, you should avoid crowding questions together to make the questionnaire look shorter. Overcrowded questions with little blank space between questions can lead to errors in data collection. Moreover, they give the impression that the questionnaire is complex and this can result in a lower cooperation and response rate. Finally, the paper for printing should be of high quality and the printing itself must be clear and easy to read. Remember that a questionnaire with a professional look can not only minimize the respondent's fatigue, boredom, and effort, but also increase the response rate.

Questionnaire design process

The design of a questionnaire can be described in terms of a series of steps that can be roughly divided into three stages (See Figure 6.1). At Stage One, where the researcher gets prepared for developing a questionnaire, he/she is expected to accomplish three major tasks: (1) select the mode for collecting questionnaire data; (2) specify what kind of data he/she intends to collect; and (3) determine the way of processing, i.e. the researcher needs to decide whether questionnaire items will be processed individually or as categories. At Stage Two, where the researcher constructs a questionnaire, he/she undertakes three important tasks: (1) decide on the content of individual items; (2) choose the question structure; and (3) check the wording of each questionnaire item. At Stage Three, the researcher needs to complete three essential tasks: (1) arrange the questions in proper order; (2) decide on the format of the questionnaire and print it; and (3) pretest the questionnaire (Malhotra, 1993). In the following parts, each of the steps at each stage will be discussed in detail.

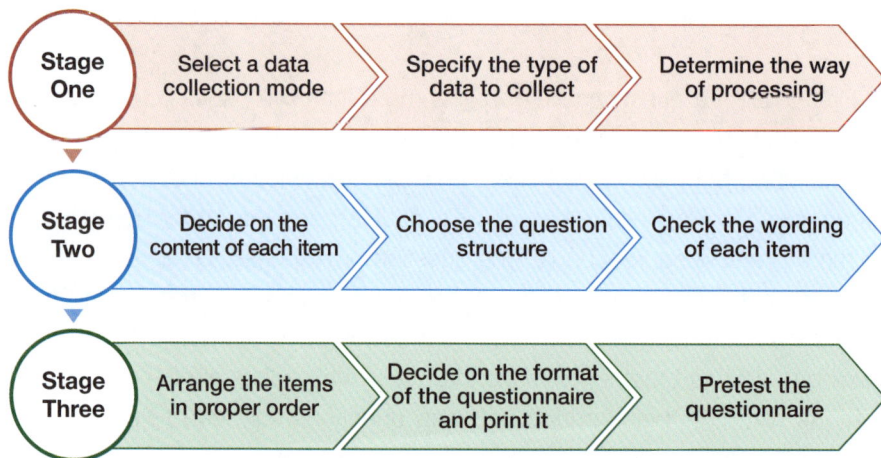

Figure 6.1: The process of constructing a questionnaire

Stage One: Preparing

Selecting the mode of administration

The mode of administration refers to the way in which questionnaires are distributed to the respondents. In the Chinese context, there are two common modes: (1) by person; and (2) by email. The first mode means that questionnaires are distributed to the respondents by an organizer rather than through the internet. The organizer can be the researcher himself/herself or other people the researcher has asked for help. By this mode, a group of subjects usually answer the same questionnaire together. The organizer gives the respondents instructions on how to respond to the questionnaire and clarifications if there are any ambiguous items. The organizer can also check whether the respondents have responded to all the items and thus the rate of missing data can be greatly reduced.

If the respondents are spread out in different cities or even in different countries, it is difficult to employ the first mode. What you can do is to disseminate questionnaires to the targeted people through the internet. By doing so, the researcher cannot control the overall response rate and the rate of missing items. Even if a questionnaire is returned, he/she cannot be sure whether the questionnaire is filled out by the targeted people and under what circumstances the questionnaire is completed.

The instructions of and the length of questionnaires vary depending on whether questionnaires are distributed by person or by email. The e-questionnaire should contain more explicit and simpler instructions than the person-administered questionnaire. Furthermore, the e-questionnaire should be shorter and easier to answer than the person-administered questionnaire because it is next to impossible to get the respondents to fill out an e-questionnaire for one or two hours unless you are prepared to pay well for their time.

Each of the modes of administration has its own strengths and weaknesses. Your choice of a mode will depend on your own consideration of cost, convenience, and the nature of the questions you are asking. I highly recommend the person-administered mode since it allows you to clarify ambiguities and check whether all the questions are answered by the respondents.

Specifying what kind of data you intend to collect

At this stage, you have to understand what kind of data you really want to collect. At the very general level, there are basically five types of information.

The first type of information at the center of Figure 6.2 is about the respondents' background (such as age, gender, and marital status). This is almost included in every questionnaire. The difference only lies in the choice of which information your study is to be focused on. For example, in a questionnaire for students, you might expect to know for how many years they have learned a foreign language and when

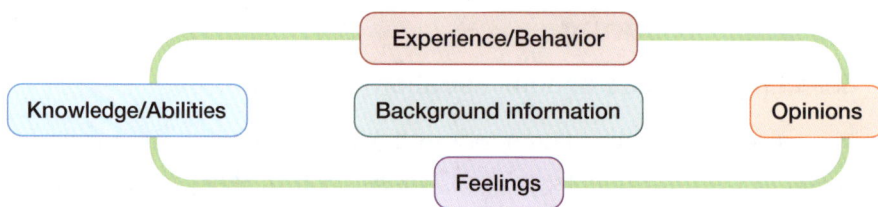

Figure 6.2: Five major types of information included in a questionnaire

they started their learning. The information about experience/behavior is to find out what participants do, such as "I read English newspapers every day." The verb "read" is a performance verb indicating an action. The information about opinions is to investigate what participants think, such as "I believe that repetition is very important for learning a foreign language." The verb "believe" indicates the idea or opinion the participants have rather than their actual performance. The information about feelings is to understand the affective aspect of the participants, such as "I feel anxious whenever I am asked to answer a question in class." The verb "feel" indicates the participants' emotion rather than an action or opinion.

In the following part, the Language Learner Factors Questionnaire, designed by myself and implemented in my doctoral study, is used as an example to show how different types of information can be gathered through questionnaire items.

The research intended to study the relation between L2 modifiable learner variables and English achievement. The questionnaire I constructed included three types of information: (1) background; (2) opinions, i.e. beliefs; and (3) behavior, i.e. learning strategies. The following is a shortened version of the original questionnaire (Wen, 1993, pp. 294-302).

Language Learner Factors Questionnaire

The following questionnaire is designed for research on the way Chinese students study English. The questions have been carefully selected to cover the more important aspects of English learning. Please answer each question honestly and frankly in your own opinion or according to your own learning experience. There are no "correct" answers. All the data collected will be highly confidential and will be used for the research only.

Part A: Background information
A01 Name: _____ ; Date of birth: _____ ; Sex: _____
A02 Scores on entrance examination (English): _____
A03 Scores on entrance examination (Chinese): _____

Part B: Beliefs

Below are some beliefs that people have about learning foreign languages. There are no right or wrong answers. We are simply interested in your opinions. Please write the number which best indicates your opinion in the parentheses at the end of each statement. The numbers stand for the following responses:

1=I strongly disagree with this statement.
2=I disagree with this statement.
3=I neither agree nor disagree with this statement.
4=I agree with this statement.
5=I strongly agree with this statement.

B01 Planning your study time is important for success. (   )
B02 Learning a foreign language requires painstaking effort. (   )
B03 It is important to repeat a lot. (   )
…

Part C: Learning strategies

Below are some strategies that people use when learning a foreign language. Please read each statement and write down the number that best describes your behavior in the parentheses at the end of each statement. Please indicate what you really do, not what you think you should do, or what other people do. Remember there are no right or wrong answers. The numbers stand for the following responses:

1=This statement is never or almost never true of me.
2=This statement is usually not true of me.
3=This statement is somewhat true of me.
4=This statement is usually true of me.
5=This statement is completely or almost completely true of me.

C01 When reading a text, I try to understand everything in it. (   )
C02 I memorize texts. (   )
C03 I talk to myself in English outside class. (   )
…

You can relate the five types of information in Figure 6.2 to the time frame: past, present, and future. For example, an item about one particular behavior may refer to the respondents' action in the middle school, or at the university now, or in the future when they take a postgraduate program.

Very often, novice researchers cannot clearly differentiate belief items from behavior items. The structure of a belief item is "I think/believe that..." For example, the statement "Learning a foreign language requires painstaking effort" is to find out the respondents' opinions or views rather than behaviors. In contrast, the statement "I put a lot of effort into learning an L2" is to investigate the respondents' behaviors rather than their views. Unfortunately, novice researchers more often than not mix up the two types of information and that certainly confuses the respondents. When the respondents take beliefs for behaviors or behaviors for beliefs, the validity of the data is then called into question.

Determining how to process the questionnaire data

Once you have decided in which mode to administer the questionnaire and what type of information you intend to collect, then you need to determine whether your questionnaire data are eventually analyzed in terms of individual items or in terms of categories. If the basic unit in the data analysis is an individual item, such as describing the frequency and the mean of one isolated item, then such a questionnaire is called an individual-item-based questionnaire. The construction of such a questionnaire is comparatively simple and easy because it does not involve setting up conceptual categories. However, this kind of questionnaire has very limited value because its results are less generalizable.

If your data analysis is to be based on categories, each of which contains a few questionnaire items, you must establish conceptual categories either by a top-down approach or by a bottom-up approach. By a top-down approach, you construct conceptual categories based on logical arguments or existing theories before you design specific items. By a bottom-up approach, you simply write down whatever items that come into your mind. You then try to classify these items into categories. Obviously, constructing a category-based questionnaire is very demanding and challenging on the part of designers. Yet all M.A. students need to grasp this skill. For example, I designed a category-based questionnaire to find out second-year English majors' beliefs about and strategies for L2 learning. The conceptual categories constructed are presented in Table 6.1.

Approach	Traditional	Non-traditional
Beliefs	Form-focused beliefs Mother-tongue-reliance beliefs Accuracy-focused beliefs	Function-focused beliefs Mother-tongue-avoidance beliefs Fluency-focused beliefs
Strategies	Form-focused strategies Mother-tongue-reliance strategies Accuracy-focused strategies	Function-focused strategies Mother-tongue-avoidance strategies Fluency-focused strategies

Table 6.1: Categories of beliefs and strategies

The above two types of learning approaches, Traditional vs. Non-traditional, are based on three major controversies in L2 learning proposed by Stern (1975, 1983, 1992): the L1-L2 connection, the explicit-implicit option, and the code-communication dilemma. Each controversial issue could be perceived as a continuum. Take the issue of the L1-L2 connection as an example, which is about the role of the learner's mother tongue in L2 learning. Generally speaking, there are two contrasting views. One is the view that learning a second language should exploit the first language and thus the learner is encouraged to use translation in learning the target language. The other is the view that learning the target language should be entirely within and through the target language and so the learner is exhorted even to think in the target language. Centering around the issue, I set up two contrasting categories about beliefs and strategies respectively: mother-tongue-reliance beliefs and mother-tongue-avoidance beliefs; mother-tongue-reliance strategies and mother-tongue-avoidance strategies.

Furthermore, an approach is regarded as a combination of beliefs and strategies. Such a conceptual definition is based on the theory of educational psychology proposed by Marton and Saljo (1976), who advocate that students' actual learning behaviors are influenced by their conceptions of learning. In other words, students' beliefs about learning will affect their choice of learning strategies.

Chen (1996), one of my B.A. students, used a category-based questionnaire to investigate senior middle school students' degree of anxiety for the purpose of discovering to what extent teachers' attitudes affected students' degree of anxiety. When he first constructed questionnaire items, he did not have any preconceived categories. He just wrote down all the items he could think of and then tried to classify them into categories. Through repeatedly examining the items in relation to the research questions, he decided to group them into two categories: the environmental anxiety and the inherent anxiety. The first type of anxiety referred to anxiety induced by the L2 learning environment, which included the classroom atmosphere and teachers' attitudes toward students; the second type referred to anxiety caused by students' personality.

Stage Two: Constructing

Deciding on the content of individual items

Once you are clear about what type of information is needed, you start thinking of the content of each individual item. You should not sit in the room thinking alone. The sources of questionnaire items are varied. One source is the items in previous studies which are related to your research topic. For example, if you want to investigate university students' strategies used in L2 learning, you may refer to Oxford's Strategy Inventory for Language Learning (1990) or Wen's Language Learner Factors Questionnaire (1993). Or you may interview some typical university students and ask them how they go about their L2 learning. The interview data may provide you with a lot of details on their strategies.

If a questionnaire is intended to contain several categories, you have to consider whether the items designed cover all the categories and whether each category contains an adequate number of items. In order to answer these two questions, you can draw a table which has two columns. In one column, you write down the categories, and in the other column, you write down the sequential number of each questionnaire item (See Table 6.2).

Category name	Item no.
Form-focused beliefs	2, 4, 5, 7, 9
Meaning-focused beliefs	1, 3, 6, 8, 10
Form-focused strategies	11, 13, 16, 18, 20
Meaning-focused strategies	12, 14, 15, 17, 19

Table 6.2: Checking questionnaire items within each category

Then you have to read the items within the same category again and again to make sure that all the items logically go together. If you find some items do not fit into the category, you don't need to feel frustrated since it is a very common problem at this stage. However, you cannot ignore it. What you should do is to revise them or construct new ones.

Checking the wording of each questionnaire item

Next, you have to check question wording very carefully. If a question is worded poorly, respondents may fail to understand the item or misunderstand it. Their answers under this circumstance tend to contain more missing values[1] or to be misleading. To avoid poorly worded questions, you can follow some of the suggestions made by Malhotra (1993) and Bernard (1994):

Use ordinary words. Ordinary words should be used in writing a question and they should be suitable to the vocabulary level of the respondents. Suppose the respondents involved in your research are primary school students. The words used in the questions must be within their range. Otherwise, they are not able to answer the questions or the answers given are of low validity.

Avoid leading questions. A leading question is one in which a hint is given so that respondents are biased toward a particular choice. Obviously, the following statement would bias respondents toward a "Strongly agree" answer since the word "unpopular" is a biased word.

The **unpopular** course of Intensive Reading should be revised.

Strongly disagree	Disagree	Uncertain	Agree	Strongly agree
1	2	3	4	5

---

[1] Missing values result from questionnaire items that were not answered by respondents.

Use dual statements. Using dual statements means that positive and negative statements should be roughly balanced in a questionnaire. In other words, the total number of positive statements should be more or less the same as the total number of negative statements. For example, in one of my own studies, I intended to investigate students' attitudes toward using a language laboratory to teach spoken English. The following are the statements from my questionnaire[1], and three are positive and five are negative marked with a star:

1=This statement is never or almost never true of me.
2=This statement is usually not true of me.
3=This statement is somewhat true of me.
4=This statement is usually true of me.
5=This statement is completely or almost completely true of me.

1. I like to have a speaking class in a language laboratory.
2. I am not clear about why we have a speaking class in a language laboratory.*
3. In a language laboratory, I cannot concentrate on what I want to say because so many people talk to microphones at the same time and they make a big noise.*
4. I don't like the teacher monitoring my conversation with others.*
5. I think it is easier to combine listening with speaking when a speaking class is undertaken in a language laboratory.
6. I think in a speaking class listening practice should be kept to a minimum.*
7. I think talking to other people through a microphone in a language laboratory lacks communicative authenticity.*
8. I feel talking to people through a microphone in a language laboratory is the same as talking to people over the phone in our daily life.

From the above examples, you may find that negative statements often contain explicit negative markers such as "not clear" in No. 2, "cannot" in No. 3, and "don't like" in No. 4, but sometimes they use implicit negative terms such as "lacks" in No. 7.

Why do we need to do so? Because research shows that the way respondents answer a questionnaire is affected by whether statements are positive or negative.

Be cautious in translation. The last suggestion is made for cross-cultural studies where in most cases two or more different languages are involved. Very often apparent equivalents in two different languages actually contain different meanings. How can we make sure our translation does not distort the original meaning? The best way to do this is through back translation. For example, I once conducted a study on Chinese and Swedish students' conceptions of learning. The first questionnaire was in English which was a common language shared by my

---

[1] The original questionnaire items were in Chinese and the English items presented here result from translation.

partner and me. But both of us needed to translate the questionnaire into our native languages for data collection. What we did was back translation. First we asked bilinguals to translate the English version into Chinese and Swedish respectively. We then asked another two bilinguals to translate the Chinese and Swedish versions back into English. By comparing the initial and final English versions, we could easily detect the problems and make further modifications until a satisfactory back translation result was achieved.

Choosing the question structure

Basically, there are two types of questions: open-ended questions or unstructured questions vs. closed-ended questions or structured questions. Now we are going to deal with these two types of questions.

Open-ended questions refer to those whose answers are in respondents' own words and are difficult to predict. The following are some examples:

Why don't you like to read simplified English novels?
When do you consult a dictionary?
What do you read outside class?
Why do you study English?

From the above examples, we can see that open-ended questions usually begin with "wh-" words such as "what," "when," and "why." In fact, this type of question is typically used to collect qualitative data. Therefore, open-ended questions are not further discussed in this chapter.

In closed-ended questions or structured questions, the researcher provides respondents with a set of response alternatives. In other words, respondents have to select one response out of the alternatives provided. They do not have the freedom to use their own words to express their response. A closed-ended question may be a multiple-choice question, a dichotomous question, or a scale.

Multiple-choice questions. In multiple-choice questions, the researcher offers a set of answers and respondents are expected to choose one or more of the alternatives given. Let's look at the following two examples that are taken from C. X. Wu's questionnaire (1998) with some modifications.

1. How do you learn the cultural differences in your daily life? Please check as many as you like.
   (1) Read English magazines and books on Western customs and etiquette

Dichotomous questions. A dichotomous question has only two alternatives to choose from, such as "yes" or "no," "important" or "unimportant," and "disagree" or "agree." Often, the two choices provided are supplemented by "don't know" as a neutral alternative. Consider the following examples.

1. Do you talk to yourself in English outside class?
   —Yes   —No
2. Do you often read English newspapers?
   —Yes   —No
3. Do you think people with talents for language learning can learn an L2 without effort?
   —Yes   —No   —Don't know

Scales. A scale is a continuum upon which a set of alternative choices are placed. The following are the examples of scales:

1. Do you guess the meanings of new words when reading English novels for pleasure?

Never	Occasionally	Sometimes	Often	Very often
1	2	3	4	5

2. Do you think the best way to understand an English text is to translate?

Strongly disagree	Disagree	Uncertain	Agree	Strongly agree
1	2	3	4	5

Scales are apparently similar to multiple-choice questions since both provide a set of response alternatives but they are different in nature. The alternatives in a multiple-choice question cannot form a continuum. (Note: Detailed information about scales will be presented later in this chapter.)

Stage Three: Post-writing questionnaire items

Determining the order of questions

The order of questions often affects respondents' answers. Therefore, we need to arrange them with great caution. The following are some tips:

Background information first. Questions concerning background information in the Chinese context are usually placed before questions about basic information such as respondents' opinion, behavior, knowledge, etc. However, according to Malhotra's view (1993), in the Western context, basic information should be obtained before background information.

General questions before specific questions. General questions usually go before specific questions. This can help prevent the answers to specific questions from influencing the responses to general questions. For example, if you want to find out what strategies students use in their reading, a general question like "I read an English text while translating it from English to Chinese" with five choices (never, occasionally, sometimes, often and very often) should be asked before the specific question "I learn new English words by translating them into Chinese."

Deciding on the format of the questionnaire

Before you print out questionnaires, you need to decide on the format, space, and position of questions. This is particularly important for person-administered questionnaires. Research findings show that questions placed at the top of the page receive more attention than those placed at the bottom. Questions that are divided into several sections tend to increase the response rate. Furthermore, all the questions must be numbered and the way the answers are recorded should be convenient for respondents to write.

Conducting a pilot study to test the questionnaire

A pilot study is one in which a questionnaire is tested on a small sample of respondents to detect and overcome potential problems. As normal practice, no questionnaire should be used in a formal study without being tested since even a questionnaire designed by an experienced researcher can always be improved through the pilot study. The potential problems may lie in all aspects of a questionnaire, such as the question content, wording, sequencing, question difficulty, instructions, and format. The respondents selected for the pilot study should be similar to those who will be involved in the actual survey. The best pilot study is done through personal interviews in which you can observe the respondents' reactions and attitudes, and check whether their interpretations of the questions are the same as you expected. Finally, the results of the pilot study should be analyzed to see whether your research questions are set up properly and whether the conceptual categories, if there are any, are supported by empirical data.

≡ SCALING TECHNIQUES

Scaling involves creating a continuum along which people's responses can be recorded and eventually each response can be assigned a number. For example, you might like to label people's attitudes toward L2 learning as "unfavorable," "neutral," or "positive"; or you might like to classify the frequency of using strategies into "frequently," "sometimes," and "occasionally." Here, unfavorable-neutral-positive and frequently-sometimes-occasionally are two continua. The process of establishing these two continua is scaling. The scaling techniques used in applied linguistics include comparative and non-comparative scales. In this section, these two types of scales will be described in detail.

Comparative scaling techniques

Comparative scales involve the direct comparison of choices. For example, respondents might be asked whether they prefer speaking in public or speaking in a small group. Or respondents might be asked to rank order a list of items. For example:

> How do you improve your reading skills? Rank order the following items according to the frequency of your actions.
> 1. Reading English magazines
> 2. Reading English newspapers
> 3. Reading simplified English novels
> 4. Reading English novels without simplification

Comparative scales can only yield ordinal data and thus they are interpreted in relative terms. As shown in Figure 6.3, comparative scales include paired comparison and rank order.

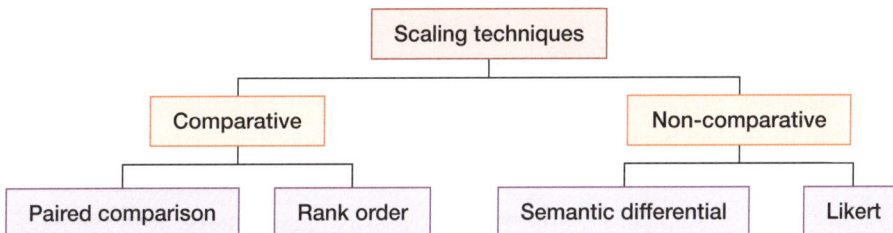

Figure 6.3: Classification of scaling techniques (adapted from Malhotra, 1993, p. 282)

Paired comparison scaling

Paired comparison scaling, as its name suggests, only offers two choices to respondents who are asked to compare them according to some criterion. For example:

1. When you speak English, which of the following two aspects do you pay more attention to?
   (1) Accuracy   (2) Fluency
2. When do you feel more nervous?
   (1) When talking to native speakers of English
   (2) When talking to your English teachers
3. When do you want to speak more?
   (1) When speaking in a group   (2) When speaking in pairs

Rank order scaling

Unlike paired comparison scaling, rank order scaling expects respondents to order or rank more than two choices with reference to some criteria. For example:

1. Why do you want to learn English?
   (1) I am interested in learning a foreign language.
   (2) I want to get a highly-paid job after graduation.
   (3) I plan to study abroad.
   (4) I like to know more about foreign culture.
   Order: _____
2. When do you want to put more efforts into learning English?
   (1) When I get higher scores on an English test
   (2) When I am praised by my English teacher in class
   (3) When I obtain a prize in an English speaking competition
   Order: _____

According to Malhotra (1993), the major advantage of comparative scaling is that small differences between two or more choices can be listed since respondents are forced to choose between them. Furthermore, respondents undertake the rating task from the same known reference point and thus comparative scales can be easily understood. Another advantage is that designing such items does not require any theoretical assumptions.

Non-comparative scaling techniques

In non-comparative scales, each item is scaled independently from the others. The resulting data are generally assumed to be intervally scaled. There are two kinds of non-comparative scales: semantic differential scale and Likert scale, as shown in Figure 6.3.

Semantic differential scale

The semantic differential scale is a five- or seven-point rating scale with end points associated with bipolar labels that have opposite semantic meanings. Subjects mark the blank that best indicates their views or behaviors. For example, Gardner and Lambert (1972, pp. 156-157) employed such a scale to investigate parental encouragement:

How much do your parents encourage you to study French?
Not at all _____ : _____ : _____ : _____ : _____ : _____ : _____ Very much

They also used a similar method to find out the subjects' impressions of French people:

Interesting _____ : _____ : _____ : _____ : _____ : _____ : _____ Boring
Prejudiced _____ : _____ : _____ : _____ : _____ : _____ : _____ Unprejudiced
Brave _____ : _____ : _____ : _____ : _____ : _____ : _____ Cowardly
Handsome _____ : _____ : _____ : _____ : _____ : _____ : _____ Ugly
Colorful _____ : _____ : _____ : _____ : _____ : _____ : _____ Colorless
Friendly _____ : _____ : _____ : _____ : _____ : _____ : _____ Unfriendly
Honest _____ : _____ : _____ : _____ : _____ : _____ : _____ Dishonest
Stupid _____ : _____ : _____ : _____ : _____ : _____ : _____ Smart

One thing that has to be emphasized here is that negative adjectives or phrases sometimes appear on the left side of the scale and sometimes on the right. This controls the tendency of some subjects, particularly those with very positive or very negative attitudes, marking the right- or left-hand sides without reading the labels.

Likert scale

The Likert scale was first introduced by Rensis Likert. For example, in one study, the subjects were asked to evaluate their reasons for learning English on a four-point scale (1=not important; 2=somewhat important; 3=important; 4=very important). This is called a Likert scale. To conduct the analysis, each response is assigned a numeric score, ranging from 1 to 4. When we use this approach to determine the total score for each subject, it is important to use a consistent scoring procedure so that a high (or low) score consistently reflects a favorable or an unfavorable response. This requires that the numeric values assigned to the negative statements by the subjects be scored by reversing the values. Note that for a negative statement, an agreement reflects an unfavorable response, whereas for a positive statement, an agreement reflects a favorable response. Accordingly, a "strongly agree" response to a positive statement and a "strongly disagree" to a negative statement will both receive the same score. (This will be further discussed in Chapter 10.)

≔ SELECTING SUBJECTS

Usually, people do not study the whole population. The reason is very straightforward: "You cannot study everyone everywhere doing everything" (Miles & Huberman, 1994, p. 27). The common practice is to select a sample from the population to study, hoping the findings from the sample can be applied to the whole. In this section, I will explain to you how to select subjects.

Selecting subjects for a survey study is neither less difficult nor less important than constructing an instrument. If the subjects are not properly selected, the data collected will certainly be of poor quality. In the worst case, where the subjects selected are not cooperative or even do not turn up, the data collection will either be spoiled or be jeopardized. In this section, we will first discuss standardized procedures for selecting subjects, and then focus on some practical concerns.

Random sampling techniques

There are three basic random sampling techniques: simple random sampling, systematic random sampling, and stratified random sampling.

Simple random sampling

Simple random sampling is the basis for the other two random sampling techniques. In simple random sampling, each unit is numbered from 1 to N (N is the size of the population). Next, a table of random numbers is used to select n items to the sample. Table 6.3 presents some random numbers (The whole set of random numbers is presented as Appendix Five). These numbers are random in the sense that for each number, any of the 10 digits (0-9) is equally likely to occur and so getting the same digit twice or more is possible. In the process of selecting, a number that is bigger than the population size *N* or a number that has been chosen for the second time has to be ignored.

91567	42595	27958	30314	04024	86385	29880	99730
46503	18584	18845	49618	02304	51038	20655	58727
34914	63976	88720	82765	34476	17032	87589	40836
57491	16703	23167	49323	45021	33132	12544	41035
30405	83946	23792	14422	15059	45799	22716	19792
09983	74353	68668	30429	70735	25499	16631	35006
85900	07119	97336	71048	08178	77233	13916	47564

Table 6.3: Random numbers (Black, 1992, p. 256)

The following is an example in which the use of the simple random sampling technique will be illustrated. Suppose you want to select 10 out of 20 universities by simple random sampling for your study. First of all, you number every university of the population (See Table 6.4). How many digits you use for the first number depends on the digits of the population size. That is to say, if the population size is in two digits, you start with 01; if the population size is in three digits, you start with 001.

01 Peking University	11 Liaoning University
02 Tsinghua University	12 Sichuan University
03 Beijing Normal University	13 Wuhan University
04 Fudan University	14 Nankai University
05 East China Normal University	15 Sun Yat-sen University
06 Nanjing Normal University	16 Henan University
07 Shanghai University	17 Shantou University
08 Southeast University	18 Zhejiang University
09 Nanjing University	19 Shandong University
10 Beijing Foreign Studies University	20 Xiamen University

Table 6.4: The numbered population of 20 universities

Secondly, select as many digits as there are in the sample. In this case, since the sample size is 10 out of 20, what we need to do is to look at two digits as a unit each time in the table of random number. All the numbers greater than 20 must be ignored. Now let's look at every two-digit unit of all the numbers in Table 6.3. In the first row of digits, the first two-digit unit is 91. This number is out of range, so it has to be ignored. The next two-digit unit is 56. Next is 74, followed by 25, 95, 27, 95, and 83. All these numbers are beyond the range. The two-digit unit after 83 is 03, which is usable. Continuing the process, we will get 14, 04, and 02, all of which are within the range of 20. Continuing along the first row, we have to ignore 48, 63, 85, 29, and 88. The next number is 09, which can be used. The remaining two numbers 97 and 30 are not usable, either. By the same method, we will move on to the second row and of all the numbers 46, 50, 31, 85, 84, 18, 84, 54, 96, 18, 02, 30, 45, 10, 38, 20, 65, 55, 87, 27, except 18, 10, and 20, the other numbers cannot be used because they are out of the range of 20 or because they have already been used before such as 02. Up to now, we have 02, 03, 04, 09, 10, 14, 18, and 20. Continuing the process, we will get another two numbers: 08 and 11. The following universities (See Table 6.5) are the ones chosen by simple random sampling.

02 Tsinghua University	10 Beijing Foreign Studies University
03 Beijing Normal University	11 Liaoning University
04 Fudan University	14 Nankai University
08 Southeast University	18 Zhejiang University
09 Nanjing University	20 Xiamen University

Table 6.5: The universities selected by simple random sampling

In the above example, we check the random numbers in the table row by row. You can also do it column by column. Such a decision is made purely based on your personal preference. But once you have made a decision, you have to stick to it all the way through. Furthermore, you are not allowed to skip over any number unless they are out of the range or they have been chosen already.

Systematic random sampling

If a population is large but the intended sample size is small, simple random sampling is not suitable because the sample selected might not be evenly distributed among the population. Suppose the total population consists of 900 students and you would like to select 30 students out of them as a random sample. Following the technique of simple random sampling, you might get 30 students when you only reach half of the 900 subjects. To avoid this problem, you can use another random sampling technique, i.e. the systematic random sampling technique which can make sure that the subjects selected are evenly spread out among the population. As with simple random sampling, the systematic random sampling technique also requires the numbering of all the subjects. Then, the following formula is used to calculate the interval:

$$\text{Interval} = \frac{\text{The total number of the population}}{\text{The size of the sample}}$$

Once the interval is decided, the subjects are selected according to the interval. How can you get 30 out of 900? The interval is 30 resulting from 900/30. Then one subject is chosen at every 30th interval. What number do you start with? You have to use a table of random numbers to select a number between 1 and 900 as a starting point. According to Table 6.3, the first number is 915, which is bigger than 900, and thus is skipped over. The next number is 674 and can be used in this case. The second number is 704 (i.e. 674+30), and the third one is 734 (i.e. 704+30). Following the same procedure, you will get 764, 794, 824, 854, and 884. Once you get 884, you will have a difficulty. Adding 30 to 884, you will get 914 which is beyond 900. What should you do now? The solution is simple: Just subtract 900 from 914, you will get 14 which is the ninth number in the following list. The tenth number is 44 resulting from adding 30 to 14. Eventually, the subjects which are chosen are the following:

674, 704, 734, 764, 794, 824, 854, 884, 14, 44, 74, 104, 134, 164, 194, 224, 254, 284, 314, 344, 374, 404, 434, 464, 494, 524, 554, 584, 614, 644

If the interval happens to be a decimal, you need to round it off to a whole number. For example, 29.4 will be rounded off to 29, and 29.5 to 30.

Stratified random sampling

Suppose there are 900 first-year students majoring in science in a university. Among them, there are only 90 female students. Suppose you want to get a sample of 30 students in which females and males are balanced. If you use systematic random sampling, the female students may be far less than 10%. In this case, you may try out another random sampling technique, that is, stratified random sampling. First of all, you need to group students into females and males. These two groups of subjects are called subpopulations or strata. And then you extract a random sample from each subpopulation by systematic random sampling. You may choose 15 out of the 90 females and 15 from the 810 males.

If you want your sample of 30 students to represent the original gender distribution of the population, i.e. 10% females and 90% males, in this case, stratified random sampling can be employed, too. First of all, you divide the students into males and females. Then by systematic random sampling, you get 3 out of the

90 females and 27 out of the 810 males. Stratified random sampling is widely used in applied linguistics. For example, you might want to obtain a sample of students to represent different levels of L2 proficiency, or with different family backgrounds, or with different mother tongues. Remember that in stratified random sampling, each unit of the population must be assigned to a stratum before the random selection process begins. Therefore, it is more complicated than the other two techniques.

The number of the subjects for a survey study is normally no less than 30. A smaller sample will cause difficulty in statistical analysis. What kind of sample do you select? How many times do you collect data from the subjects? These two questions will be answered in the following part.

Convenience sampling

Despite our best efforts, it is often impossible to do strict random sampling in our actual research especially for individual researchers. Often, instead of using strict random sampling techniques, we simply use convenience sampling, in which elements are selected for the sample for the convenience of the researcher. In other words, the researcher tends to choose subjects that are readily available. Convenience sampling is useful for exploratory research, and for pretesting questionnaires to make sure that the items are unambiguous and not too frightening. In other situations, however, convenience sampling tends to have inherent limitations.

What needs to be considered in subject selection?

Once you move on to the stage of selecting subjects, you should first remember that subject selection always depends on the other elements of the research, particularly the research questions. Therefore, whatever decisions you make for selecting subjects, you need to justify them in relation to the whole project. Generally speaking, you have to address the following three questions:

1. How many subjects will be involved in the study, and why?
2. How will the subjects be selected and to what extent can the chosen subjects represent the population, and why?
3. How many times will the subjects be involved in the study, and why?

A large sample size or a relatively small one

If the survey study is a major part of your project and the main purpose of your study is to reveal a general pattern or a tendency in L2 learning or teaching, then you have to choose a large sample. However, if the survey study is only part of your project and it is exploratory in nature, you can select a relatively small sample. A legitimate question is what is meant by saying "large" or "small." It is true that these two adjectives are used in a relative sense. According to my understanding of the statistical requirement, the smallest sample size for a survey is no less than 30 while a large sample size is no less than 500. If your study needs to compare two or three groups, then the size of each group is required to be no less than 30.

A random sample or a convenience sample

When representativeness is a compulsory requirement for your research, you must have a random sample which may be obtained through one of the standardized sampling techniques: simple random sampling, systematic random sampling, and stratified random sampling. As a graduate student, you more often than not cannot obtain a random sample due to many practical constraints. Very often, you have to take a convenience sample "where the researcher takes advantage of an accessible situation which happens to fit the research context and purposes" (Punch, 1998, p. 105). For a convenience sample, you need to decide on the procedures by which subjects are chosen. For example, is your sample obtained on a voluntary basis or based on subjects' L2 proficiency levels or through teachers' recommendation? Obviously, subjects who voluntarily join the study won't have any cooperation problems in data collection but they may be less representative because volunteers are more likely to be among the more motivated ones. Taking an intact class as a sample will be better than taking volunteers if you want the study to be more generalizable. Furthermore, in the selection of subjects, you have to consider the demographic attributes of them. For example, how many subjects are males or females? If all of them are the same gender, you have to justify such a decision. Some studies, for example, are interested in the age difference in learning. Then the age will be a key variable in subject selection.

Longitudinal or cross-sectional

If a study is to detect changes or reveal developmental patterns in certain variables, then the subjects need to be studied at several points of time. In this case, the subjects form a longitudinal sample. Suppose you want to find out whether English majors' strategies for learning a foreign language have changed or not through tertiary education and thus you ask some English majors to respond to the same questionnaire twice: the first time when they just start their undergraduate studies and the second time upon their graduation. The responses to the questionnaire at the two points of time are then compared. However, sometimes, the researcher cannot afford the time to follow up the same group of subjects for several years. Therefore you can choose a cross-sectional sample in which the subjects who are selected from the first year through the fourth year are studied only once. Take the study on strategy change as an example again. Instead of studying the same group twice, you may ask a group of the first-year students and a group of the fourth-year students to respond to the same questionnaire together. Then the responses given by the two groups are compared. The advantage of such a cross-sectional sample is that it is economical. The disadvantage is that the changes detected from the two groups may be due to other differences between the two groups besides their tertiary education experience.

☰ ADMINISTERING THE QUESTIONNAIRE

Very often, we are willing to spend as much time and effort as is needed for constructing a good instrument, but the same amount of time and effort has not been put into actual data collection. Obviously, constructing the instrument and administering the instrument are equally important in determining the quality of data. This section is about practical suggestions on administering a questionnaire.

Approaching the subjects professionally

It is very important to approach the subjects in a professional way. When the subjects are called to meet together in a classroom to get ready to answer a questionnaire, the researcher should give them a brief but clear introduction before the questionnaires are administered. Such a talk can make them feel that they are fully informed about the study and their cooperation is important and meaningful.

The introduction consists of two parts. The first part is about the background of the project and the second part about the requirement for responding to the questionnaire. In the first part, you should try to give the subjects a very clear explanation of the research purpose, the context, and the way the data will be used. The research purpose, however, in some cases, is a sensitive issue and must be explained in a very tactical way. Suppose the real purpose of the research is to find out the relationship between the use of L1 and L2 proficiency. In this case, the purpose cannot be revealed to the subjects in a frank manner since it may directly affect their responses to the questionnaire. Thus, you have to talk about the purpose in a very general way by saying that the study wants to find out how L1 functions in learning an L2. Furthermore, you should not only assure the subjects of the confidentiality of the data but also ensure that the data are in fact confidential. Finally, you need to express very sincerely your deep gratitude to them for their time spent and effort exerted in answering the questionnaires.

In the second part, you need to give them specific instructions. You might think it is not necessary to repeat them if the written instructions are simple and easy to understand. However, I still suggest you emphasize some important points since some subjects may be rather careless or simply don't read the instructions. Finally, don't forget to remind them that they should answer all the questions and ask them to put up their hands if they have any difficulty in understanding the items.

If your resources permit, you had better give the subjects each a small gift as a sort of appreciation of their work. The gift of a pen or a folder can be an incentive for the subjects to answer all the items in the questionnaire seriously.

Trying to have face-to-face administering

The way a questionnaire is administered does make a difference to the quality of data. If possible, I strongly recommend face-to-face administering instead of the mailing of the questionnaire. Furthermore, I strongly suggest, if possible, you should administer the questionnaire personally. By doing so, you can guarantee that the subjects are professionally approached.

If your survey is a large-scale one in which the subjects are spread out in several universities that are located in different cities, you usually cannot afford to go personally from one university to another. What you have to do is to ask other people for help. When this is necessary, these helpers need training so that they can administer the questionnaire in a standardized way.

A good environment and suitable timing

Where and when a questionnaire is administered will also affect the quality of data. For example, the quality of questionnaires answered in a classroom is different from that of those responded to in a dorm. Similarly, the quality of questionnaires responded to near lunch time is different from that of those answered just after breakfast. Obviously, a quiet environment and suitable timing are important if you want the data to be reliable and valid. The best arrangement, according to my previous experiences, is to have the subjects answer the questionnaire during normal class time upon the consent of their course teacher. With their teacher's presence and during normal class time, students are usually more cooperative and more serious about the questionnaire.

▶ SUMMARY

A survey study usually involves a relatively large sample and employs a questionnaire with closed-ended questions to collect quantitative data. A good questionnaire must be of high internal validity with a professional look. To design a questionnaire, you have to undertake a series of tasks: (1) deciding on the mode of administration; (2) specifying what kind of data to collect; (3) determining how to process the data; (4) deciding on the content of individual items; (5) choosing the question structure; (6) checking the questionnaire wording; (7) arranging the questions in proper order; (8) determining the questionnaire format; and (9) pretesting the questionnaire.

Scaling is used as a technique in a questionnaire to create a continuum upon which people's responses can be recorded in the form of numbers and eventually can be calculated statistically. The scaling techniques can be divided into comparative and non-comparative ones. Comparative scales involve direct comparison of choices. When a comparison is made between two items, it is called paired comparison scaling; otherwise, it is called rank order scaling. In non-comparative scales, each item is scaled independently from the others with an equal interval between every two adjacent items. There are two kinds of non-comparative scales: semantic differential scale and Likert scale. The semantic differential scale is usually a five- or seven-point rating scale with endpoints associated with bipolar labels that have opposite semantic meanings. A Likert scale contains a few choices which can form a continuum with every two adjacent choices having an equal interval.

If the number of subjects who are asked to answer a questionnaire is less than the whole population, they can be selected through randomization.

There are three random sampling techniques: simple random sampling, systematic random sampling, and stratified random sampling. When you are administering a questionnaire, you must approach the subjects professionally and have them answer the questionnaire in a comfortable environment at a suitable time.

AFTER-READING ACTIVITIES

Reviewing

1 What are the basic criteria for a good questionnaire?

2 What are the procedures for designing a questionnaire?

3 What is the difference between a random sample and a convenience sample? When is it acceptable for a researcher to use a convenience sample?

4 What should be considered in selecting subjects?

Exploring

1 Select one questionnaire from an international journal to evaluate its internal validity.

2 Construct questionnaire items by using different scaling techniques.

3 Decide which random sampling technique will be better used in the following studies.

(1) Researcher A wants to divide 106 Senior Two middle school students into two random groups for a comparative study.

(2) In 2019, 180 students were enrolled in the School of Foreign Studies at one comprehensive university. Among them, 70 were majoring in English, 25 in French, 24 in German, 26 in Japanese, 20 in Russian, and 15 in Spanish. How can we get a representative sample of 30 to represent the 180 students?

(3) In one university, there are 1,000 freshmen in the science stream and 860 in the arts stream. Among the science students, 80% are males and 20% are females, while among the arts students, 52% are males and 48% are females. Now how can we get a random sample of 100 in which the science and arts students are evenly divided and so are the females and males?

Chapter 7

An experimental study

Like a survey study, an experimental study typically collects quantitative data. Compared with a survey study, however, it is much more difficult to implement but much more powerful for establishing the cause-effect relation. In this chapter, I will start by explaining what an experimental study is, and then discuss two important concepts in an experiment: causality and validity. Next, I will describe various types of experimental studies and procedures for conducting an experiment. A paper that reports on an experimental study is presented as Appendix Two.

A BRIEF DESCRIPTION OF AN EXPERIMENTAL STUDY

Experiments were first used in natural sciences. All of us have had the experience of undertaking either a physical or chemical experiment in a laboratory. What have left in your memory by these experiments, I am afraid, are tubes, chemicals, wires, and other materials. What is an experiment in social sciences? I will answer this question first by a conceptual definition and then by examples. Before defining what an experimental study is, I would like to have your personal answer to the following question.

> **?** • What is the major difference between an experiment in natural sciences and that in social sciences?

The answer to the above question is rather complex, but there is one thing I hope you keep in mind: Applied linguistics is part of social sciences which study activities always related to human beings. All the humans vary from one person to another and have their own agency so that they are difficult to be manipulated. Furthermore, some manipulations cannot be operated on humans due to ethical requirements.

Definition

An experimental study is a study in which the researcher manipulates one or more independent variables and measures their effects on one or more dependent variables while controlling the effects of extraneous variables (Rogers & Révész, 2020). The basic elements of an experimental study include:

1. A treatment in which one or more independent variables are manipulated
2. A comparison which involves at least two groups of people or two conditions
3. The measurement of one or more dependent variables as the result of the treatment
4. Measures that are used to control the effects of extraneous variables

If the comparison is carried out between two groups of people, then one group is called a control group and the other one, an experimental group. These two groups are assumed to be alike in all respects except for differential exposure to the treatment. The former does not receive the treatment while the latter does. Once the treatment is accomplished, the dependent variable is measured. The differences that are found between the two groups can be attributed to the independent variable(s).

The essential difference between a survey study and an experimental one is that the former one is carried out in natural surroundings but the latter one is undertaken in a human-manipulated environment. The manipulation typically involves a treatment to some subjects but not to the others, and makes the treatment meet the specified conditions. The more manipulation the researcher engages in, the more convincing the inferred causal relation is.

Illustrations

The following are examples of experimental studies.

Example 1

A comparison between two groups of people

Bejarano (1987) intended to determine whether the cooperative learning approach was more effective than the traditional, whole-class learning approach. An experiment was conducted in Israel, where 665 seventh-grade students were involved. Classes were randomly assigned to use either the cooperative learning approach or the whole-class learning approach. After four and a half months' instruction, their performance on listening and reading comprehension tests was measured respectively. The results of the comparison of the two groups' performance indicated that the cooperative learning method was more effective than the whole-class learning method for the development of listening comprehension but not for the development of reading comprehension.

In Example 1, the treatment is the use of different learning designs and the result of the treatment is the students' performance on listening and reading comprehension tests. The control group is the classes that stick to the traditional approach and the experimental group is the classes that employ the cooperative learning method. Randomization is used to control the effects of the extraneous variables.

Example 2

A comparison between two conditions

In the study conducted by Pica, Young, and Doughty (1987), they intended to find out whether negotiated interaction would facilitate L2 comprehension. They constructed a small-scale experiment in which two ways of providing linguistic input were compared. Altogether 16 adults at the intermediate level were involved. Their comprehension was checked by placing objects on a board under two conditions. Under the first condition, a native speaker of English read instructions that were modified by simplifying syntactic structures, using more words to paraphrase each instruction, and repeating each content word several times. While listening, the subjects were not allowed to interact with the native speaker. Under the second condition, the native speaker read instructions without any modifications. However, the subjects were encouraged to communicate with the native speaker to obtain comprehension. It was observed that the input was modified through interaction. The results showed that the subjects placed more objects correctly on the board under the second condition than under the first condition. It was concluded from the results that negotiated interaction can facilitate L2 comprehension.

In Example 2, the treatment involved two ways of providing linguistic input that were, however, tried out on the same group of people. The results of the treatment were measured by placing objects on a board according to instructions. A comparison was made between the results produced under two conditions. Many extraneous variables were controlled since only one group of people were involved.

?

- The two examples show that an experiment may involve two or more groups of people or two or more different conditions. What are the differences between these two kinds of experiments?

CAUSALITY

The concept of causality is very essential for experimental studies. However, this concept can be interpreted differently. Therefore, this section will first discuss the meaning of causality and then the conditions for causality.

The meaning of causality

A statement such as "X causes Y" is interpreted by scientists as:

1. X is only one of many possible causes of Y;
2. X can account for the variance in Y;
3. The cause-effect relation between X and Y can never be proved but inferred.

The above interpretations are different from our daily understanding in a number of ways (Malhotra, 1993). An ordinary person tends to think of a causal relation in an absolute and deterministic sense. The statement "X causes Y" would mean that X is the sole cause that can determine the occurrence of Y and such a causal relation can be observed and testified.

Evidently, the scientific interpretations of causality are more appropriate for applied linguistics research. L2 teaching and learning are complex and bound to be linked with multiple variables. The cause-effect relationships existing in the field of L2 teaching and learning tend to be probabilistic rather than deterministic. Moreover, we can never directly perceive or verify causality. What we can do at most is to infer a cause-effect relationship. Consequently, it is possible that the genuine causal relation, if it exists, may not have been identified. The following part will further clarify the concept of causality by identifying conditions for a cause-effect relation.

Conditions for causality

Three conditions are generally proposed, i.e. temporal precedence, necessary connection, and the absence of spuriousness within the cause-effect relationship (Maxim, 1999; Punch, 1998). The three conditions should be present simultaneously if a causal relation is to be proposed since none of them alone is enough to define causality (See Figure 7.1).

Temporal precedence is regarded as essential for the occurrence of causality. It means that X must occur before Y but not the other way around if we want to claim that X is a cause of Y. This view seems to be clear enough and can account for many instances of causality. For example, language aptitude can account for the differences in L2 achievement; L1 proficiency can affect L2 performance. Temporally speaking, language aptitude and L1 proficiency evidently occur before L2 learning. However, this condition is easily challenged. For example, summer always follows spring, and winter always follows autumn, yet we won't say that spring is a cause of summer, or autumn is a cause of winter. Therefore, the temporal precedence alone does not seem to be enough to define causation.

The second condition is necessary connection. It means that the two variables concerned must show a necessary link if they form a causal relation. In other words, the changes in X should be related to the changes in Y. Or we say that the two variables must be co-varied. The problem with this condition is that many co-varied variables possess reciprocal relations in which the cause and the effect are not easily teased out. For example, L2 motivation and L2 achievement are such a pair of variables. However, if we can establish the time order of these two co-varied variables, we are in a better position to identify causality since logically speaking, something that occurs later cannot become a cause of something that happened earlier. Even if the above two conditions are satisfied, we still cannot conclusively establish a causal relation since it is possible that variables other than the ones under investigation are the real causes that, however, have not been noticed.

The third requirement is that other plausible causes can be ruled out. That is to say, the researcher should be able to explain why causes other than the ones proposed are not possible. There are two ways to eliminate the plausible causes. One is called physical control, in which the experimental group and the control group are divided through randomization on the assumption that the differences between the two groups are not systematic and they can cancel each other out. The second way is called statistical control, in which the effects of extraneous variables are removed in the process of data analysis. However, the justifiable explanations are not always easy to provide since phenomena in applied linguistics are complex in nature. This topic will be further discussed when we deal with the measures for controlling extraneous variables.

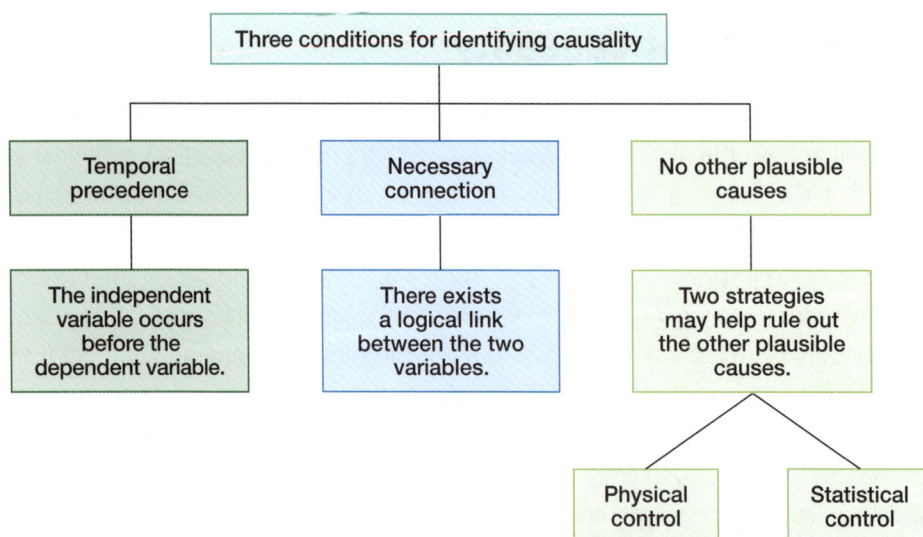

Figure 7.1: Conditions for identifying causality

⊟ VALIDITY IN EXPERIMENTATION

The basic criterion for evaluating the quality of an experimental study is validity. What is validity in an experiment? What factors may affect validity? How do we ensure high validity in experimentation? These questions will be dealt with in this section.

Focus highlight

- Validity is essential for experimental studies. However, it is a bit difficult to have a clear conceptual understanding of the term. Furthermore, it is even more demanding to meet the requirements of validity in an actual experiment.
- I suggest that you read the following part from time to time when you conduct an experimental study. It takes time for you to comprehend the concept of validity. Your understanding can be deepened particularly when you link the concept with your practice.

Internal and external validity

There are two kinds of validity in experimentation: internal validity and external validity. Internal validity concerns the question "To what extent can the claimed cause-effect relation be justified?" In an experiment, if the researcher succeeds in constructing an environment where only the independent and dependent variables are working while the other variables are controlled, the changes in the dependent variable can thus be attributed to the treatment only. Such an experimental design shows high internal validity. In other words, it ensures that the independent variables in question in fact induce the effects in the dependent variables rather than some other variables that are not investigated. Those variables that are not targeted for investigation are called extraneous variables or intervening variables (Read Chapter 2). Controlling extraneous variables is a key to success in achieving high internal validity.

External validity concerns the question of the generalizability of research findings. Bracht and Glass (1968) indicate two major aspects of generalizability: people and environment. The question for "people validity" is: How far can the findings be applied to other populations? The question for "ecological validity" is: To what extent are the findings transferable to other settings or contexts?

Factors affecting internal validity

The factors which can influence the internal validity of research are varied (Bryman, 2016). Among them, some are related to the environment, some related to the subjects themselves, some related to the way variables are measured, some related to the selection of subjects, and some related to the treatment. In the following parts, each type of factor will be described.

Factors related to the environment

Environmental factors refer to the factors occurring in the environment when the research is progressing. For example, Brown (1988) once conducted a study in China and part of the study was to compare two groups' performance on a listening comprehension test. The first group took the test with windows open, but it was reasonably quiet outside. However, when the second comparison group was tested several hours later, there arose a big noise produced by diesel tractors outside. Even with the windows closed, the noise was still disturbing. Obviously, any comparison of these two groups would be meaningless. In addition to noise, the variables such as temperature, time of day, adequacy of light, ventilation, comfort of seats, etc. are also important environmental factors that should be considered by the researcher when he/she is designing an experiment. Otherwise, they will function together with independent variables to confound the results.

Factors related to the subjects

The important factors related to the subjects include maturation, mortality, and the Hawthorne effect.

Maturation refers to changes in subjects themselves that are, however, not caused by the impact of independent variables but by natural changes over time. In L2 learning, maturation takes place as L2 learners become older and more experienced. Such experiences might include other simultaneous learning, or psychological and physical changes. In other words, their L2 proficiency will be improved as their learning experience accumulates. If you undertake a study that lasts for several months or several years, you should keep maturation in mind when you interpret the results.

Mortality refers to the loss of subjects while the experiment is in progress. This happens for many reasons. For example, the subjects may refuse to continue the experiment because the experiment is boring, time-consuming, or too demanding, or it is held at a time that is not convenient for the subjects. Mortality confounds the results because it is difficult to determine if the lost subjects would respond in the same manner to the treatment as the remaining ones.

The Hawthorne effect was first found when Mayo, Roethlisberger, and Dickson carried out their study at the Hawthorne branch (Chicago) of the Western Electric

Company (cited by Brown 1988). They noted that whenever they were present, the productivity was increased although working conditions varied from time to time. In social sciences, the Hawthorne effect refers to a situation where the subjects are so pleased to be chosen for the study that they behave better than usual. In this case, the findings may be related more closely to this pleasure than to the independent variables you intend to investigate. Consider, for instance, a hypothetical study of the effectiveness of a task-based approach in which you tell the students that they are selected for an experiment in order to see whether this new method is better than the traditional one. At the end of the study, you find the students in the experimental group outperform the students in the control group. It is not clear whether the results are due to the greater effectiveness of the method or due to the Hawthorne effect. Consequently, this will pose a problem: How do we separate the Hawthorne effect from the effects of the task-based approach?

> **?**
>
> • **Do you have any strategies to tease out the Hawthorne effect from the effects of the task-based approach?**

Factors related to the measurement

Another set of factors which may affect the internal validity of a study is related to measurement. For example, we use tests, questionnaires, interviews, or any other means to measure one or more variables. The way we measure the variables may affect the internal validity by testing effects and the instability of the measures.

Firstly, testing effects occur in the process of data collection. They may happen in various ways. For example, if the time interval between the pretest and posttest is too short, the subjects may remember the answers they give in the pretest. Some of the subjects might try to select the same responses in the posttest in order to show their consistent views, while others might try to select different answers in the posttest when they think they have figured out what the study is about and try to "help" the researcher. In this way, the validity of the responses in the posttest is affected.

Secondly, testing effects may happen in a situation where the items in the pretest might make the subjects become aware of the variable you intend to investigate. As a result, their sensitivity to the variable will lead to better learning results. For example, once Brown (1988) attempted to examine the effectiveness of teaching reduced forms. Two equivalent groups took a pretest on reduced forms before the teaching started. Then, one group (the experimental group) was explicitly taught reduced forms while the other (the control group) was not. At the end of the study, both groups were again tested on reduced forms. It was not surprising to find that the experimental group outperformed the control group in the second test. However, he was not certain whether the high scores obtained by the experimental group were also affected by the subjects' high degree of awareness of the reduced forms through the pretest.

Thirdly, testing effects may be found when the same test of language proficiency is administered repeatedly to determine how much progress students have made in their performance through a certain period of teaching. The progress in the second test may not be solely caused by teaching. For example, if the same grammar test is given to students twice, some of the problems occurring in the first test may be cleared up in the second test simply because students learn from their mistakes. Thus, the results are ambiguous and difficult to interpret.

In addition to testing effects, inconsistency or instability of instrumentation is another factor related to measurement. Consider two different tests which are administered to the same group of students. One test is used before the experiment and the other one after the experiment for the purpose of checking whether there is any progress in L2 performance. If the second test is actually much more difficult than the first one, then it is not clear whether the differences in the scores on the two tests reflect a real failure of the experiment or are simply due to the different degrees of difficulty of the two tests.

Factors related to the selection of subjects

Subject selection may influence the results of research studies. Suppose you selected two groups to investigate the effectiveness of two teaching designs: the task-based approach and the traditional method. Actually, the two groups were not the same at the beginning of the study since one group had already received instructions on the teaching method for quite a long time. Thus, the differences between the two groups' performance on the posttest might not be caused by the instruction given this time but by preexisting differences. Sometimes, the subjects selected are volunteers who are most likely better motivated in learning than those who do not want to participate in the experiment. The findings are then ambiguous because they might also be affected by the subjects' strong motivation.

Factors related to the treatment

The last set of factors that may affect the internal validity of an experimental study is related to the treatment. For example, how long does the treatment last? Suppose you intended to measure the effects of peer-correction on the development of L2 writing. Your treatment lasted four weeks and the result was that the experimental group did not do better than the control group in their post-writing task. According to such a result, you concluded that peer-correction was not more effective than teacher-correction. However, it can be argued that the ability of L2 writing develops slowly and gradually, and the drastic improvement in L2 writing cannot be made within four weeks. Along this line of argument, the internal validity of your study is called into question.

In addition to the length of the treatment, the way the treatment is given can also threaten the internal validity of an experiment. For example, suppose you wanted to find out whether students' annotating their compositions was an effective method in improving their L2 writing ability. The experiment lasted one year. Two groups of students were taught in the same way except for one difference. That is, the experimental group was asked to write each composition with their annotations while the control group was asked to write each composition without annotations. The result was that the experimental group did outperform the control group in the posttest. Therefore, you attributed the superior performance of the experimental group to the method of writing annotations. However, the students in the experimental group actually spent more time on each composition than those in the control group because it took time for the experimental group to annotate their compositions. By adding all the time spent in annotating in a year, we would immediately find that the experimental group had spent much more time in learning L2 writing than the control group. It is thus uncertain whether the better performance produced by the experimental group was caused by the method of writing annotations or by having more learning time or by both.

Finally, the internal validity of an experiment can also be affected by the people who implement the treatment. Suppose you asked two teachers to carry out your experimental study, and one teacher taught the experimental group while the other taught the control group. What were the characteristics of these two teachers? Did they have similar teaching experience? Did their L2 proficiency reach the same level? Consider the situation where the more experienced teacher taught the experimental group and the less experienced teacher taught the control group. The final result was that the experimental group did better than the control group. Obviously, it is not certain whether the superior performance of the experimental group was due to the effect of the experiment or due to the teacher's rich teaching experience.

Factors affecting external validity

When you run an experiment, you hope that the results will be generalizable to other students or settings. However, factors related to the environment and subjects may affect generalizability.

Suppose you are investigating the effectiveness of a particular method of teaching /r/ vs. /l/. If you conduct the study in a language laboratory with highly sophisticated equipment and tightly controlled procedures, you won't be able to interpret the results of your study in terms of teaching those items in an ordinary classroom. The reason is that the setting in which you carry out the research is not that of the real world.

Subject selection is another factor influencing external validity. For example, if you want to find out about English reading strategies of Chinese middle school students, you should not select students from a foreign language school as a sample. If you want to be able to generalize your findings, you need to choose your sample carefully.

Relationship between the two types of validity

Internal validity and external validity are extremely important if you hope your results will be useful to you and to others in the same research field. However, there is a trade-off between maximizing internal validity and external validity. In order to have the most valid results, you restrict the experimental procedures as carefully as possible, often to laboratory procedures. Consequently, the results are not generalizable to real classroom situations. Similarly, maximizing external validity will be at the expense of reducing internal validity. Once you conduct your experiment in a natural environment to enhance external validity, many extraneous variables coexist with the variables you are examining. Thus, internal validity is threatened. What you are expected to do is to try your best to keep a balance and select procedures that will maximize both types of validity. However, in reality, it is not easy to balance the two. I suggest that you give priority to internal validity since without internal validity, external validity will be meaningless.

Controlling extraneous variables

Extraneous variables represent alternative explanations of experimental results. They pose a serious threat to the internal and external validity of an experiment. Unless they are controlled, they affect the dependent variable and thus confound the results. For this reason, they are also called confounding variables. There are two general ways of controlling extraneous variables: physical ways and statistical ways (Punch, 1998). In physical control, variables are controlled in the process of designing an experiment while in statistical control, variables are controlled in the process of analyzing data. Figure 7.2 shows various strategies.

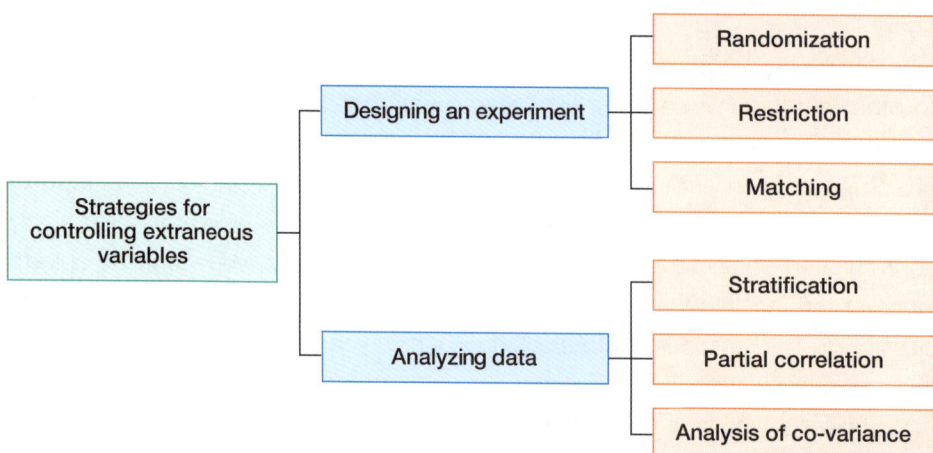

Figure 7.2: Strategies for controlling extraneous variables (Punch, 1998, p. 83).

Physical control

If you want to control extraneous variables when designing an experiment, you employ any one of the three strategies: randomization, restriction, and matching.

Randomization refers to the random assignment of subjects to an experimental group and a control group by using one of the randomization techniques. This technique does not guarantee that the experimental group and the control group are identical but it does make sure that extraneous factors are represented unsystematically in the two groups. Their effects are assumed to cancel each other out. Therefore, randomization is the preferred procedure for ensuring the prior equality between the experimental group and the control group. However, randomization may not be effective when the sample size is small because randomization merely produces groups that are equal on average. It is possible, though, to check whether randomization is effective by measuring the possible extraneous variables and comparing them across the groups.

Restriction refers to the avoidance of the variance of one or more variables by keeping the variables concerned constant. Keeping a variable constant means that the variable has no variance in the experiment. For example, if the researcher thinks that gender may affect the dependent variable as an extraneous variable, he/she may select the subjects who are of the same gender to participate in the experiment. Thus, gender cannot have any relation with the dependent variable. However, by keeping gender constant, the research findings are not generalizable to both sexes. Furthermore, keeping one variable constant does not guarantee that the findings are not affected by other extraneous variables.

Matching involves comparing subjects on the basis of a set of key background variables before assigning them to treatment. For example, in a study on the effectiveness of teaching reading strategies, two groups could be matched on the basis of motivation, L2 reading proficiency, and gender. Then one group could be assigned to be an experimental group and the other to be a control group. Matching has two obvious weaknesses. First, subjects can be matched according to only a few characteristics. As a result, the subjects may be similar in terms of the variables selected but unequal in others. Second, if the matched characteristics are irrelevant to the dependent variable, then the matching effort is wasted.

Statistical control

Instead of making the differences between the groups non-systematic or keeping the variance constant, we may allow natural groups to participate in the experiment. In this way, two groups may have systematic differences before the experiment. However, if we are aware of such differences, in the analysis of the data, we can use some strategies to measure the differences. We can then adjust their effects through statistical adjustments. In other words, we may remove the effects of extraneous variables from the overall effects of the independent variable on the dependent variable. This process is called statistical control and is an alternative to physical control. Specifically speaking, we may employ the following three strategies to exercise statistical control.

Strategy 1

Stratification

Stratification (Rosenberg, 1979) refers to the situation where one extraneous variable is selected as a moderator variable and then the analysis is carried out in groups partitioned according to the moderator variable. For example, if you think the level of L2 proficiency is a possible extraneous variable, you select it as a moderator variable. The subjects are then separated according to their levels of L2 proficiency. Further analyses are carried out within the same level of L2 proficiency. It is no longer possible that the resulting relationships from such analyses between the independent and dependent variables are influenced by the level of L2 proficiency since all the subjects within each group are at the same level.

Strategy 2

Partial correlation

Partial correlation is used to tease out the effects of extraneous variables from the overall effects of the independent variable on the dependent variable. For example, there are three variables involved in your study: motivation, learning strategies, and L2 learning outcomes. You intend to find to what extent learning strategies can affect L2 learning outcomes. In this case, you believe that motivation can work together with learning strategies to influence L2 learning outcomes. In order to tease out the effects of motivation, you may carry out a partial correlation between learning strategies and L2 learning outcomes in which motivation is controlled.

Strategy 3

Analysis of co-variance

Analysis of co-variance functions when the effects of co-variate(s) are removed from the dependent variable before mainstream analysis. Suppose your experiment intended to find out the effectiveness of reading strategy training. The students who comprised a control group and an experimental group were two natural intact classes. The control group was having a reading lesson as usual while the treatment group was taught reading strategies in addition to the normal reading activities. They had pretests and posttests of reading comprehension. Since these two groups were not formed through randomization, they had significant differences in their pretest scores before the experiment. In order to control the extraneous variable of previous reading ability, their reading comprehension test scores were adjusted by removing the differences shown in their pretest reading scores. The formal comparison was made between the two groups after this adjustment.

The three strategies by nature are the same in the sense that they all aim at removing the effects of extraneous variables from the dependent variable. Therefore, the rival hypotheses or alternative explanations to the preferred causal relation are eliminated. The assumption in doing this is that through statistical control, we are able to approximate to the ideal conditions for demonstrating causality.

TYPES OF EXPERIMENTAL STUDIES

Experimental studies are classified as pre-experimental, quasi-experimental, and true-experimental, and can be placed on a continuum in terms of the degree of the researcher's control. Pre-experimental studies are the least controlled and true-experimental studies are the most controlled. The critical feature that separates these three types of experimental studies is the extent to which comparison groups look alike in all respects.

The best strategy to make the comparison groups similar is random assignment of subjects. True-experimental studies are characterized by randomization while randomization is absent in the other two types of experimental studies. Quasi-experimental studies involve naturally occurring treatment groups that are fairly clear-cut. In this sense, although randomization is not present, the differences between the two groups can be identified and measured and eventually their effects can be extracted statistically. Such a statistical control may enable the treatment conditions to approximate to the ideal experimental conditions. Pre-experimental studies are less controlled than quasi-experimental studies since there are no two identifiable groups to compare as such.

Table 7.1 shows three different types of experimental studies with their different designs and features. We will discuss them one by one.

	Pre-experimental	Quasi-experimental	True-experimental
Various designs	One-group posttest-only design	Posttest-only nonequivalent groups design	Posttest-only equivalent groups design
	$X \quad O_1$	EG: $X \quad O_1$ CG: $\quad\quad O_2$	EG: R $\quad$ X $\quad O_1$ CG: R $\quad\quad\quad O_2$

(to be continued)

(continued)

	Pre-experimental	Quasi-experimental	True-experimental
Various designs	One-group pretest-posttest design	Pretest-posttest nonequivalent groups design	Pretest-posttest equivalent groups design
	0_1 X 0_2	EG: 0_1 X 0_2 CG: 0_3 0_4	EG: R 0_1 X 0_2 CG: R 0_3 0_4
Different features	No control group No randomization	Having a control group No randomization	Having a control group Using randomization

Table 7.1: Different types of experimental studies
(*Note.* EG=experimental group; CG=control group; R=randomization)

Pre-experimental studies

Pre-experimental studies are characterized by the absence of randomization and a control group. Two specific designs will be described: the one-shot case study and the one-group pretest-posttest design.

One-shot case study

The one-shot case study may be symbolically defined as:

$$X \qquad 0_1$$

(where X represents a treatment and 0_1, a single measurement on the dependent variable)

Example

Is a new method better than the traditional one?

One researcher hypothesized that a new method was better than the traditional one in terms of improving scores on TOEFL. She ran a one-year training course for the TOEFL candidates for five years by using the traditional method and she recorded the students' TOEFL scores accordingly. The yearly average scores fluctuated from 540 to 575 with the mean being 567. This year she used a new method to teach her students. Once the treatment was accomplished, all the students in her class took TOEFL and their average score was 585. She compared their average scores this year with the students' average scores in the past five years. The results showed that this group did outperform the students in the past.

This type of experiment is useful when it is possible to compare a sample statistic with a known value or population parameter. Such a comparison is sufficient to determine whether the group under consideration differs from some established values. One may, for example, suspect that the students in a particular class are outstanding in their examination performance. This hypothesis can be examined by comparing the students' test scores with historical records.

The value or applicability of this design is limited, however, since it is useful only when the established value is available and the dependent variable can be measured by an authoritative test. If these two conditions are absent, the weaknesses in experiments of this type can be easily demonstrated. First of all, it is not possible to compare the level of the dependent variable to what would happen when X was absent. Secondly, the level of the dependent variable might be influenced by many extraneous variables such as history, maturation, mortality, and selection. Lack of control for these extraneous variables will pose a serious threat to the internal validity. For these reasons, the one-shot case study is more appropriate for exploratory research than for formal research.

One-group pretest-posttest design

The one-group pretest-posttest design may be symbolized as:

$$O_1 \quad X \quad O_2$$

(where X represents a treatment; O_1, the first measurement on the dependent variable; O_2, the second measurement on the dependent variable)

Example

Is reading strategy training effective?

To find out whether reading strategy training can improve students' reading comprehension ability, Researcher A decided to carry out an experiment in her class. She measured the students' reading comprehension ability before the training started. After a ten-week training, they took another reading comprehension test that was equally difficult as the pretest. The means of the two tests were then compared. It was found that the students performed much better on the posttest than on the pretest.

In this design, one group is measured twice without a control group for comparison. A pre-treatment measure is made (O_1) before the group is exposed to the treatment (X). A post-treatment measure is made (O_2) when the treatment is finished. The treatment effect is calculated as $O_2 - O_1$. Such a design can work well in natural sciences where inanimate objects remain stable over time, but it is questionable in social sciences since extraneous variables such as history, maturation, testing effects (both main and interactive testing effects), instrumentation, selection, and mortality could possibly be present. Furthermore, the longer the time between O_2 and O_1, the greater the danger of having confounding effects on the dependent variable.

Quasi-experimental studies

What separates quasi-experimental studies from pre-experimental studies is the presence of a control group, and what separates them from true-experimental studies is the lack of random assignment of group members.

Posttest-only nonequivalent groups design

This design involves two groups: the experimental group and the control group. Measurements on both groups are made only after the treatment, and subjects are self-selected or selected arbitrarily by the researcher. This design may be symbolically described as:

$$\text{Experimental group: X} \quad O_1$$
$$\text{Control group:} \quad O_2$$

(where X stands for a treatment; O_1, a single measurement on the experimental group; O_2, the same measurement on the control group)

> ## Example
>
> ### Is learning strategy training effective?
>
> To find out whether learning strategy training can improve students' English learning, Researcher A decided to carry out an experiment in the classes she was assigned to teach. One class served as an experimental class and the other served as a control class. In the experimental class, the students received learning strategy training in addition to normal class teaching while the control class had English lessons as usual without any strategy training. After the 15-week training for the experimental class, the students in the two classes took the same English proficiency test. The two test means were then compared. It was found that the students in the experimental class outperformed on the test than the students in the control class.

It seems that the experiment looks sound. The same teacher taught the same English lessons to two classes. The difference only lies in presence or absence of strategy training. However, this treatment effect could also be attributed to a series of extraneous variables since without randomization, the two groups may differ before the treatment.

Pretest-posttest nonequivalent groups design

Compared with the posttest-only nonequivalent groups design, this design requires pre-measurement. It can be symbolically described as:

$$\text{Experimental group: } 0_1 \qquad X \qquad 0_2$$
$$\text{Control group:} \qquad 0_3 \qquad\qquad 0_4$$

(where X stands for a treatment; 0_1 and 0_3, a measurement before the treatment on the experimental group and on the control group respectively; 0_2 and 0_4, a measurement after the treatment on the two groups respectively)

The experimental effect is measured as $(0_2-0_1)-(0_4-0_3)$. In this way, the differences between the two groups before the treatment can be taken into consideration to a certain extent. However, one pretest score cannot represent all the differences between the two groups before the treatment. Suppose the treatment is gender-sensitive, or personality-sensitive. Obviously, the pretest score does not reflect such differences. Therefore, without randomization, the confounding effects cannot be fully controlled.

Quasi-experimental studies are inevitably the second best choice to test hypotheses and should be used only where true-experimental studies are clearly impossible to carry out.

True-experimental studies

The essential difference between quasi-experimental designs and true-experimental designs is the use of randomization. Otherwise these two types of experimental designs are the same.

Posttest-only equivalent groups design

The posttest-only equivalent groups design and the posttest-only nonequivalent groups design share one common feature, i.e. the absence of pre-measurement. The difference between them is that the former employs randomization but the latter does not. This design may be described as:

$$\text{Experimental group: } R \qquad X \qquad 0_1$$
$$\text{Control group:} \qquad R \qquad\qquad 0_2$$

(where R stands for randomization; X, a treatment; 0_1, a single measurement on the experimental group; 0_2, the same measurement on the control group)

In this design, the treatment effect is calculated as 0_1-0_2, i.e. the results on the posttest of the experimental group minus the results on the posttest of the control group. Although random assignment of group members allows the strong assumption that the two groups are identical in terms of all relevant features before the experiment starts, this identity is assumed and is not further checked without pre-measurement. Therefore, this design is still sensitive to selection bias, mortality, the Hawthorne effect, etc. Apart from its limitations, this design possesses significant advantages in terms of time, cost, and sample size requirements. It involves two groups and one measurement per group.

> ## Example
>
> ### Are multiple revisions more effective than writing multiple compositions?
>
> The hypothesis that was tested in the experiment was that multiple revisions were more effective than writing multiple compositions in developing L2 writing skills. Two randomly assigned classes participated in the experiment in which one class was required to do multiple revisions and the other class to do multiple writing. Specifically speaking, the students in the first class wrote six compositions with each revised three times while the students in the second class wrote 18 different compositions without revising. With the exception of the difference in this requirement, the writing lessons were the same for the two classes. At the end of the semester, the students in the two classes were measured on their ability in writing in English. Against the researcher's expectation, these two classes did not show any significant differences in their writing ability.

Pretest-posttest equivalent groups design

In the pretest-posttest equivalent groups design, subjects are randomly assigned to either the experimental or the control group and a pre-measurement is taken on each group. This design is formally described as:

$$\text{Experimental group: R} \quad 0_1 \quad X \quad 0_2$$
$$\text{Control group:} \quad R \quad 0_3 \quad 0_4$$

(where R stands for randomization; X, for a treatment; 0_1 and 0_3, a pre-measurement on the experimental and control groups respectively; 0_2 and 0_4, a post-measurement on the experimental and control groups respectively)

In this design, the assumption of random assignment is logically justified if 0_1 and 0_3 are statistically equivalent, and it is not possible to have any systematic bias. While, in reality, such an assumption can hardly be perfectly realized. The use of pre-measurement is a good way of further controlling any differences between the two groups that may exist before the experiment. Let's look at the following example with a slight modification to the previous example.

A modified version

Suppose we have modified the experiment on the effectiveness of multiple revisions mentioned in the posttest-only equivalent groups design by measuring the writing ability of the two groups before the treatment. The pretest and posttest scores are the following:

Pretest: $O_1=75$; $O_3=80$

Posttest: $O_2=85$; $O_4=85$

Without the pretest scores, no experimental effects ($O_2-O_4=85-85=0$) could be found. In contrast, by having the pretest scores, the experimental effects could be obtained as:

$(O_2-O_1)-(O_4-O_3)=(85-75)-(85-80)=5$

PROCEDURES FOR AN EXPERIMENTAL STUDY

If your research questions need to be answered in an experimental study, what procedures should you follow? Logically speaking, the researcher should make a plan for an experiment first and then implement it. At the stage of planning, he/she has to make a series of decisions concerning subject selection, pretest, treatment, and posttest. With the plan fully justified, the researcher can start implementing the experiment in which monitoring, modification, and recording are important tasks. In the following parts, I will describe these two stages one by one.

Planning an experiment

At the stage of planning an experiment, the researcher needs to answer a series of questions as follows:

1. What is the number of subjects and how are they selected?
2. How is the pretest administered if there is any?
3. How is the treatment implemented?
4. How is the posttest administered?

I will use a hypothetical study as an example in our later discussion to illustrate how to answer the above questions. The hypothetical study runs like this: The researcher intends to find out whether L2 writing taught in a computer laboratory is more effective than that taught in a traditional classroom. The researcher decides to conduct an experiment to compare the effects of these two ways of teaching writing.

Subject selection

To have an experiment, you must decide on the number of subjects and the number of comparison groups. The ideal number of subjects within one group should be no less than 30 according to the statistical requirement and the number of comparison groups, no less than two. Where can you get these subjects? Should you randomly select them from all the students, or from one level of students? Or should you simply take intact classes? If an experiment is carried out during normal teaching time, random assignment of subjects may disturb the normal teaching schedule, or may not be possible at all since the English lessons of different classes are usually not at the same time. Therefore, randomization is very often not a feasible decision in real life although it is the best solution for controlling confounding effects. In this case, what you can do is to take naturally occurring classes by matching a few important features. The comparison groups should be similar in terms of their L2 writing ability, L2 overall performance, and major (in science or arts). Altogether two or more classes are involved as shown in Table 7.2.

Control group	Experimental group
One arts class (30)	One arts class (30)
	One arts class (30) (optional)

Table 7.2: Classes for the control group and the experimental group

Suppose you think science and arts students may have different gains from computer-assisted learning since science students are more familiar with the computer. You may add one more dimension for comparison. That is, you may compare two more classes: one science class as a control group and one science class as an experimental group.

If your experiment is conducted in the summer holiday when there is no requirement to follow the national syllabus, teachers will have more freedom to assign the students randomly into comparison groups.

Pre-measurement

The purpose of a pre-measurement is to identify differences in comparison groups prior to the introduction of intervention. Thus, the measurement should cover the essential differences that may confound the effects of the treatment. In the case mentioned above, you need at least to test the students' overall English proficiency, including their English writing ability. If an authoritative test already exists, you had better use it since it can avoid the trouble of justifying the validity and reliability of the test. If subjects are university students, the College English Test for non-English majors and the Test for English Majors are the best tests available in China.

The conditions for a pretest should be the same. Suppose one class has the test in the morning and the others in the afternoon, or one class in the first period in the morning and the others in the last period in the morning. Such variations could lead to differences in the students' performance on the test.

How pretest papers are scored could be another factor that affects the internal validity of the experiment. For multiple-choice questions that usually have only one correct answer, fair scoring is beyond question. However, scoring a composition involves subjective judgement. To increase the reliability of scoring, you had better take the following measures:

1. At least two raters score each paper independently.
2. The compositions of the control class and of the experimental class(es) should be mixed up so that the raters cannot show bias in marking.
3. A marking scheme should be provided so that raters can follow the same criteria to evaluate a composition.

If comparison groups are formed by strict randomization, a pretest can be avoided. However, by having a pre-measurement, you have an opportunity to further check whether there is any difference between the compared groups. If you can show that there is no significant difference between groups on the pretest, differences obtained in the posttest gain far more credibility.

Treatment

Let's look at the example of the L2 writing experiment with multiple revisions again. To design a treatment, you have to consider many things, for example:

1. How will an L2 writing lesson be taught to an experimental group and how will it be taught to a control group?
2. Should these two groups finish the same number of take-home assignments? Should they be taught by the same teacher or two different teachers?
3. Do the two groups have the writing lesson under similar physical conditions (e.g. the time schedule, the environment)?

No matter what kind of decision you make, you have to notice that the differences in learning content, the number of take-home assignments, and the variations in teachers may all influence the changes in the dependent variable. If insufficient attention is paid to these differences, the final result is more difficult to interpret. For example, it could be questionable whether the difference between the two groups is induced by the use of computer-assisted learning or by other extraneous variables.

The issue of controlling extraneous variables could be rather complicated when you come to make decisions. Let's look at the following two examples.

Example 1

Does the researcher choose one or two teachers to instruct the two groups?

If the same teacher is asked to be responsible for the two groups (the experimental group and the control group), the apparent advantage is that there seems to be no variation in teachers. However, in this case, it may not be certain whether this teacher has any bias toward either way of teaching. Even without any bias at the conceptual level, it is difficult to guarantee that he/she can manage the two ways of teaching equally skillfully. After considering the problems, you will most likely decide against having one teacher for the two groups. What can you do now? The alternative is to choose two teachers, each responsible for one class. It is usually difficult to find two teachers who are similar in all respects. The logical solution would be to choose two teachers who are considered to be experts in using their own teaching methods. However, who can guarantee these two teachers are identical in L2 proficiency, teaching experience, and attitudes toward teaching?

The above example shows the advantages and disadvantages of asking one or two teachers to give the treatment. In fact, more often than not, we cannot find a perfect solution. A researcher has to take many factors into consideration. The decision to be made is usually a result of compromise. Then in the thesis/dissertation, the researcher has to admit its limitations.

Example 2

How long will the treatment last?

Some treatments can produce immediate effects but some can only produce delayed effects. Obviously, the improvement of the students' L2 writing ability cannot be achieved within a short period of time. Identifiable effects on L2 writing can be shown, according to our experience, only after at least one semester's treatment. However, one semester's treatment might be too long if we think of the effects of the experiment on the students. If the treatment could produce positive effects, it would be unfair for the control class. Otherwise, it would be harmful to the students in the experimental class.

In Example 2, we may find that it is not a simple decision on the length of the treatment particularly when the treatment involves human beings. At least we have to consider two factors. One is the minimal time of treatment that possibly shows the experimental effects and the second is the ethical concern about the students' learning.

Post-measurement

Pre-measurement is optional but post-measurement is obligatory for all experimental studies. Planning a posttest in the study where a pretest is absent is simpler than the other way around since the researcher does not need to consider testing effects. How does the researcher design a proper posttest to evaluate the effects of the treatment?

Example

The same writing topic or a different topic in the posttest?

Let's look at the previous example again (Are multiple revisions more effective than writing multiple compositions?). Suppose that in the pretest, the subjects were asked to write a composition based on the given topic "Should Chinese university students be allowed to live outside the campus?" Do you want to ask the students to write on the same topic or a different one in the posttest? Using the same topic can eliminate variations in the difficulty level of writing tasks. The danger is that some students who have a good memory may simply write down what has been retrieved from their memory. Using a different topic, you have to make sure it is more or less similar to the one used in the pretest in terms of writing difficulty. The common practice is to use a different topic which is at the same difficulty level as the previous one.

In the above example, the researcher is faced with a tough question of whether in the posttest, the same topic in the pretest or a totally different topic should be chosen. In fact, neither choice can avoid all the weaknesses. The wise decision is to discuss this issue in the research design part and to show that as a researcher, you are aware of the design's limitations.

The scoring procedures, no doubt, should be the same as those followed in pre-measurement. Ideally, the raters who score the pretest papers also score the posttest papers. This can increase comparability between the two tests. If possible, the pretest and posttest papers should be scored together. This arrangement can increase consistency in scoring the two sets of test papers.

Implementing an experiment

The more careful and meticulous your plan is, the fewer problems you may come across when you implement an experiment. However, no matter how perfect your plan looks, you cannot avoid dealing with unexpected problems since situations change. Furthermore, no plan can be perfect and it is common that you find out flaws in the plan afterward. Therefore, making modifications in the process of implementation is normal rather than exceptional.

The difficulty in the process of selecting subjects is often related either to the size of the sample or to the assignment of the subjects into comparison groups. For example, you may find the two intact classes show great differences in the total number of students: one class with 20 students and the other one with 30 students. If you change one class into another one, you will have a problem in matching two teachers. In this case, you had better give up the idea of having a new class since matching two teachers is even more difficult. If possible, you had better try out a new method on a bigger class rather than on a smaller one. Then, in the process of analysis, you can use the strategy of randomization to make the two classes have the same number of students.

The pretest should be taken before the actual teaching starts. Furthermore, the pretest should be held for the two groups at the same time. By doing so, you want to avoid the case where information about the test will leak out before the second group takes it. The difficulty is that the actual teaching schedule is often not arranged according to your own needs. Then, you have to rearrange the class schedule before the pretest. Meanwhile you should inform the students of such a change. Otherwise, a substantial number of students may be absent in the test simply due to being uninformed. The quasi-experiment cannot afford the absence of the pretest scores. Another problem you might come across is that the students may not be serious about the pretest and posttest. To avoid this problem, you had better take the scores on the tests as part of the final score on the course.

Once the treatment starts, the researcher should keep a close eye on progress. If possible, he/she should sit in on the classes and take field notes. Through observation, the researcher may gain a better understanding of what is happening in the treatment. Furthermore, he/she could detect problems and make necessary corrections if the treatment does not strictly follow the original plan either due to an incomplete understanding of the plan or due to the occurrence of some unexpected difficulties.

In regard to the posttest, the researcher has to deal with the same problems as those in the pretest. First of all, the experimental group and the control group should take the test at the same time. Secondly, the students' absence from the test should be prevented. In addition to the above requirements which control potential differences between the two groups, the posttest and the pretest should be taken in the similar environment. By doing so, the possibility of attributing differences between the two groups to factors other than the treatment can be reduced.

?

- Some people think experimental designs have very limited values in doing research on L2 teaching. First of all, an experiment can focus on one or a few variables which cannot capture the complexity of a real life situation. Secondly, the results of the experiment only show the performance of a group rather than individual behavior. However, L2 teaching should cater for individual needs. Thirdly, it very likely violates the ethical rules when you treat the experimental and control groups differently. What is your opinion? Do you agree with the above views? Why?

≡ SUMMARY

An experimental study is a study in which the researcher manipulates one or more independent variables and measures their effects on one or more dependent variables while controlling the effects of extraneous variables for the purpose of establishing a causal relation. The researcher's manipulation is typically in the form of a treatment in which two or more comparisons are made to measure the influence of the hypothesized cause on the assumed effect.

The meaning of the term "causality" used in an experimental study is different from our daily understanding. It is characterized by probability. There are two kinds of validity in experimentation: internal validity and external validity. Both are extremely important for an experiment. Internal validity concerns the question "To what extent can the claimed cause-effect relation be accounted for by the variables investigated?" External validity concerns the question "To what extent can the research findings be applied to contexts beyond the group investigated?" The factors that can reduce internal validity are various; some factors are related to the environment, some to the subjects, some to the measurement, some to the selection of subjects, and some to the treatment. External validity can also be affected by a variety of factors related to the environment and the selection of subjects. In order to increase the validity of an experimental study, you may take various measures to control the effects of extraneous variables. They include physical control and statistical control.

Experimental studies are classified as pre-experimental, quasi-experimental, and true-experimental in terms of the degree of the researcher's control. The true-experimental study is characterized by two features: having a control group and randomly assigning the subjects into the control and experimental groups. In the case of the quasi-experimental study, randomization is absent although there is a control group. The pre-experimental study has the least control by the researcher. In real life, the quasi-experimental study is more commonly used by M.A. and Ph.D. students because of practical constraints.

To implement an experiment, the researcher needs to consider with great caution the number of subjects and the way of selection, the format in which the pretest and posttest are carried out, and the manner in which the treatment is given.

AFTER-READING ACTIVITIES

Reviewing

1 What are the differences between a survey study and an experimental study?

2 Under what conditions can we claim a causal relation between two or more variables?

3 What factors may threaten the internal and external validity of an experiment?

4 When you carry out an experiment, what should you take into consideration?

Exploring

1 Use hypothetical examples to illustrate the three different types of experimental studies.

2 Identify the type of experimental design employed in each of the following studies and compare the designs to explain their differences and similarities.

(1) The study investigated whether pretask planning promotes focus on lexical items or grammatical accuracy during task-based interaction. In the study, 110 South Korean EFL learners were randomly assigned into one of the two groups: having pretask planning and without pretask planning. The students under the two different conditions were all asked to complete two oral picture narrative tasks in dyads over two weeks during their regularly scheduled classes. The findings revealed that regardless of the pretask planning opportunity, the learners focused on vocabulary. (Modified from Park, 2010)

(2) The study investigated whether pretask planning promotes focus on vocabulary or grammatical accuracy during task-based interaction. In the study, 110 South Korean EFL learners were randomly assigned into two groups: One was an experimental group and the other was a control group. The experimental group had three minutes for pretask planning while the control group had no planning time. All the students were asked to complete two oral picture narrative tasks in dyads over two weeks during their regularly scheduled classes. The findings revealed that the two groups did not show any significant differences in their performance. They all focused on vocabulary rather than grammatical accuracy. (Modified from Park, 2010)

3 Find an experimental study from an international journal and evaluate it in terms of internal and external validity.

8

A case study

Unlike survey studies and experimental studies, a case study typically involves a small number of subjects/participants[1] and aims at qualitative data. Since the beginning of the 21st century, case-study research has become increasingly popular due to more extensive acceptance of qualitative studies by researchers (Duff, 2020). In this chapter, I will first explain what is a case study, and then describe how to select participants and collect data in a case study. A paper reporting on a case study is presented as Appendix Three.

A BRIEF DESCRIPTION OF A CASE STUDY

Case studies are extensively used by applied linguists to gain an in-depth understanding of L2 learning and teaching. Particularly, they can reveal complexities and non-linearity in L2 development. In this section, I will first give you the definition of a case study together with illustrative examples. Secondly, I will discuss with you the possibilities of having a case study as an independent study or as part of a mixed design.

Definition and examples

What is a case study? Let's begin with a very simple definition: A case study is a study that examines one or more cases in detail by using multiple sources of data. Let's look at some examples first. Example 1 and Example 2 involve a single case. The first case is about a six-year-old boy while the second case is about a joint online course, which shows that a case can be human or non-human.

---

[1] In the field of research, subjects for a case study can refer to humans or non-humans while participants only refer to humans. The emphasis of this chapter is on selecting humans, and therefore I will use the word "participants."

Example 1

Chen (2000) studied a six-year-old boy whose way of learning English words was particularly interesting. Unlike other children, he tried to remember new words through pictures. Chen observed how he learned new words for a period of six months and took down a lot of notes.

Example 2

Dong (1999) studied a case of a joint online course in which the students from Nanjing University and Randolph-Macon Woman's College read selected writings of Pearl S. Buck and then communicated online about what they read. She observed the classes, and collected the emails and assignments for the purpose of examining the advantages and disadvantages of the course.

A case study may also involve two or more people.

Example 3

In order to illustrate and supplement the results from a survey study, Wen (1993) examined two students who entered Nanjing University with similar matriculation scores but differed greatly in TEM4. Through interview scripts, observation notes, and the students' diaries, she intended to find out why these two students showed such a huge difference in their achievement after two years' study in university.

Example 4

Li (2015) conducted a case study aiming to explore the professional learning space of three highly-motivated university English teachers and the influencing factors of their learning. Through the qualitative data such as interviews, observations, self-reflective journals, she intended to answer the following research questions: (1) What learning activities have the three teachers participated in? How have their professional abilities changed in the process? (2) How do their meta-professional abilities and learning needs interact with these changes?

Of the four examples, the first two can be called single-case studies where the focus is within the case. The last two are multiple-case studies where the focus is both within and across cases.

What is a case? It is difficult to give a short and clear answer since any phenomenon can be qualified as a case (Duff, 2020; Miles & Huberman, 1994; Theodorson & Theodorson, 1969). It could be an L2 learner, an L2 teacher, or a class, or a school. It could be a decision such as a language policy, an L2 curriculum, a teaching approach, or an L2 course. It could also be an attribute of an individual such as vocabulary learning strategies, motivation, etc. or an attribute of an institution.

According to Stake (1988, p. 258), a case study is "a study of a bounded system, emphasizing the unity and wholeness of that system, but confining the attention to those aspects that are relevant to the research problem at the time." This definition reveals several important features of a case study. First of all, a case study does not investigate all the details of each case. Instead, a case study has a clear focus which serves as a lens through which the researcher studies the case. Secondly, the focused aspects should be examined within the context. Thirdly, the focused aspects have to be viewed as part of a system rather than as isolated factors.

SELECTING PARTICIPANTS

Unlike participants for a survey study or an experimental one, participants for a case study are not required to be selected by randomization. Such a requirement is waived not because of the difficulty or impossibility of doing so; rather, it is simply because randomization is not meaningful for a small number of participants. However, the absence of randomization does not mean that the participants can be chosen without careful thinking. In this section, I will introduce to you how to select participants for case studies.

A single case vs. multiple cases

Do you select a single participant or several participants for your study? The decision to be made is no doubt based on research questions. In research on medicine, a single patient whose disease is extremely rare is worth documenting and reporting to other people. Similarly, in the field of applied linguistics, a single L2 learner or teacher is worth investigating if he/she has something unique. However, for an M.A. or a doctoral thesis, it is common to have multiple cases rather than a single case.

Considerations for participant selection

When participants are to be chosen, you first have to think clearly about how to select them. Success in selection results from quite a few factors. I will discuss with you two major factors: (1) the participants' attributes; and (2) the participants' attitude.

In the selection of participants, the first factor you need to consider is their attributes. To be specific, you have to decide in which attributes you want the participants to be varied and in which ones to be similar. The simple answer to this question is except the attributes you are to investigate, you should try to neutralize as many attributes as possible. Now, my own study (i.e. Example 3) that has been introduced at the beginning of this chapter will be taken as an example. As mentioned before, my purpose was to find out why some students with almost identical scores on their matriculation tests showed great variations in their scores on TEM4 after two years of university learning. My speculation was that Strategy Use could account for the variations in L2 achievement in some cases if not in all. With such a research purpose, two participants were deliberately chosen from the same class in order to keep the effects of teaching quality constant and furthermore, they were almost similar in terms of family background, L1 proficiency, previous L2 proficiency and learning purpose as shown in Table 8.1. The essential differences were displayed only in Efforts and their scores on TEM4.

ID	Gender	Age	Parents	L1P	L2P	LP	Efforts	TEM4
01	F	19	F: university teacher M: university teacher	75	95	2.67	20.5	90.50
06	F	20	F: doctor M: nurse	75	96	2.67	40	64.25

Table 8.1: Information about the participants involved in the case study
(*Note.* L1P=Scores on the National Matriculation Chinese Test; L2P=Scores on the National Matriculation English Test; LP=Purposes of learning English; Efforts=Amount of time spent on self-initiated study per week; TEM4=Scores on TEM4)

First of all, you might have noticed that I tried to keep constant as many variables as possible except the variables of scores on TEM4 and Efforts. Why should I do so? In this way, the differences identified later in Strategy Use could be regarded as the major cause of their varied L2 achievement without too much disagreement. Otherwise, even if the differences in their use of strategies did exist, we might have strong reasons to believe that there were many other factors working together with the use of strategies. Secondly, you might be curious about differences in the variable of Efforts. I intentionally selected the cases where the high achiever spent less time studying outside class than the low achiever rather than the other way around. The reason is that my interest was in the role of Strategy Use and I did not want other people to challenge my conclusion by saying that the more important reason was Efforts rather than Strategy Use which led to Participant 01's better L2 learning outcome.

The second factor you have to take into account is the participants' attitude toward the study. By contrast with survey studies and experimental studies, a case study only involves a few participants and therefore we cannot afford to lose any of them. Furthermore, compared with survey studies and experimental studies, a case study is much more demanding on the time and effort of participants who are often required to undertake a series of tasks individually. Obviously, without their sound cooperation, it is not possible to conduct any case study. How can we make sure that the participants to be chosen will have a positive attitude? First of all, all the candidates should be well informed of what they are expected to do in the study and in which way you will compensate for their time and effort, if you plan to, before they make their own decisions on whether they are willing to join the study or not. It is not uncommon for a few of them to refuse to participate in it. The refusing rate is about 20% on average, and it is higher for poor learners than for good learners. Therefore, you had better select more poor learners if a balance between these two types of learners is essential for your study. After all, all the participants who are eventually involved in the study must be volunteers. To motivate them to cooperate with you, it is often best to find a way to show your appreciation of their work. The simplest way is to give them some gifts such as dictionaries, books, or stationery. As an alternative or an additional incentive, you may promise to help them analyze their problems in learning and provide them with constructive suggestions once the study is finished. This is more effective sometimes, particularly for the poor learners who are anxious to improve their study.

COLLECTING DATA

In a case study, the researcher more often than not needs to collect data from multiple sources by different techniques. Widely used techniques include interviews, think-aloud, and diaries/journals. Very often the researcher employs two or more techniques in one study. In this section, I will introduce to you these common techniques one by one.

Interviews

In this part, we will discuss a very useful technique for collecting qualitative data, i.e. interviewing (Bryman, 2016). What is an interview? It may simply be defined as a talk through which the researcher asks the interviewee a series of questions to find out some information about the interviewee. As mentioned before, questionnaires may contain closed-ended questions or open-ended questions. Similarly, interviews may be conducted by using open-ended questions or closed-ended questions. However, only truly open-ended questions can lead to qualitative data. Therefore, the interviews discussed only contain open-ended questions.

- When you conduct a case study which involves a single case or multiple cases, the interview you carry out intends to collect qualitative data rather than quantitative data.
- Therefore, the interview questions are always open-ended in the sense that the answers given by the interviewee are not designed by the interviewer.

Advantages and limitations

There are various advantages of interviewing. It can elicit information which is impossible to obtain by other data collection techniques. For example, using other data collection techniques, you cannot observe feelings, thoughts, and intentions. You cannot observe situations that occurred at some previous points of time. You cannot observe situations that preclude the presence of an observer. You have to ask people questions about those things. The purpose of interviewing, then, is to allow us to enter another person's perspective. The assumption we have for interviewing is that the perspective of others is meaningful, knowable, and that it is possible to make such a perspective explicit. However, we have to be cautious about such self-reported data resulting from interviewing. In an interview, people may understate or overstate something due to their unreliable memory or their personal bias. Furthermore, people are not able to report things which are not consciously noticed. Finally, poor interviewing skills of the researcher may greatly reduce the validity and reliability of the interview data.

Three types of interviews

There are three types of interviews in terms of the degree of freedom on the part of the interviewer: (1) unstructured interviews; (2) semi-structured interviews; and (3) structured interviews.

Unstructured interviews

Unstructured interviews are also called open interviews. They provide interviewers with a lot of freedom. The interview questions are generated spontaneously in the natural flow of an interaction. Typically, the interviewee may not even realize an interview is being conducted. For example, a teacher may have a talk with his/her students individually, discussing the problems in their mid-term exams. Actually, one of the purposes of such a talk is to find out to what extent the students differ in their ability to identify their own problems.

Semi-structured interviews

Semi-structured interviews are conducted according to an interview schedule which is prepared before the interviews begin. The questions in the schedule do not need to be in any particular order and the actual wording of the questions is not determined in advance. The interview schedule presumes that there is common information that should be obtained from each person interviewed. The interviewer is thus required to adapt both the sequence and the wording of questions for specific participants in the context of the actual interview. Such an interview requires the interviewer to have a high level of skills.

Structured interviews

Structured interviews consist of a set of open-ended questions carefully worded and arranged with the intention of asking each interviewee the same questions in the same sequence with essentially the same words. Flexibility in probing is more or less limited, depending on the nature of the interviews and the skills of the interviewers. Structured interviews are particularly appropriate when several interviewers need to conduct interviews on the same topic. By controlling and standardizing the interview questions, the interviewer obtains data that are systematic and thorough about each interviewee, but the process reduces flexibility and spontaneity.

The common characteristic of all three types of interviewing is that the interviewees respond in their own words to express their own personal perspectives. While there are variations in strategies concerning the extent to which the sequencing and wording of questions ought to be predetermined, there is no variation in the principle that the response format should be open-ended. In other words, the interviewer never supplies the phrases or categories that must be used by interviewees in their responses.

The classifications of interviews appear to be clear-cut. However, in an actual study, it is not uncommon that the researcher moves back and forth from one type of interview to another depending on his/her purpose.

Preparing an interview guide/schedule

For semi-structured and structured interviews you should prepare an interview guide or schedule which consists of a series of questions. The interviewer must decide what questions to ask, how to sequence questions, how much detail to solicit, how long the interview should last, and how to word the actual questions. Generally speaking, preparing the interview guide mainly involves the following tasks: (1) decide what type of information you want to obtain; (2) determine the sequence of questions; (3) choose the wording of questions.

Types of information

Like a questionnaire, interviews can generally obtain five types of information: (1) experience/behavior; (2) feelings; (3) opinions; (4) knowledge/abilities; (5) background. You can put the five types of information in the time frame: past, present, and future. Once you have decided on the general types of information, you need to determine exactly which research questions your interview data intend to address.

The sequence of questions

There are no fixed rules about the sequence in organizing an interview. Unstructured interviews are flexible so that a fixed sequence is seldom possible. However, structured interviews must establish a fixed sequence of questions due to their structured format. Here are some suggestions about sequencing:

1. Easier questions first;
2. Questions about "here and now" first;
3. Interesting questions first.

The wording of questions

An interview question is a stimulus that aims at creating or generating a response from the person being interviewed. The way a question is worded is one of the most important elements determining how the interviewee will respond. Asking questions is an art. For the purposes of qualitative inquiry, good questions should be at least open-ended.

What questions can be regarded as open-ended? A truly open-ended question allows interviewees to take whatever direction and use whatever words they want in order to respond in their own way. For closed-ended questions, the participants are asked to choose one as their answer out of a limited and predetermined set of alternatives given. In other words, for closed-ended questions, the response possibilities are clearly stated and made explicit in the way the question is asked. Many interviewers think that the way to make a question open-ended is simply to leave out the structured responses. Such an approach does not, however, guarantee a question is truly open-ended. It can only make predetermined response categories implicit and disguised.

Consider the following "open-ended" question: How satisfied are you with the speaking class in the language laboratory? On the surface, this appears to be an open-ended question. On close inspection, however, it is clear that the dimension along which the interviewee can answer the question has already been identified, that is, the interviewee is being asked for some degree of satisfaction. It is true that the interviewee can use a variety of modifiers for the word "satisfied," saying he/she is "pretty satisfied," "kind of satisfied," "mostly satisfied," and so on. But, in effect, the possible response set has been narrowly limited by the wording of the question.

A truly open-ended question does not presuppose which dimension of feelings or thoughts will be salient for the interviewee. A truly open-ended question permits the person being interviewed to select from among that person's full repertoire of possible responses. Examples of truly open-ended questions might take the following formats:

1. How do you feel about the speaking class in the language laboratory?
2. What is your opinion of the speaking class in the language laboratory?
3. What do you think of the speaking class in the language laboratory?

Moreover, a truly open-ended question cannot be phrased as a Yes/No question. The purpose of an in-depth interview is to get the interviewee to talk—to talk about experience, feelings, opinions, and knowledge. Far from encouraging the interviewee to talk, Yes/No questions create a dilemma for the interviewee because he/she is frequently not sure whether he/she is being asked for a simple response. Let's look at the following example which shows what happens in an interview if Yes/No questions are asked.

The interview between a novice researcher and a university student as an interviewee:
R: Do you like learning English?
S: Yeah.
R: Do you think your English classes are interesting?
S: Yeah.
R: Is your English teacher good?
S: Yeah.
R: Do you love your English teacher?
S: Yeah.
R: Do your classmates like your English teacher?
S: I don't know.

Yes/No questions can turn an interview into an interrogation or quiz rather than an interactive conversation. The information obtained from the interviewee is not very useful for your research.

Interviewing strategies

In order to obtain data with high quality and use them effectively, you may employ various kinds of strategies listed in this part.

Recording the interview

Don't rely on your memory in interviewing and use electronic recording devices in all cases[1]. However, some researchers do not record their interviews not because they do not know that recording is better than personal memory and taking notes manually, or because they have difficulties in getting high-quality technical devices. The common reason is that they are afraid that the interviewees may feel nervous or even decline their request.

It is true that the interviewees may not feel at home when they are told the interview will be recorded and sometimes they may not allow you to do it. I suggest that you only select the interviewees who are willing to cooperate with you. How can you have enough cooperative interviewees? You are advised to use several strategies when you approach the potential interviewees before a formal interview. Firstly, you give them a clear explanation of the purpose of your research. Secondly, you assure them that you will keep the interview data confidential. To be specific, anything written in your thesis/dissertation concerning the interview will be checked by them and their names will never be revealed to other people in any case for any reason. Finally, you need to obtain a written consent from the interviewees and at the same time, you also give them a written promise. Thus, both parties are ensured that the recording of the interview will be dealt with by strictly following research ethics. In fact, the process of selecting the interviewees should be described in detail, which is an academic requirement.

Probing

The key to successful interviewing is learning how to probe effectively—that is, how to stimulate an interviewee to produce more information, without injecting yourself so much into the interaction. There are many kinds of probes that you can use in an interview. In this part, I will introduce to you some probes recommended by Bernard (1994).

The silent probe

The silent probe is apparently the easiest yet the most difficult. It simply means remaining quiet and waiting for an interviewee to continue. The silence may be accompanied by a nod, or by a mumbled "uh-huh." The silent probe sometimes produces more information than direct questioning does. Some interviewees are more talkative than others and require very little probing to keep up the flow of information. Others are more reflective and take their time. Inexperienced interviewers tend to jump in with verbal probes as soon as an interviewee goes silent. However, the interviewee may be just reflecting, gathering thoughts, or preparing to say something important. You can kill those moments

---

[1] You have to gain permission from the interviewee before you record the interview.

with your interruptions. On the other hand, the silent probe is a tricky technique to use, and that is why beginners should avoid it. If an interviewee is genuinely at the end of a thought and you don't provide further guidance, your silence can become awkward. You may even lose your credibility as an interviewer. It takes a lot of practice to use the silent probe effectively, but it's worth the effort.

The echo probe

The echo probe is another kind of probe that is simply repeating the last thing an interviewee has said and asking them to continue. This echo probe is particularly useful when an interviewee is describing a process, or an event. Suppose you ask an interviewee to describe his/her reading process. Once the interviewee stops describing, you might say, "I see. You read the title first to predict the general idea about the text. Then what do you do next?" This probe is neutral and doesn't redirect the interview. It shows that you understand what has been said so far and encourages the interviewee to continue with his/her narration. If you use the echo probe too often, though, you'll hear an annoyed interviewee asking you, "Why do you keep repeating what I just said?"

The uh-huh probe

The uh-huh probe is the third kind of probe. You can encourage an interviewee to continue with his/her talk by just making affirmative sounds, like "uh-huh," or "Yes, I see."

Using the conversational style

Using the conversational style means that an interviewer and an interviewee should talk to each other in a natural manner. That is to say, a question you ask should be related to the previous answer given by the interviewee. This is a difficult task. On the one hand, as an interviewer, you have prepared a set of questions to ask and you have to keep the conversation on track. On the other hand, you should talk in such a manner that the interviewee does not feel that he/she is being interrogated. What is required is flexibility and spontaneity.

Common problems in interviewing

By observing graduate students' simulated interviews, I have found several common problems. The first one is that many interviewers who cannot put up with a single second's silence interrupt the interviewee's thinking by more questions. The second problem is that they often ask Yes/No questions to which the interviewee only offers a short answer. They then do not know what should be asked next. The third problem is that the interviewers do not know how to draw the interview back to the right track when the interviewee digresses. The last problem is that the interviewers talk too much and they basically give the interviewee the answer they are hoping to get.

These problems cannot be overcome overnight. Developing an effective interview technique requires a lot of reflective practice. In reflective practice, you have to make an evaluation of each of your simulated interviews and try to overcome the weaknesses identified in the next one. If possible, you may invite your supervisor or experienced researchers to listen to your pilot interview together and identify the problems. I am sure such reflective practice will enable you to become a skillful interviewer.

Think-aloud

Think-aloud, as a technique of data collection, has gained its legitimate status since the 1980s when cognitive research gained favor. Quite a few researchers (for example, Cohen, 1987; Flower et al., 1990; Guo, 1997, 2007; Hosenfeld, 1984; Hudelson, 1989; Lauer & Asher, 1988; Lu, 1997; Raimes, 1985; Wen & Guo, 1998; Zamel, 1983, 1987) probed into the process of students' L2 writing and reading by this technique. The findings from their studies provide insights into students' cognitive processes. In this part, the following questions will be answered: (1) What is think-aloud? (2) How is think-aloud carried out? (3) What are the limitations of think-aloud?

What is think-aloud?

When a child is at the age between 3 to 7, he/she likes to talk while playing a game. Through this talk, we may know what is going on in his/her mind. The talk the child does is think-aloud. Similarly, in L2 research, think-aloud requires participants to speak out their inner thoughts which are otherwise not accessible to outsiders. By contrast with children who do think-aloud naturally, L2 learners have to be trained to do so. In other words, think-aloud is no longer a natural behavior for an adult L2 learner. Therefore, without proper training, think-aloud as a data collection technique cannot work effectively on people who are no longer young children.

In the following part, I will describe two studies, which were both conducted by my M.A. students using think-aloud in 1997. Their theses are not published.

Example 1

Guo's study

Guo (1997) used the think-aloud method to investigate to what extent L1 is involved in students' picture composition. In his study, the participants were 20 Senior 2 and Senior 3 students from a high school, who were recommended by their teachers as students who were extrovert and talkative, and more likely to be cooperative in accomplishing the task of thinking aloud.

The training in think-aloud lasted two weeks. It started with the researcher's demonstration in which he spoke out what was going on in his mind while reading a piece of classical Chinese prose. Then all the selected participants were asked to accomplish two tasks by thinking aloud: (1) Read some classical Chinese prose pieces and show their understanding by thinking aloud; (2) Describe a process in which they understood distorted or blurred pictures or words. These two tasks were well selected because they did not involve the use of two languages, which would not make the participants think they had to use Chinese mixed with English in their later L2 writing.

Once everyone understood what think-aloud was and knew how to carry it out, they each were asked to write a story in English of about 100 words based on a series of pictures while trying to say aloud anything occurring in their minds in the whole process of writing. The language used in think-aloud data was not specified but they were told that their think-aloud should be natural in the sense that the language used should be the same as the form through which their thoughts were expressed. To put it simply, if inner thoughts were in Chinese, then Chinese should be employed; if in English, then English should be used.

Altogether they were given eight pictures in a sequence describing how a student saved the life of a blind man on his way to school and he was late for his class. A tape-recorder was used to record each participant's composing-aloud process and at the same time the stories written down were also collected from the participants as the data of product.

Once the data collection was finished, all the tapes were transcribed and the transcripts were called protocols. The researcher first made a statistical comparison between the quantitative use of L1 and L2. Secondly, he identified the different functions of the use of L1 by qualitative analysis. Finally, he hypothesized two L2 writing models with a focus on L1 use.

Example 2

Lu's study

Lu (1997) intended to investigate the relationship between L2 proficiency and EFL learners' strategy use in L2 reading. Four junior non-English foreign language majors in Nanjing University were selected for this study. Among them, two were Japanese majors and the other two, Russian majors. One Japanese major and one Russian major formed a pair of beginners who had only studied English for one year and the other two formed a pair of intermediate readers who had studied English for seven years. They were all successful learners in their own majors.

Two passages were chosen according to the readers' proficiency levels. They were asked individually to read the given passage while reporting verbally as much as possible about how they understood the text. Their verbal reports were recorded. The researcher remained silent and observed their performance. An interruption by the researcher only occurred when the participant kept silent for more than a minute. No time limit was set for reading.

To make sure they knew how to go about think-aloud, the researcher asked the participants to read a sample passage after the researcher's instruction. Since they were university students, it did not take long for them to understand the think-aloud procedure.

The verbal reports were transcribed and then the protocols were coded on the basis of Block's classification of strategy categories (Block, 1986) with some necessary modifications. The results revealed from the study are the following: The relationship between L2 proficiency and comprehension strategy use is rather complicated. L2 proficiency, on the one hand, does not prevent the beginners from making use of some higher-level comprehension strategies and using them effectively. On the other hand, L2 proficiency is indeed a constraint on the use of strategies. Compared with more proficient L2 learners, less proficient L2 learners tend to use fewer varieties of reading strategies and use some categories less frequently and/or with poorer quality. Furthermore, lower L2 proficiency more likely produces a higher level of anxiety and frustration in dealing with new words and difficult sentences.

In the two examples, both M.A. students tried out the think-aloud technique in data collection as pioneers in the Chinese context. Guo (2007) wrote a book on think-aloud based on his cumulated experience in using this technique for his research. If you are interested in using it for your research, I strongly advise you to read his book and get detailed information about it. The following part only deals with this technique very briefly.

How is think-aloud carried out?

Think-aloud is much more difficult than it appears to be. To make sure think-aloud is working successfully, you have to at least meet the following four requirements. First of all, the participants you select should be very cooperative in the sense that they are willing and able to think aloud as required. Secondly, the training you provide must be sufficient and adequate. Thirdly, the quality of recording has to be guaranteed. Finally, the researcher should behave professionally when a participant is undertaking a task using think-aloud. Next, we will discuss how the above criteria can be met.

Selecting "ideal" participants

By saying "ideal" participants, I do not refer to the participants who can provide you with the information that can support your assumption. In this context, "ideal" participants are those who are talkative, and capable of thinking aloud after proper training. In fact, not all participants feel at ease to think aloud even after good training. For example, some L2 learners who are not good at articulation are quiet and hardly utter anything to their classmates in daily life; some L2 learners, although they are talkative, don't show a positive attitude toward the technique of think-aloud. Therefore, the "ideal" participants are those who are talkative and are also able to think aloud without too much uneasiness. This, of course, is a constraint on the researcher's data.

The participants eventually involved in your study are usually chosen through three stages. At the first stage, you select the participants for training. The initial criterion for the first selection is the participants' personality, i.e. being talkative. Hence, the students who are obviously introverted and reserved are not candidates for training. The second selection is made after well-constructed training. At this stage, you are only interested in the participants who feel at ease in think-aloud and are also willing to be cooperative with you. According to our previous experience, nearly 40% of the trainees are screened out because they are not happy with think-aloud. The third selection is made once you have collected all the data by using the technique of think-aloud. You try to eliminate the participants whose noticeable pauses comprise more than 10% of the total amount of time of think-aloud. The third selection often reduces 10%-20% of the participants. Since about half of the participants are screened out from the second and the third selections, you have to choose more than the required number of participants for initial training and for think-aloud data collection.

Providing effective training

To provide participants with effective training, the normal procedure is that the researcher first demonstrates how think-aloud is carried out and then gives the participants at least two opportunities to practice it. In order to save time, the demonstration can be made in a group and the first think-aloud tryout can be undertaken in a laboratory where their think-aloud process can be recorded. Furthermore, the participants might be less nervous when they are doing it together and no one is able to hear the others. However, the second tryout is better done individually. By doing so, the researcher can easily offer help if they have any misunderstanding about think-aloud. Moreover, the researcher can easily identify the participants who are not suitable for this kind of study.

One potential problem in the training is that the researcher's demonstration may be misleading in the sense that the researcher's think-aloud illustrates how a certain type of data is produced. For example, suppose you want to find out to what extent L1 is involved in L2 writing. In your demonstration, you speak out what is going on in your mind sometimes in Chinese and sometimes in English. The participants might then think this is the way they should do it. Thus, to avoid this problem, your demonstration should be carefully designed. In this case, it is often best to choose a task that is not related to language learning at all, for example, to guess the missing part of a Chinese character, or to resolve a puzzle.

Having an electronic recording device of high quality

First of all, the recording devices used for think-aloud should be checked more carefully than those used in interviews where the researcher asks the participants one question after another and the interviews can be stopped if the devices do not work properly. Furthermore, the interview questions are usually discrete and are not necessarily linked logically. By contrast, in think-aloud, once the flow of the participant's thoughts is interrupted, it is difficult, if not totally impossible, to resume.

Secondly, it is often best to make sure the batteries of the recording devices do not run out of power in the process of think-aloud. Finally, you should make sure that the device is set in the mode of recording when the participant starts the task. One problem I once came across was that the student felt unhappy with what had been said and stopped the recording. If this happens, you have to ask him/her not to do it again and remember to push the recording button when he/she resumes the task.

Behaving professionally

How should a researcher behave when a participant is undertaking a task using think-aloud? In general, the researcher should behave professionally. Behaving professionally means that whatever the researcher does should be conducive to the participant's completion of the task. I suggest that you sit quietly in a corner that is out of the sight of the participant while observing the participant's performance. If necessary, you may take some notes. Remember that any movement and noise you make will certainly disturb the flow of thought of the participant.

How do you deal with the situation where the participant keeps silent for a while? Should you ask him/her a question such as "What are you thinking now?" to push him/her to speak? In my opinion, instead of asking him/her a question, you had better make a sound signal indicating that he/she has to stop pausing. Of course, you need to tell your participant about the signal before the data collection starts.

Limitations

Think-aloud has gained its legitimate status in research on L2 learning in the past few decades. As a result, a growing number of studies using this method have gained some valuable insights into L2 learners' mental processes which are not accessible by other data collection techniques. However, this method has some unavoidable weaknesses which a researcher must keep in mind when interpreting the results.

As mentioned before, the think-aloud technique can only be effective for participants who are eventually able to accomplish the task of think-aloud successfully. Therefore, it is doubtful that the data reported by such a highly selective group are the same as those reported by people who are screened out. As a result, we have to admit the participants selected in the study are biased to a certain extent.

No matter how effective the training is, think-aloud is not a normal behavior of an adult. When an adult is required to do it, his/her mental process is likely to be distorted in one way or another. It is not clear to what extent the data elicited by think-aloud can reflect natural thinking. However, the more effective the training is, the more natural the data will be.

Although the participants are required to speak out all that is going on in their minds, some mental activities inevitably go unreported verbally since thinking is always faster than speaking. Also, you can speak out something while thinking about other things. In this sense, think-aloud can never report all of the inner thoughts. To compensate for these inadequacies, the researcher may conduct an immediate follow-up interview to elicit more information.

Although we are aware of the limitations of think-aloud, this technique is the best available one to date for us to gain access to the inner thoughts of the learner. Along with the development of cognitive research, people become more curious about the mental activities involved in L2 learning. So far, we have not reached the stage where scientific instruments are capable of examining inner thoughts of humans. Think-aloud, in my opinion, can at least partially satisfy our curiosity.

Diaries/journals

A diary or journal is also an important tool in the research on L2 learning and teaching, which can record the learner's or the teacher's feelings, attitudes, behaviors, reflections, and conscious awareness of cognitive process in a language class or other L2 learning/teaching contexts. The difference between a diary and a journal primarily lies in their frequencies. A diary is a record of personal experiences written every day, while a journal is also a personal written record of things the participant sees, does, or thinks about but without the requirement on writing every day. In this sense, journals are used more often than diaries in our research.

Definition

According to Bailey's definition (cited by Nunan, 1994, p. 120), the diary used in research is "a first-person account of a language learning or reading experience, documented through regular, candid entries in a personal journal and then analyzed for recurring patterns or salient events." Her definition emphasizes three important requirements. First of all, the participants have to keep the diaries themselves. Secondly, the participants need to keep their diaries regularly and honestly. Thirdly, the purpose of having the participants keep diaries is to find out either similarities or unique features displayed by diary keepers.

However, in my opinion, Bailey's definition does not capture the essential differences between a diary in daily life and a diary used as a research tool. Firstly, a diary kept by a person in daily life is an account of personal feelings, views, random thoughts, etc. which is not meant for any public purposes. Therefore, it can be fragmentary, illogical, and ungrammatical. However, once a diary is used as a research tool, it has lost the characteristic of being private. The diary keeper must write in a way that other people can understand without much difficulty. Secondly, the diary in daily life can record anything occurring in people's minds, while the diary for research has to contain information relevant to the research purpose. Finally, the diary in daily life primarily keeps an account of things that have just happened whereas the diary for research can record not only the activities that have happened now and here but also then and there. When a diary is used to record the then-and-there experiences, I will call it a reflective diary.

In view of the above differences, I would like to define a diary or a journal in research as "a comprehensible written account of one's own experiences in L2 learning and teaching which are however confined to aspects relevant to specific research problems."

Illustrations

A few L2 researchers have recorded their own experiences of learning languages other than the first language in an attempt to have a better understanding of the process of L2 learning. For example, Rivers (1983) in her diary described how she strove to learn a sixth language. Bailey (1983) also recorded through a diary her rich experiences in learning French.

However, many more researchers ask their participants to keep diaries according to the given instructions so that they can investigate their language learning. In the following part, two examples are given to show how data collection can be conducted through diaries/journals.

Example 1

Wen's study

In my study on the role of controllable learner factors in L2 learning (Wen, 1993), 10 participants out of the 242 participants were selected for case studies. As part of the case studies, they were required to keep one-week diaries to record their self-initiated English learning activities in order to find out the differences in the use of learning strategies between high and low achievers.

The diary instructions were given as follows.

> Please keep a diary for a week. In the diary, you are required to record the English learning activities you undertake after class every day. Your writing should address the following aspects:
> 1. What type of activities are you undertaking? And why?
> 2. How much time do you spend on each activity?
> 3. What is your physical and psychological state when carrying out the activity (e.g. physical state: tired or energetic; psychological state: attentive or absent-minded)?
> 4. What do you think of the activity? (Is it important for improving your language proficiency?)
> 5. What strategies have you adopted in undertaking the activity? (Please try to give as many details as you can.)

Since my purpose of asking them to keep a diary this time was not to test their language proficiency, they were allowed to use any language (English, Chinese, or the mixed code) they feel that can best express themselves (Wen, 1993, p. 309).

By examining the questionnaire and interview data provided by the 10 participants, we concluded that both low and high achievers were active strategy users. However, the diaries displayed quite a few qualitative differences between high and low achievers, which made me think why such differences were not present in the questionnaire and interview data. The reason I found was that the high achievers tended to set up higher demands on themselves than the low achievers so that the high achievers were more likely to blame themselves for not doing well in responding to questionnaire items and interview questions. In contrast, the low achievers tended to overvalue themselves since their expectations were not that high. For example, through diaries, I found that the low achievers tended to have poorer performance in the use of management strategies than the high achievers. The following are excerpts from the one-week diaries written by one low achiever (Participant 10).

Wednesday, Oct. 23, 1991
After class I went to the library, sitting in the section of "Language and words." There were many books in this section. I often chose different books to read. But today, I was interested in the book *Idioms for Everyday Use*. The idioms were arranged in alphabetical order. Most of them were useful, such as "Nothing ventured, nothing gained..." So I copied down some sentences I liked and memorized them at the same time. I copied down more than 20 sentences. But I found I only reached the letter "c." It took me too much time and I did nothing else this afternoon. I often do things like this. I do not care whether something is helpful or not; so long as I like it, I will spend time on it. As with my English study, even though it seemed that I learned little this afternoon, "many a mickle make a muckle." As time goes on, I believe I will feel at home in English.

Obviously, the two reading activities recorded in her diary were ad hoc decisions. Furthermore, in her outside reading, she habitually or automatically employed the strategies she used in reading prescribed texts. Since she followed the same method to continue these two reading activities, it would be extremely difficult for her to accomplish them because she could not afford the time. Even if she finished them, it could be imagined that she would not have fruitful results. Unfortunately, given such ineffective learning strategies, she still showed satisfaction with them.

Example 2

The study by Schmidt and Frota

Schmidt and Frota (1986) conducted a case study in which a participant, a native speaker of English, was asked to keep a diary documenting his learning experience of learning Portuguese in Brazil. The diary indicated that the participant's learning could be divided into three stages: (1) learning through natural communication with local people; (2) learning through formal instruction; and (3) learning through natural communication with subsequent self-reflection. The following three extracts selected by Nunan (1994, pp. 121-23) can illustrate the participant's cognitive as well as affective experiences at these three stages of L2 learning.

Extract 1

Journal entry, Week 2
I hate the feeling of being unable to talk to people around me. I'm used to chatting with people all day long, and I don't like this silence. Language is the only barrier, since it is certainly easy to meet Brazilians. I've noticed that it is acceptable to ask anyone on the street for a cigarette. It...appears to have no relationship to age, sex, or class. Last night, an attractive and obviously respectable young woman, accompanied by her boyfriend, stopped me and bummed a cigarette. If I take a pack to the beach, it disappears within an hour, so that's 20 people I could have met...Today when P and I were at the beach, a

guy came up for a cigarette, sat down, and wanted to talk. He asked if I were an American and I said *sim*. He said something I didn't comprehend at all, so I didn't respond. He said, "Well, obviously communication with you would be difficult," (I did understand that, though I can't remember any of the words now) and left. (p. 242)

Extract 2

Journal entry, Week 4

P and I started class yesterday. There are 11 in the class (of various nationalities). The teacher is young and very good. She introduced herself to us (in Portuguese). I am X, my name is X, I am your teacher, I am a teacher, I am a teacher of Portuguese, I'm also a teacher of English, I'm from [place], I'm single, I'm not married, I don't have children, I have a degree in applied linguistics, etc. She went around the class, asking the same kinds of questions: What's your name? Where are you from? What kind of work do you do? Do you have any children? etc. Most of the students could answer some of the questions, e.g. I know what my title is at the university. Everyone was rapidly picking up new things from the others' answers. For the rest of the class, we circulated, introducing ourselves to each other and talking until we exhausted the possibilities. At the end of the class, X put the paradigm for SER on the blackboard, plus a few vocabulary items. Great! This is better than *bom dia* and then silence...I'm sure I'll be asked all those questions thousands of times before I leave here. So I went out last night and talked to four people. It worked, and they invited me to a party tomorrow night. Of course, I quickly ran out of things to say and quickly stopped understanding what people said to me, but that just made me eager to get back to class. (p. 243)

Extract 3

Journal entry, Week 11

H and I ate dinner at Caneco 70. He complained nonstop about his job. I tried to say "you don't seem comfortable" (with the job): *sinto que você não está comfortável*, and his face showed complete non-comprehension. I grabbed my dictionary. "Comfortable" is *comfortável*, but it flashed through my mind that perhaps you can only say chairs are comfortable, not people. A few minutes later H said something with *não deve*. I was taught DEVER means "have to" or "must," so I thought that *não deve* + Verb would mean "don't have to" and *deve não* + Verb would mean "must not," but H's remark obviously meant "should not." So I learned something, but in general H is a terrible conversationalist for me. He doesn't understand things I say that everyone else understands. When I don't understand him, all he can ever do is repeat. (p. 246)

In the examples given, we may get some general ideas about what a diary/journal for the research purpose looks like and how a diary/journal can reveal insights into processes of L2 learning.

Advantages and limitations

The use of diaries/journals is more convenient and easier than interviewing and think-aloud. First of all, it does not take so much time on the part of the researcher as that required by interviewing and think-aloud since the latter methods have to be conducted on an individual basis and have to be transcribed afterward. Secondly, it is less technically demanding than interviewing and think-aloud. Using think-aloud, the participants must be cautiously selected and effectively trained before data collection. In the case of interviewing, in addition to having a carefully designed interview schedule, the quality of the data also very much depends on the interviewing skills of the researcher. For diaries/journals, there is only one thing you need to pay great attention to, i.e. the quality of instructions given to the participants. Otherwise, the advantage can be easily turned into a disadvantage since the data of poor quality due to unclear instructions can only be known when they have been collected, which is too late to remedy.

Although diaries/journals sometimes can provide us with the data which would be difficult to gather in other ways, diaries/journals' data face challenges and criticism. First of all, people doubt their validity. To put it in simple words, people are not sure to what extent the recorded data in diaries/journals can reflect the reality. Obviously, once the participants describe their experiences and attitudes toward L2 learning activities after the activities occur, they might distort them unintentionally. Furthermore, diaries/journals usually document the things the participants are conscious of. Finally, diaries/journals are sometimes not clearly written or are difficult to understand.

Problems in using the technique of diaries/journals

Although the use of diaries/journals is easy and convenient, it can be a total failure which goes unnoticed until the diaries/journals are submitted to you. By contrast with interviewing and think-aloud, in the process of which you may notice the problems, problems occurring in diaries/journals can only be realized after data collection. Therefore, you must anticipate the problems the participants may have and try to prevent them from happening by giving the participants clear oral instructions as well as written ones or checking the diaries/journals while they are in progress.

One problem postgraduate students may encounter is that in the participants' diaries/journals, much information is irrelevant and the relevant information is far less than needed. The cause of the problem is that the researcher does not explain to the participants explicitly what they are expected to write.

Another problem is that if instructions are biased, the participants' diaries/journals will contain the information that reflects the bias. For example, in the students' diaries in one study, they all discussed the reasons why they overused textual connectives and attributed this to the teacher's teaching. After I read their diaries, my first question was: Did all the participants involved here overuse textual connectives? When the researcher admitted that this was not the case, I asked the second question: Why did they say so? Later I found that one of the instructions given by the researcher was the following: Please try to explain in your diaries why you overused textual connectives. Obviously, the instructions were biased.

⊟ SUMMARY

A typical case study involves a few participants and aims to collect qualitative data. It may study a single case or multiple cases depending on the research purpose. In the selection of participants, two questions need to be answered: (1) What attributes of the participants need to be neutralized and what attributes need to be varied? (2) Are the participants willing to cooperate with you?

With regard to collecting data in a case study, three techniques are discussed: (1) interviews; (2) think-aloud; and (3) diaries/journals. An interview is an interaction through which the researcher asks the interviewee a series of questions to find out some information about the interviewee. It can elicit information that cannot be obtained by other data collection techniques, such as the interviewee's feelings and opinions in the past, at present, and in the future. Its most obvious weakness is that self-reported data by the interviewee are only confined to those at the conscious level and can be distorted intentionally or unintentionally. There are three types of interviews in terms of the degree of freedom on the part of the researcher: (1) unstructured interviews; (2) semi-structured interviews; and (3) structured interviews. For semi-structured and structured interviews you should prepare an interview guide or schedule which consists of a series of questions that must be truly open-ended. In order to conduct an interview effectively, you are advised to use a variety of strategies, such as using electronic recording devices, probing, and using the conversational style.

Think-aloud is a technique to get inner thoughts of the participants while they are performing a language activity. The use of this technique is time-consuming and skill-demanding. The participants to be selected to do think-aloud need to be talkative, be comfortable with this task, and be capable of completing it after training. Effective training is very critical to the success of think-aloud.

A diary/journal is also an important tool in collecting data in a case study. It may be used to record what has just happened in L2 learning and teaching or reflect on what happened long before. The use of diaries/journals is more convenient and easier than the use of interviews and think-aloud, but the data reported may not truly reflect the reality.

AFTER-READING ACTIVITIES

Reviewing

1. What is a case study? Find an example to illustrate your understanding.
2. What are the differences between semi-structured interviews and unstructured interviews?
3. What are the advantages and limitations of interviews?
4. Conduct an interview using an electronic recording device. Play the recording in a small group and ask the other members to make critical comments on it.
5. How do you collect data by think-aloud? How can you make sure that the data are of high quality?
6. Under what conditions can think-aloud be effective?
7. What are the advantages and limitations of think-aloud?
8. When can you use a diary/journal as a data collection technique? Give some examples.
9. What are the advantages and disadvantages of a diary/journal as a data collection technique?
10. What are the common problems in the use of a diary/journal as a research tool?

Exploring

1. Find one paper from an international journal which reports a single-case study and then answer the following questions.
    (1) Why does the researcher focus on one case in the study?
    (2) What is the value of such a single-case study?
    (3) What are the questions the study intends to answer?
    (4) What types of data did the researcher collect?
    (5) What are the research findings?
2. Find a multiple-case study reported in an international journal and then answer the following questions.
    (1) What is the difference between the single-case study mentioned above and this multiple-case study?
    (2) What are the research questions in this study?
    (3) How did the researcher collect the data?
    (4) What are the research findings?

Chapter 9

Basic statistics

Being lucky to live in a computer age, we don't need to analyze quantitative data manually with painstaking efforts. There are various statistical procedures available that can provide us with findings within seconds. However, to select an appropriate procedure to process data effectively, we must have a good understanding of basic concepts and formulas used in statistics. This chapter serves this purpose.

A BRIEF DESCRIPTION OF STATISTICS

There are two branches in statistics, namely descriptive statistics and inferential statistics. In this section, I will first briefly describe what are descriptive statistics and inferential statistics respectively and then discuss two important terms: "parameter" and "statistic."

Definitions

If a researcher is interested only in describing a group from which the data are gathered, the statistics involved is called descriptive statistics. In many cases, data in the field of applied linguistics are primarily descriptive in nature.

If his/her interest goes beyond describing the group from which the data are collected and he/she tries to draw conclusions about the population from which the group is selected, the statistics needed in this case is inferential statistics. The advantage of using inferential statistics is that it allows the researcher to make decisions about the population without studying the entire population. The use and importance of inferential statistics are ever growing.

Parameter and statistic

A descriptive measure of the population is called a parameter. Parameters are usually denoted by Greek letters such as μ and σ. Examples of parameters are population mean (μ), population variance (σ^2), and population standard deviation (σ). A descriptive measure of a sample is called a statistic and is usually denoted by a Roman letter. Examples of statistics are sample mean ($\bar{x}$), sample variance (S^2), and sample standard deviation (S).

Differentiation between parameters and statistics is important only in the use of inferential statistics. A statistician often wants to estimate the value of a parameter. However, the calculation of a parameter is usually either impossible or not feasible because of the amount of time and money required to take a census. In this case, the statistician can take a random sample of the population, calculate a statistic on the sample, and infer by estimation the value of the parameter.

Suppose you are an English teacher at one comprehensive university and you want to know the relationship between the use of strategies and the English proficiency of all the students in the university. There are more than 10,000 students on two campuses. Obviously, you cannot afford the money and time to take a census. What you may do is to survey 400 students as a sample by a questionnaire. Then you use descriptive statistics and inferential statistics to analyze the data. For example, you use descriptive statistics to get to know which strategies are more frequently used by these 400 students. The results you get are statistics on the sample. You may use inferential statistics to examine the relation between the use of strategies and English achievement, or to see whether the male students differ from the female students in their use of strategies based on the notion of probability.

Descriptive analysis or statistics, as its name suggests, simply describes the general pattern or tendency emerging from the data collected, while inferential analysis or statistics, which is more complicated, aims at predictions beyond the sample data.

DESCRIPTIVE STATISTICS

The statistics used to summarize data is called descriptive statistics. Once data have been coded and checked, descriptive statistics will be used to organize data in terms of frequencies, central tendency, and variability.

Frequency

The simplest way to organize data is to describe their frequency distribution which can reduce and summarize data effectively and efficiently. The frequency distribution can be presented in a table or in graphic forms such as a histogram, a polygon, or a pie chart.

First of all, you will learn how to present the frequency distribution in a table form. It is easy to construct the frequency distribution if the total possible values are very limited. For example, if students' responses to questionnaire items are no more than five: 1, 2, 3, 4, 5, the frequency distribution can be obtained simply by tallying up all the responses, as shown in Table 9.1.

Choice	Frequency	Percentage (%)
1. Strongly disagree	30	30
2. Disagree	45	45
3. Neither disagree nor agree	10	10
4. Agree	5	5
5. Strongly agree	10	10

Table 9.1: The frequency distribution

However, when the total possible values are many and various, such as people's ages and students' test scores, we need to group the raw data into classes. In this case, the frequency distribution is concerned with classes rather than with each individual age or score. Then, how do we describe the frequency distribution in terms of classes? There are no hard-and-fast rules to follow. Very often, the final shape and design of the frequency distribution vary from researcher to researcher even if the original data are identical. The following are the scores on the mid-term exam taken by a group of freshmen:

58, 65, 84, 70, 90, 75, 86, 76, 80, 82,

83, 84, 69, 84, 85, 86, 72, 89, 75, 92

Generally speaking, we may construct the frequency distribution of the above data in terms of classes in three steps.

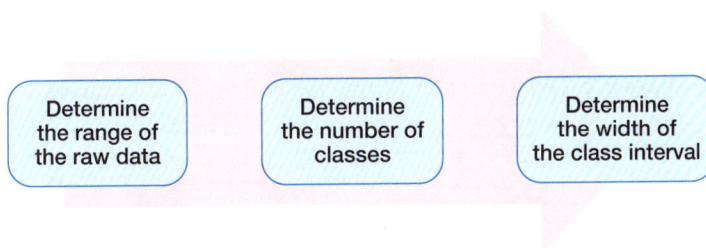

Figure 9.1: Three steps in constructing the frequency distribution

The range of the raw data is defined as the difference between the largest and smallest numbers. The range (92–58) here is 34. The number of classes should not be too many or too few. If there are too many classes, we might not be able to achieve generalization. If there are too few classes, we might not be able to see the important differences. One rule of thumb is that the number of classes selected is between 5 and 10. However, it is your personal decision and the final number of classes must serve your research purpose. An approximation of the size of the class width can be calculated by dividing the range by the number of classes. Usually we will choose a round number such as 5 or 10. If not possible, we might use 15, 20, 25, 50, and so on.

The frequency distribution must include all the data given. Therefore, the frequency distribution should start at a value equal to or lower than the lowest number of the ungrouped data and end at a value equal to or higher than the highest number. Class endpoints are selected so that no value of the data can fall into more than one class. We may use the word "under" to indicate the endpoint of each class.

Table 9.2 shows that the number of classes is 5 and the class width is 10. Once the data are presented in Table 9.2, you may offer a reasonable explanation without difficulty. You may say that 12 students did quite well on the exam while 8 students still needed more efforts. In general, the performance of the whole class was not unusual.

Class	Frequency
50-under 60	1
60-under 70	2
70-under 80	5
80-under 90	10
90-under 100	2
Total	20

Table 9.2: The frequency distribution in terms of five classes

We may also present the same set of data in an alternative way as shown in Table 9.3:

Class	Frequency
50-under 65	1
65-under 80	7
80-under 95	12
Total	20

Table 9.3: The frequency distribution in terms of three classes

Frequencies sometimes do not make much sense. Percentages are more straightforward as shown in Table 9.4.

Class	Frequency	Cumulative frequency	Percentage (%)
50-under 60	1	1	5
60-under 70	2	3	10
70-under 80	5	8	25
80-under 90	10	18	50
90-under 100	2	20	10
Total	20	20	100

Table 9.4: The frequency distribution with cumulative frequencies and percentages

If you want to know the relative standing of any particular score in a group of scores, you can show it by a percentile score. The following formula can be used to calculate the percentile score:

$$\text{Percentile} = \frac{\text{Cumulative } F \times (100)}{N}$$

In the above formula, cumulative frequency (F) refers to the frequency of the score or the scores within a class plus the frequency of the score or the scores within the class just below. As shown in Table 9.4, the scores within the class 60-under 70 occur twice and thus the frequency is 2, while their cumulative frequency is 3 that is the result of 2 plus 1, which is the frequency of the score within the class 50-under 60. The letter N represents the total number of scores.

A percentile can be defined as a number which represents the percent of scores that a particular raw score exceeds. For example, suppose one of your students received a score in the 67th percentile on TOEFL. It means that 67% of the students who took the test scored lower than that level. Or we say that his/her score was higher than the scores of 67% of the students taking the test but lower than the scores of 33% of the students.

To help you have a correct understanding of the definition of percentiles, Table 9.5 presents more percentiles and their interpretations.

Percentile	Interpretation
95th	The score concerned exceeds 95% of the scores.
90th	The score concerned exceeds 90% of the scores.
75th	The score concerned exceeds 75% of the scores.
60th	The score concerned exceeds 60% of the scores.
50th	The score concerned exceeds 50% of the scores.

Table 9.5: Percentiles and their interpretations

To visualize differences in the frequency distribution, you can display the frequency distribution in a graphic form. The common forms include a histogram, a polygon, and a pie chart. For example, the frequencies in Table 9.1 can be shown in figures (See Figure 9.2, Figure 9.3, and Figure 9.4).

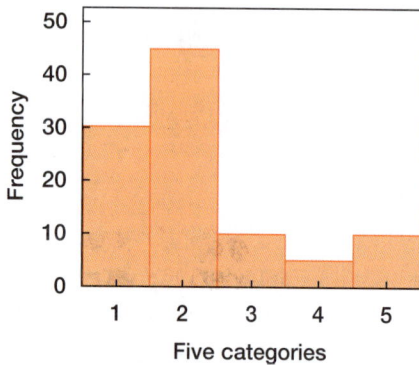

Figure 9.2: A histogram

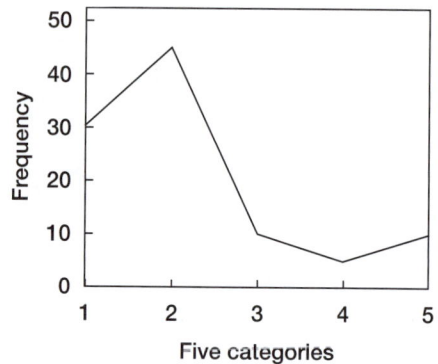

Figure 9.3: A polygon

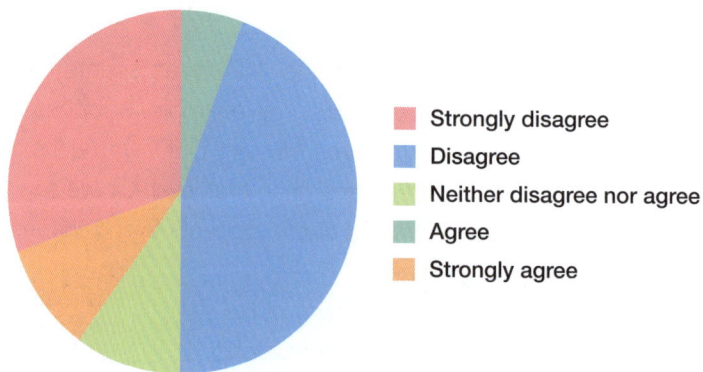

Strongly disagree
Disagree
Neither disagree nor agree
Agree
Strongly agree

Figure 9.4: A pie chart

Central tendency

With regard to central tendency, you may describe it in terms of the mode, median, and mean.

The mode is the most frequently occurring number in the data. For example, in the following data set, the mode is 84:

58, 60, 65, 70, 80, 84, 84, 84, 84, 90, 92

Sometimes you may have two modes if there are two values which occur equally frequently. For example, the following set of data has two modes, i.e. 65 and 84:

58, 60, 65, 65, 65, 65, 84, 84, 84, 84, 90

Using a mode to describe central tendency is the easiest since it doesn't require any calculations. However, it has an obvious limitation: It is very sensitive to accidental scores. Let's look at the following example.

The mode of the scores 58, 64, 65, 65, 65, 85, 85, 86, 86, 88, 90 is 65. However, if one of the students who scored 65 just by chance had scored 64 while one of the students who scored 86 had scored 85 instead, then the mode would change from 65 to 85. The difference would be 20. Therefore, we have to take such a limitation into serious consideration.

The median is the value which serves as a mid-point of a series of numbers. To find out the median value, you first arrange the given values in rank order. If the number of values is odd, the value at the center is the median. If the number of values is even, you use the mid-point between the two middle values as the median. The median value is often used as the measure of central tendency when the number of values is small and/or when the data are obtained by ordinal scales.

The mean is the most frequently used indicator of central tendency because it is better than the mode and median in the sense that it takes all the values into account. The formula for calculating the mean is:

$$\bar{x} = \sum x / n$$

In the above formula, $\bar{x}$ is the symbol for the mean of a sample; $\sum$ means adding up all the individual observations x; n refers to the total number of observations. In other words, to calculate the mean, you have to add up all the individual scores and then divide the sum by the total number of the scores. "In any case, the mean is the best, most practical, most useful measure of central tendency" (Hatch & Farhady, 1982, p. 55). However, the mean is not appropriate for nominal and ordinal data.

Variability

Once you have decided on your measure of central tendency and found the most typical value, there are some reservations to keep in mind about the typical score. Suppose we look at the mean scores of two different classes and they turn out to be the same. Does this imply that the two classes have the same performance? No, of course it doesn't. The variability among the values, i.e. how they are spread out from the central point, may be quite different in the two groups. Therefore, to be able to talk about data more accurately, we have to measure the degree of variability of data apart from the central tendency. Just as there are three ways of talking about the central tendency in data, there are three major ways, too, to show how data are spread out from the middle point: range, standard deviation, and variance.

Range

The easiest way to talk about the spread of the distribution of values is the range. Suppose in addition to the mean score of your class on the final exam, you also told the head of your department the range of the scores. This would give him/her an idea of the spread of the scores. To calculate the range, you first arrange the values from the highest to the lowest and then subtract the lowest score from the highest score.

The weakness in using the range as an indicator of variability is that it is easily affected by extreme scores. For example, if one student in your class scored zero, then the range would increase drastically just due to that one particular score. Therefore, it is not a precise measure and is thus rarely used in a formal study.

Standard deviation

The most frequently used measure of variability in a formal study is the standard deviation. Before I explain what a standard deviation is, let me first give you an example to show you what an individual deviation is.

Example

When the mid-term exam of English was over, by calculation, you told your students the mean score of the exam was 82. Naturally, each individual student was concerned with the difference between his/her score and the mean. Suppose Student A got 90 and thus her score was 8 points above the mean; Student B scored 65, and thus his score was 17 points below the mean. Then such a difference is the individual deviation from the mean.

As researchers, our concern goes beyond an individual deviation. What we want to know is the average deviation of all scores from the mean. The word "standard" is used simply because it looks at the average variability of all the values around the mean. Then how do you calculate a standard deviation? The following is the formula:

$$S = \sqrt{\frac{\Sigma(x-\bar{x})^2}{n-1}}$$

To apply the above formula, you may follow the steps listed below:
1. Calculate the mean $\bar{x}$.
2. Subtract $\bar{x}$ from each score to get the individual deviation scores (standing for the deviation of the individual score from the mean).
3. Square each individual deviation and then add them up.
4. Divide the sum by $n-1$. (Mathematicians have determined that it is more accurate to divide the sum by $n-1$ with a small sample.)
5. Take the square root of the result obtained at Step 4.

Consider, for example, the scores of 10 students on a dictation test: 10, 9, 9, 8, 7, 7, 6, 6, 5, 3. The mean is 7. The following table shows you how to get the standard deviation of all the scores:

x (Score)	x−x̄ (Individual deviation)	(x−x̄)²
10	3	9
9	2	4
9	2	4
8	1	1
7	0	0
7	0	0
6	−1	1
6	−1	1
5	−2	4
3	−4	16
Σ=70 n=10 $\bar{x}$=7	Σ=0	S=2.11

Table 9.6: An illustration of calculating a standard deviation

The concrete example in Table 9.6 can help you have a better understanding of how a standard deviation is obtained. However, if you are not good at calculation, you don't need to worry about it since with the help of the computer program, you can obtain the standard deviation of values without any difficulties.

What can a standard deviation tell us? A standard deviation can tell us the average deviation of all the scores from the mean. The larger the standard deviation, the more deviant the scores from the central point in the distribution; the smaller the standard deviation, the closer the scores to the central point. Suppose you were a new English teacher and the head of the department told you that you could select one class from the three of Band 3 to teach. Table 9.7 presents the mean scores and standard deviations of their scores on the final exam in the previous semester.

Class number	$\bar{x}$ (Mean)	S (Standard deviation)
Class 1	83.4	5.2
Class 2	82.3	5.0
Class 3	84.1	8.4

Table 9.7: Descriptive statistics about the exam scores of the three classes

Based on the information provided in the table, how can you make a better decision? If you simply look at their mean scores, Class 3 got the highest and Class 2, the lowest. However, the differences among their mean scores are rather small. Then you look at the standard deviations. You immediately find that the scores for Class 3 are much more widely spread than those for Class 1 and Class 2. What kind of class do you want to teach? Do you want a more homogeneous class or a more heterogeneous class? The larger the standard deviation, the more heterogeneous the class is; the smaller the standard deviation, the more homogeneous the class is. In this sense, the standard deviation gives you information which the mean score cannot give. Therefore, in data analysis, we need to calculate both the mean score and the standard deviation.

Variance

The variance (S^2) is one of the three measures of variability. It is defined as "the sum of the squared deviation scores divided by $n-1$" (Hatch & Farhady, 1982, p. 60).

$$S^2=\Sigma(x-\bar{x})^2/(n-1)$$

You must have noticed that the standard deviation is the square root of the variance. Thus, to obtain a standard deviation, the variance is computed first.

⋮≡ INFERENTIAL STATISTICS

Unlike descriptive statistics which is only concerned with describing sample data, inferential statistics goes beyond sample data to predict to what extent the sample can represent the population from which it is drawn. Before we discuss the details of inferential statistics, we must understand two important concepts: normal distribution and probability.

Normal distribution

Before we come to a theoretical explanation of what is a normal distribution, let's draw graphs to present the frequency distribution of two data sets listed below:

Data Set 1:
80, 81, 81, 82, 82, 82, 83, 83, 84

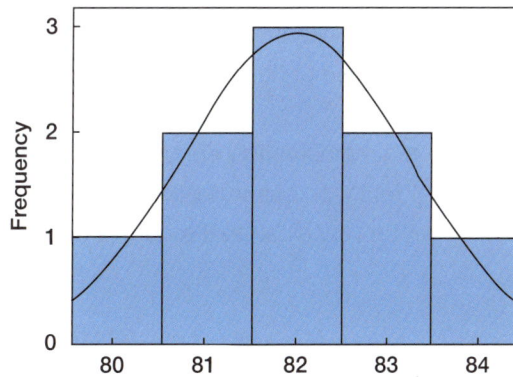

Figure 9.5: A polygon of Data Set 1

Data Set 2:
100, 99, 99, 99, 99, 98, 98, 98, 98, 98, 98, 98, 98, 98, 98, 98,
98, 98, 98, 98, 98, 97, 97, 97, 97, 96

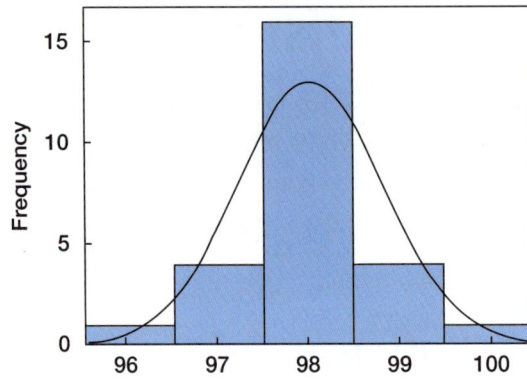

Figure 9.6: A polygon of Data Set 2

I think by drawing the polygons yourself, you must have got some idea of the shape of a normal distribution, which is symmetrical. You must also have noticed that the two polygons are somewhat different. The first one has a much lower peak while the second one has a much higher peak. However, they are both normally distributed since they both possess the following three distinct properties:

1. The mode, median, and mean are the same.
2. The range is symmetrical. The lowest value and highest value have exactly the same distance from the mean.
3. The normal distribution does not have a zero score; the two tails never meet the X axis.

The normal distribution is a mathematical concept which is used to describe an ideal distribution. However, it rarely occurs in reality. If a sample is extremely large, the distribution you obtain will be very close to the normal distribution.

Probability

What is probability? It is difficult to define but it is easy to understand. Let's start with some examples. Every year before the Spring Festival, all the shopping centers try their best to promote their sales. One of the measures taken is to offer prizes to the winners. I remember once the first prize was a new flat. I could not resist such a temptation and like many other customers, went there to buy goods. Eventually, it turned out that there were altogether 250,000 customers. Then what was the probability that I could get the first prize? That was 1 out of 250,000. It was almost next to impossible for me to get the first prize. In an examination, very often there are multiple-choice questions. If each question has four choices and there is only one correct answer, then what is the probability of guessing the right answer? 25%. If each question has five choices, the probability of guessing the right answer is 20%.

The formula for assigning probabilities is the following:

$P=n_e$ (number of desired events)/N (number of possible outcomes)

The number of desired events can never be greater than N. The highest value of any probability is 1. If the probability of an event occurring is 1, it means that the event is 100% certain to occur. The smallest value of any probability is 0, meaning an event is 100% certain not to occur. Therefore, the value of any probability is never negative and is never bigger than 1. The value falls between 0 and 1. Probability values may be converted to percentages by multiplying them by 100. For example, we may say that there is a 50% chance of guessing the correct answer in true-or-false questions. Or we say, the probability of guessing the correct answer in true-or-false questions is .50.

Practical uses

Normal distribution together with probability can help us decide on the following two things:

1. What is the probability that a certain score can occur? What proportion of the values falls between a certain range?
2. Can a sample drawn from the population represent the population?

Since the normal distribution is symmetrical, and the mean, median, and mode are the same, half the scores fall above and half below the mean. Mathematicians further describe the probability of getting a score in Figure 9.7 (Nunan, 1994, p. 31):

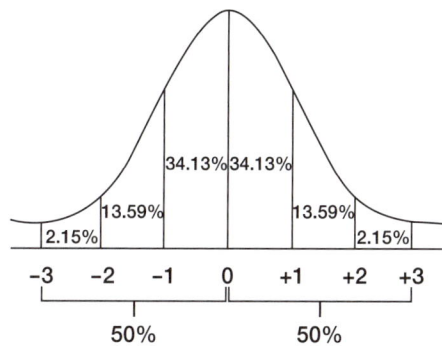

Figure 9.7: Proportions of standard deviations in a normal distribution[1]

---

[1] The probability of the scores within ±1SD is 68.26% (34.13%+34.13%); the probability of the scores within ±2SD is 95.44% (34.13%+34.13+13.59%+13.59%); and the probability of the scores within ±3SD is 99.74% (34.13%+34.13%+13.59%+13.59%+2.15%+2.15%).

According to the figure, we may say that the scores within the range of ±1SD have the area of about 68%. In other words, the probability of getting a score within the range of ±1SD is about 68%. Similarly, we may say that the probability of getting a score within ±2SD is about 95% and the probability of getting a score within ±3SD is about 99%.

With this knowledge about the probability and normal distribution, we may know whether the sample we study can represent the population from which it is drawn. If the sample can represent the population, it means that there is no significant difference between the mean of the sample and the mean of the population. When can we say there is no difference between the mean of the sample and the mean of the population? Actually, we are testing a null hypothesis.

If your sample falls in the area of the 95% probability, then your sample is the same as the population. Thus, the null hypothesis cannot be rejected.

If the sample falls in the area of the 5% probability, then your sample is different from the population. In other words, we can say that we are 95% confident that the difference between the sample and population is significant. Or we say, there are 5 chances out of 100 that we might be wrong.

The problem is that very often we cannot get the mean and standard deviation of the population. What we can do is to get as many sample means as we can and then use the sample means to estimate the population mean.

The process of hypothesis testing

In research, you are usually anxious to discover the probability of your hypotheses about research outcomes. To do this, you must first state the hypotheses in a way that allows you to compare the sample data with the data of the population from which the sample is drawn. To be specific, you need to set up a null hypothesis and an alternative hypothesis. The next decision you need to make is the significance level at which you are allowed to reject the null hypothesis. Significance levels are usually .05, .01, or .001 in the field of applied linguistics.

Let's assume that you have stated a null hypothesis, and that you have selected the level of significance of .05 for rejecting the null hypothesis. If the results fall within the area of 95% as shown in Figure 9.8a, the null hypothesis cannot be rejected, for the scores are typical of those that would normally be found in such a distribution. On the other hand, if the sample data fall in the area shaded in Figure 9.8b, you have to reject the null hypothesis since the scores are not those typically found in the distribution. If the data fall in the lower left tail, the sample is worse than the population. If they fall in the far right tail, the sample is much better than the population. In either case, you can reject the hypothesis that the sample is not different from the population from which it is drawn.

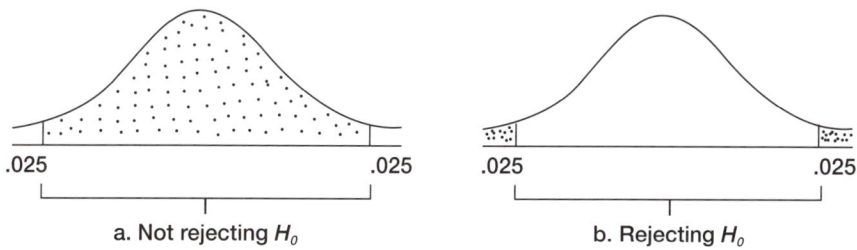

Figure 9.8: Rejecting or not rejecting H_0 (Hatch & Farhady, 1982, p. 87)

Similarly, if the chosen level of significance is .01, the null hypothesis cannot be rejected when the results fall within the area of 99%. If the selected level of significance is .001, the null hypothesis cannot be rejected when the results fall within the area of 99.9%.

You can notice in Figure 9.8 that, although you have chosen .05 as the level of significance, you have to divide the .05 into two parts, giving a .025 area to each tail of the distribution. This is because the null hypothesis you formulated did not specify where the difference might be. That is to say, when there is no direction specified for possible differences in the hypothesis, you must consider both tails of the distribution. The hypothesis is, therefore, called a two-tailed hypothesis.

▷≡ SUMMARY

Descriptive statistics and inferential statistics are two branches in statistics. Descriptive statistics is concerned with the description of a group while inferential statistics aims at drawing inferences about the entire population from the group investigated.

Parameters are used to describe a population and statistics are used to describe a group. This distinction is necessary only when the difference between a population and a group is essential. Parameters are denoted by Greek letters while statistics are denoted by Roman letters.

Descriptive statistics is used to organize data in terms of frequency, central tendency, and variability. Two important concepts underlying inferential statistics are normal distribution and probability. By having these two concepts, we can test null hypotheses. If the probability of getting the result concerned is lower than .05, the null hypothesis can be rejected and the alternative one can be accepted accordingly. This probability level is also called the significance level and varies from .05 to .001 in the field of applied linguistics and many other social sciences.

AFTER-READING ACTIVITIES

Reviewing

1 What are the differences between descriptive statistics and inferential statistics?

2 In descriptive statistics, what are the common ways to organize data?

3 What are the most important concepts in inferential statistics?

4 What is probability? Give an example to illustrate your understanding.

5 What are the practical uses of the concept of "probability"?

Exploring

1 The following are scores on TEM4 obtained by 20 second-year English majors: 50, 60, 70, 75, 55, 60, 65, 70, 80, 85, 55, 60, 80, 80, 65, 45, 70, 65, 70, 75.

(1) Divide the scores into three groups and then present the results in a table and in a graphic form respectively.

(2) Divide the scores into four groups and then present the results in a table and in a graphic form respectively.

2 The following are scores on the composition test of TEM8 obtained by 20 fourth-year English majors: 12, 14, 10, 12, 16, 18, 10, 12, 16, 18, 14, 12, 16, 10, 12, 14, 10, 18, 10, 12.

(1) Find out the mean, median, and mode of the scores.

(2) Find out the range, variance, and standard deviation of the scores.

Chapter 10

The analysis of quantitative data

As was discussed before, quantitative data can be analyzed descriptively or inferentially depending on your research purpose. A common computer software used in applied linguistics is SPSS (Statistical Package for the Social Sciences). In this chapter, I will first give you a brief description of SPSS and then focus on the analysis of questionnaire data from a survey study and an experimental study.

⊟ AN OVERVIEW OF SPSS FOR WINDOWS

SPSS is a comprehensive and flexible statistical analysis and management system which is, however, easy to operate. Most tasks can be accomplished simply by clicking the mouse. In this section you will have an overview of this statistical package.

Three main windows

SPSS uses a number of windows or screens in its operations. Each window functions to help you accomplish specific tasks and create different types of SPSS files. The following part will describe three major windows: Application Viewer, Data Editor Viewer, and Output Viewer.

Application Viewer

The Application Viewer is the default window which appears whenever you start SPSS. It contains a menu bar as shown in Figure 10.1. You use it to open files, create new files, choose statistical procedures, and ask for help whenever you encounter difficulties.

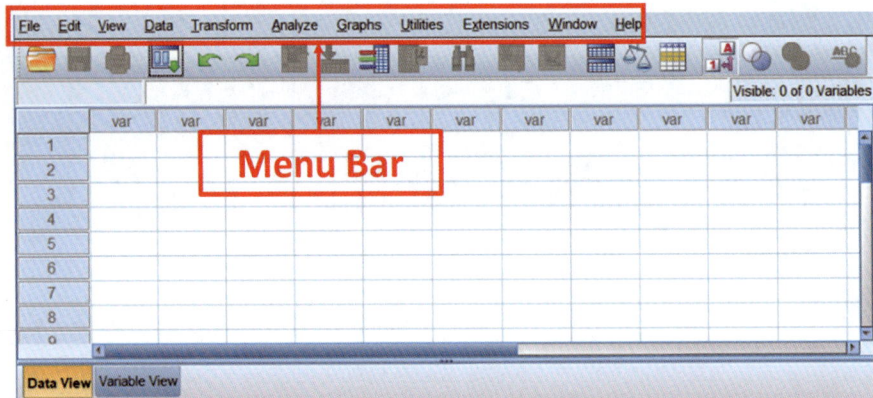

Figure 10.1: SPSS Application Viewer window

There are altogether 11 menus in the main menu bar. I will introduce 9 major ones.

File

The File menu is used to create a new SPSS file or read an existing file. It can also be used for saving a new file or an old file after editing. If you are familiar with the File menu in Microsoft Word, then there will be no problem for you to use the File menu in SPSS.

Edit

The Edit menu is also like the one in Microsoft Word, which is for modifying or copying a text from the output window.

Data

The Data menu is for defining a variable, inserting a variable, merging files, splitting files, selecting cases for analysis, etc.

Transform

The Transform menu is used to make changes in the data file, such as computing a new variable based on the values of existing variables, recoding a variable into a new variable, or recoding the same variable by changing the values systematically.

Analyze

The Analyze menu is for you to choose the various statistical procedures for your own purpose. You may select the procedures of Correlate, Compare Means, Regression, etc.

Graphs

The Graphs menu is used to produce various kinds of graphic representations.

Utilities

The Utilities menu is used to change the font, display the information about the variables, or open an index of SPSS commands.

Window

The Window menu is used to arrange, select, and control the various SPSS windows. For example, if you want to change the Data Editor Viewer into the Output Viewer, you may simply click the Window menu and then select the Output Viewer.

Help

The Help menu contains information on how to use different menus properly.

Data Editor Viewer

The Data Editor Viewer is the window which appears whenever you have already created a file and you want to do further work with SPSS. The window presents drop-down menus that allow you to modify or analyze data in an existing file. The data are displayed in a spreadsheet format which consists of columns and rows. Columns represent variables and rows represent cases. At the bottom of the spreadsheet, there are two tabs labeled "Data View" and "Variable View".

The Data View shows the data file containing rows of cases and columns of variables (See Figure 10.2). Cases represent the persons responding to a questionnaire or the participants in an experiment while variables refer to attributes (e.g. gender, age), characteristics (e.g. L2 proficiency level, the number of years of learning English), or treatment effects (e.g. posttest scores) that describe each case.

The Variable View shows you various information about each variable such as name, type, label, values, etc. This will be further discussed later in this chapter when the process of inputting data is discussed.

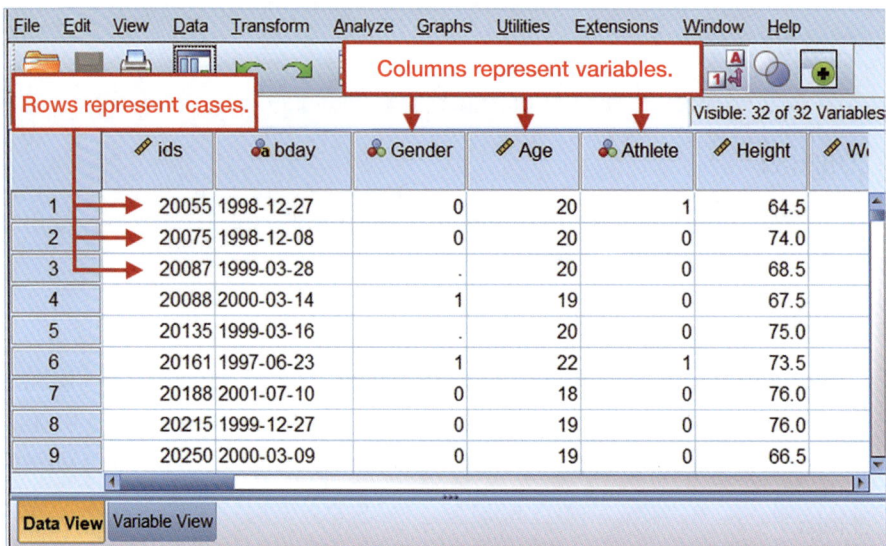

Figure 10.2: SPSS Data Editor Viewer window

Output Viewer

The Output Viewer is the window which displays results yielded by statistical procedures such as frequency distributions, means, and standard deviations. The Output Viewer has two frames as presented in Figure 10.3. The left frame contains an outline of the content in the Output Viewer window. This output outline is especially useful when you run many SPSS commands and need to locate a particular section of the output easily. The right frame contains the actual output. You can save the output as a viewer file (*.spv). By doing so, you can read it again without having to run the same statistical procedure again. To save an Output Viewer window, click File>Save As.

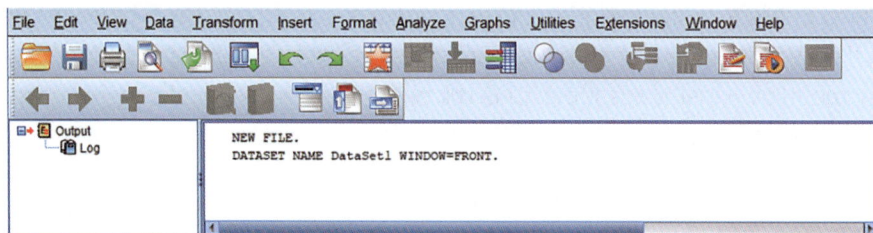

Figure 10.3: SPSS Output Viewer window

⊟ ANALYZING THE DATA OF A QUESTIONNAIRE

I will use my own study[1] as an example to illustrate the details of the analysis of questionnaire data.

A brief description of the study

The study was conducted to find out how second-year English majors study English and to what extent their way of learning is related to their learning outcomes.

In September 1997, 77 second-year English majors from three intact classes at one key comprehensive university were asked to answer the Language Learner Factors Questionnaire. The questionnaire was administered during class time and the response rate was 100%. Among the 77 participants, 59 were females and 18 were males. Their ages ranged from 18 to 20 with the average being 19.4. They took the TEM4 in May 1998.

The Language Learner Factors Questionnaire consists of three parts. Part A is divided into two subparts. The first one concerns personal details such as name, sex, date of birth, scores on the national English and Chinese matriculation tests, and an estimate of time spent in studying English outside class, which is used as the indicator of Effort. The other section of Part A establishes students' reasons for learning English. Students rated reasons listed on a five-point scale from "not important" (1) to "extremely important" (5). Part B consists of statements of beliefs about language learning. The students indicated their opinions in terms of a five-point scale from "strongly disagree" (1) to "strongly agree" (5). Part C contains statements concerning learning strategies. Some of them are management strategies, and the rest are language learning strategies. Students again responded on a five-point scale from "This statement is never or almost never true of me" (1) to "This statement is completely or almost completely true of me" (5).

There are altogether 15 variables listed in Table 10.1. Among them, English Achievement is a dependent variable while others are independent variables. The first 5 variables only have a single indicator and thus they do not need a statistical check, whereas the remaining 10 are variables with multiple indicators. The alpha value indicates the internal consistency within the multiple items. (Note: The meaning of the alpha value will be discussed in the section "Category confirmation.")

---

[1] The study described here is part of a large project.

Variable name	A brief description of the variable	No. of items	Alpha
1. English Achievement	The score on TEM4	1	
2. Sex	Biological sex	1	
3. L1 Proficiency	The score on the National Matriculation Chinese Test	1	
4. L2 Proficiency	The score on the National Matriculation English Test	1	
5. Effort	The self-estimated amount of time spent by the learner outside class in studying English	1	
6. Learning Purpose	Reasons for learning English	3	
7. Effort Belief	Views about the importance of effort in language learning	5	.51
8. Management Belief	Views about the importance of planning, setting goals, evaluating progress, etc.	5	.75
9. Traditional Belief	Opinions on the importance of repetition, memorization, and intensive study of texts	4	.59
10. Non-traditional Belief	Opinions on the importance of extensive exposure to and communicative use of the target language	4	.64
11. Mother-tongue-using Belief	Opinions on the necessity of using mother tongue in reading, listening, writing, and speaking	4	.64
12. Management Strategy	Actions in planning, goal setting, evaluating, etc.	8	.79
13. Traditional Strategy	Actions in traditional activities	11	.73
14. Non-traditional Strategy	Actions in non-traditional activities	12	.75
15. Mother-tongue-using Strategy	Actions in using mother tongue in L2 learning	5	.69

Table 10.1: Descriptions of 15 variables

An overview of a spreadsheet for a new data file

Once you have collected questionnaires, you are going to set up a new data file. When you open the SPSS program, you can see a blank sheet in Data View with columns and rows. Each of the columns is labeled "var" and each row is labeled with a number, "1," "2," and so on (See Figure 10.4). The column names represent the variables you enter into the data set and the rows represent cases that are part of your data set. When you enter values for your data in the spreadsheet cells, each value must correspond to a specific variable (column) and a specific case (row).

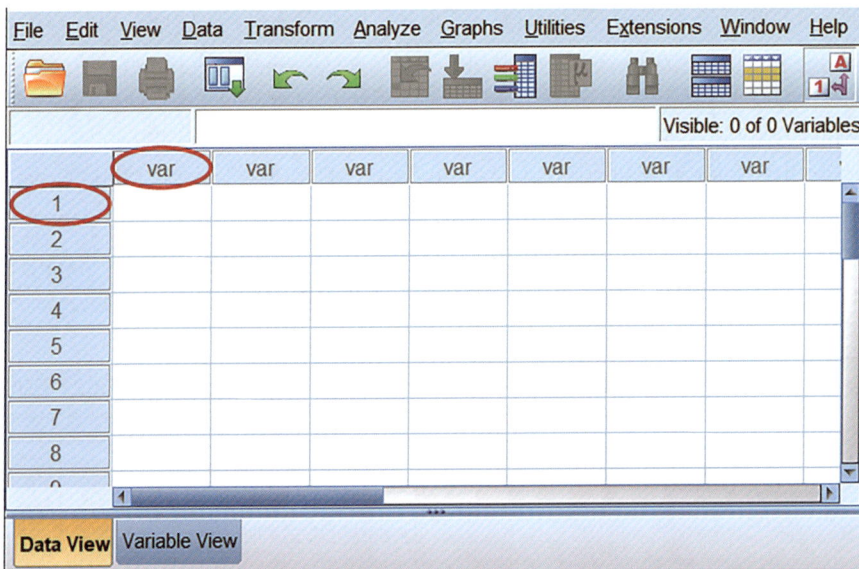

Figure 10.4: A blank spreadsheet for creating a data file

Preparations for creating a data file

In order to create a data file, you have to do preparations such as numbering the questionnaires and defining variables.

Numbering the questionnaires

Before you input the data, you should carefully number all the questionnaires. That is to say, you have to assign a unique number to each questionnaire. For your convenience, you had better use sequential numbers, i.e. 1, 2, 3, 4, 5 and so on. When you input the data, this number will be entered in the first column as an ID to represent each case (See Table 10.2). At the stage of cleaning data, when you find a mistake, this number will help you locate the original questionnaire.

Defining variables

When you click the Variable View tab (at the bottom of the Data Editor Viewer), you can see the following information, in columns, about each variable in your data such as name, type, width, decimals, label, missing values. The following part will describe each of them one by one.

Name

The name of a variable must begin with a letter. The remaining specifications can be letters or numbers. The length of the name cannot exceed eight characters. All the names of variables should be placed at the first row of a spreadsheet. Furthermore, they must be mutually exclusive since duplication is not accepted. Finally, the name of a variable should be easy to recognize. As Table 10.2 shows, ID stands for the variable of identity number, ES for the variable of the score on TEM4; L1P for the variable of the score on the National Matriculation Chinese Test; L2P for the variable of the score on the National Matriculation English Test; P01 for the first questionnaire item concerning Learning Purpose; EB01 for the first questionnaire item about Effort Belief. If you want to change the name of a variable, you can double click it.

ID	Sex	ES	L1P	L2P	P01	P02	P03	EB01	EB02	EB03

Table 10.2: A spreadsheet of the data file

Type

To correctly identify the type of each variable is very important since some statistical analyses can only operate on a particular type of variable. There are two common types of variables in research: numeric and string. Numeric variables, as the name suggests, have data values that are displayed as numbers. It seems that all the numeric values can be calculated arithmetically. However, this is not always right. For example, nominal variables such as Sex ("1" for "male" and "2" for "female") cannot be processed arithmetically. String variables are also called character variables and their values are treated as text such as the date of birth or telephone numbers. They cannot be processed arithmetically, either.

Width

Width refers to the number of digits that is allowed for numeric values or the length of a string variable. If a variable requires 11 digits, you have to specify its width correctly. Otherwise it cannot be inputted. To set a variable's width, click inside the cell corresponding to the "width" column for that variable. Then click the "up" or "down" arrow icon to increase or decrease the number of width.

Decimals

Decimals refer to the number of digits appearing after a decimal point for values of a variable. To specify the number of decimal places for a numeric variable, click the "up" or "down" arrow icon to increase or decrease the number of decimal places. Suppose you choose "2," the values of variables look like 1.00, 2.00, 3.00 which show two digits after an integer. If you choose "0," they will look like 1, 2, 3 without anything after an integer. In the study mentioned in Table 10.1, the students' responses to the questionnaire items ranged from 1 to 5. Therefore, I chose "0." By doing so, the data set looks simple without any decimals.

Label

The label of a variable refers to a brief description or display name of the variable. Once the variable's label is clearly described, it will appear in the output in place of its name. For example, the variable EB01 will be described by the label "Effort Belief 1."

Values

Value labels are useful for the variables when they are recorded as codes such as 1, 2, 3. You are strongly advised to give each value a label so that you and other researchers can understand what each value means. For example, in my study mentioned in Table 10.1, for the variable Sex, "1" represents "male" and "2" represents "female"; "1," "2," "3," "4," "5" for EB01 represents "strongly disagree," "disagree," "neither disagree nor agree," "agree," and "strongly agree" respectively.

Missing values

When you come across a case where the respondent did not answer an item or gave an ambiguous answer, you have to treat it as a missing value. Although some variables may not have missing values at all, you have to assume that there are missing values for all the variables and also decide what number to use to represent a missing value. Normally speaking, you can use "0" to represent a missing value. However, "0" may sometimes be meaningful. To avoid such an ambiguity, I suggest you use "999" to represent a missing value.

Inputting data

Some use machines to read data when responses are recorded on a standardized answer sheet. However, in the Chinese context, almost all postgraduate students input data manually. Once you have defined all the variables, you can enter data case by case. You had better find someone to read out the numbers for you while you are keying them in. Furthermore, you had better have a short break once you feel tired. Very often you don't want to stop at this moment because you are eager to get the job done. However, by doing so, the efficiency of inputting is usually low and many errors occur at this time according to my own experience. Finally, I strongly suggest that you should make a copy of your data file before you start any analysis. The original data file should be kept in a safe place, and be separated from your working data file.

Cleaning data

To clean data, you need to undertake two tasks: (1) checking whether there are errors in data entry; and (2) dealing with missing responses.

Correcting errors

Errors must be corrected because incorrect data values distort the results of statistical analyses and contaminate all the analyses. Some errors are easy to spot. For example, forgetting to claim a value as missing, using an invalid code, or entering the value 585 for age will be apparent in a frequency table. On a five-point Likert scale, the possible responses must be numbers 1 through 5. If the data file contained 34, 45, 12 as responses, they must be wrong. Sometimes, a number may not be totally impossible but rather unusual. For example, one student responded to the question "How many hours do you spend learning English outside class every week?" by writing down 100. Although such a value is not totally impossible, it raises suspicion and should be examined to ensure that it is really correct. Other errors, such as entering an age of 62 instead of 26, or entering 5 instead of 3 may be difficult, if not impossible, to detect.

Dealing with missing values

Missing responses refer to values of a variable that are unknown, either because respondents did not answer them at all or because they provided ambiguous answers. If the percentage of missing data is less than 20%, you can use a neutral value to replace the missing response.

Here a neutral value refers to the mean score of the item concerned. Such a substitution does not change the mean of the item and is helpful for further analysis. For example, you want to put together the items 2, 8, 10, 12 and 23 to form a category. Unfortunately, two respondents did not answer Item 2 and thus they have a missing value for this item. In the process of forming a category, these two respondents will be automatically excluded by SPSS from the sample for this category because of the missing value. If we use a mean to replace the missing value, the situation will be different. That is to say, these two respondents will be treated the same as the other respondents.

Category confirmation

In the section "Questionnaire design process" in Chapter 6, you are told there are two kinds of questionnaires: individual-item-based and category-based. In the latter case, you need to employ statistical procedures to confirm the categories which you justified conceptually. Specifically speaking, you need to make sure that all the items within the category are in the same direction and the category holds up by running the item-total correlation.

Recoding the responses if they are in the opposite direction

By saying that the responses are in the opposite direction, I mean that they are contradictory in meaning. Let's look at the following two sentences:

1. Accuracy is more important than fluency in L2 learning.
2. Fluency is more important than accuracy in L2 learning.

In category confirmation, the first thing you have to do is to make sure that all the items within a category are not in the opposite direction. If they are, you have to make them in the same direction by transforming the values of some items. In my questionnaire I formed a category called Effort Belief which refers to the students' opinions about the important role of effort in L2 learning. The category includes the following five items and the students were asked to respond to each item on a five-point scale (1= strongly disagree; 2= disagree; 3= neither disagree nor agree; 4= agree; 5= strongly agree).

1. Learning a foreign language requires painstaking effort.
2. A person with a high language aptitude can grasp a foreign language without hard work.
3. Learning English well is due to one's inborn ability in language learning.
4. Without hard work, no one in China can learn a foreign language successfully.
5. Effort is more important than inborn ability in learning a foreign language.

Let's examine the first three items. Logically speaking, if you strongly disagree upon the first item, you would strongly agree upon the second and third items. That is to say, a 1 on the first item is a 5 on the second and the third, and vice versa. In this sense, Item 1 and Items 2 and 3 are not in the same direction.

What should you do? Since the category which includes the five items is called

Effort Belief, responses to Items 2 and 3 have to be recoded. 1 is changed into 5, 2 to 4, 4 to 2, and 5 to 1 so that all the five items are in the same direction in the sense that they all emphasize the importance of effort. Otherwise, they are in conflict since Items 1, 4, and 5 advocate the important role of effort while Items 2 and 3 emphasize the role of language aptitude.

How do you recode a variable? You just double click the Transform menu of SPSS where you can find Recode. There are two options for you to choose from: (1) recode into same variables; and (2) recode into different variables. To be safe, you had better select the second option because if you make a mistake with the first option, you will lose your data.

Checking internal consistency by the item-total correlation

Next we have to see whether the items within the category are internally consistent by the item-total correlation. What does the item-total correlation mean? Let's look at an example. The hypothesized category Management Belief contains five items and I tested these items on 77 second-year English majors.

1. Planning your study time is important for success.
2. Selecting appropriate learning strategies is important for success in learning a foreign language.
3. Setting your learning goals and evaluating your progress are important for success.
4. It is important for success that you frequently review your progress in learning English to find out your weak areas.
5. Reflecting upon whether your learning strategies are effective or not is important for success in learning a foreign language.

My data look like this:

ID	MB01	MB02	MB03	MB04	MB05
01	x	x	x	x	x
02	x	x	x	x	x
03	x	x	x	x	x
04	x	x	x	x	x
...	...	...	...	...	...
77	x	x	x	x	x

Table 10.3: A description of the data file

In Table 10.3, x is the score given by each person on each item. For five items, scored from 1 to 5, each person could get a score as low as 5 and as high as 25. In practice, of course, each respondent in a survey will get a total score somewhere in between. With 5 items, the total score gives you an idea of where each person stands on the category you're trying to measure. Then you run the item-total correlation. Here the total score does not refer to each individual's score but the total score of 77 respondents and similarly the score for each item is not one person's score, but 77 respondents'.

To run the item-total correlation, you may use the Analyze menu where you can find Scale on the list. Once you highlight Scale, there are two choices for you: (1) Reliability Analysis; and (2) Multidimensional Scaling. You just click the first one. Table 10.4 presents the results yielded by the scale reliability analysis. Since the value of alpha is as high as .7542, the proposed category of Management Belief is confirmed. In other words, this category can be employed for further statistical analysis.

	Item-total statistics			
	Scale mean if item deleted	Scale variance if item deleted	Corrected item-total correlation	Alpha if item deleted
MB01	17.3247	3.5906	.4758	.7258
MB02	17.0000	3.4474	.6417	.6833
MB03	17.4156	3.3513	.4343	.7472
MB04	17.2468	3.1883	.6588	.6607
MB05	17.4545	3.3301	.4658	.7332
Reliability coefficients No. of cases=77 Alpha=.7542		No. of items=5		

Table 10.4: The item-total correlation of Management Belief

All the proposed categories need to go through such statistical confirmation. Very often we are not lucky. Although conceptually the items within the category hang together, they are not necessarily supported by empirical data. In a worse case, the whole category has to be thrown out. But more often than not we simply need to make some modifications such as deleting some items or rearranging some items.

Then how can you make modifications? In this case, you may look at the last column "Alpha if item deleted," which can give some information to you so that you can decide which item is thrown out to make the category internally more consistent. In the case of Management Belief, no further modification is needed since deleting any item will reduce the degree of internal consistency.

Now let's look at another example in which four items form the category "Mother-tongue-using Belief." These four items cover the students' opinions about the use of L1 in L2 reading, listening, writing, and speaking.

1. To understand a text well, the best way is to translate it.
2. The best way to memorize what you have heard in listening is to keep in your memory what you have heard in Chinese.
3. To write well in English, the best way is to organize ideas in your mother tongue first.
4. When you speak English, the best way is to think what you want to say in Chinese first.

According to the last column of Table 10.5 "Alpha if item deleted," if Item 4 is deleted, the alpha value will increase to .6661. In contrast, if Item 3 is deleted, the alpha value will drop to .4988. To make a decision on deleting or keeping one item is not simply a matter of looking at the statistical figures. The alpha value is just one factor. We also need to consider the content of each individual item. In the case of Mother-tongue-using Belief, although the deletion of Item 4 may increase the alpha value, this item describes the use of L1 in a particular area, i.e. the use of L1 in L2 speaking, and thus it is better to keep it. Of course, if the cost of keeping Item 4 is so high that the alpha value is too low for us to accept the whole category, then we have to remove this item without too much hesitation.

In addition to the statistical procedure of the scale reliability analysis, we can

	Scale mean if item deleted	Scale variance if item deleted	Corrected item-total correlation	Alpha if item deleted
MTUB01	12.7013	1.7912	.3891	.5902
MTUB02	12.7143	1.6015	.4770	.5278
MTUB03	12.5325	1.6733	.5401	.4988
MTUB04	13.2078	1.5615	.3195	.6661

Reliability coefficients
No. of cases=77   No. of items=4
Alpha=.6386

Table 10.5: The item-total correlation of Mother-tongue-using Belief

also employ a more rigorous procedure, i.e. factor analysis, to establish or confirm categories. Suppose your questionnaire contains 30 items and you intend to have 5 categories. If all these categories are discrete and unidimensional, then there will be five distinct factors on which all the items within a category should load high respectively. However, the reality is more complicated than its conceptualization. Therefore, category developers may start with a large pool of potential category items and then ask different groups of people to respond to the items. Factor analysis is run repeatedly based on the responses given by different groups of people. Each time, only those items that load high on the factor are selected. In other words, these categories must be tested repeatedly through factor analysis and in the process of testing, many inadequate items are screened out.

Although we know that forming categories through factor analysis is more rigorous than by checking internal consistency, some categories describing the L2 learning process are not identified as distinct factors by factor analysis because these categories are conceptually distinct but empirically overlapping such as Belief and Strategy used in my study.

Selecting appropriate statistics

There are a variety of statistics for you to choose from. Which one is the most appropriate to answer your research questions? You have to make a series of decisions in such a selection process. In the following part, four frequently used procedures appearing in the Analyze menu of SPSS are introduced: Summarize, Correlate, Compare Means, and Regression. Before we go to the details, one thing I have to emphasize is that all the statistical procedures except Summarize, are operated under the assumption of normal distribution.

Summarize: Frequencies and Descriptives

Once you open the Analyze menu, Summarize appears on the top of the list which includes a variety of options. Due to the limited space, only the first two options are explained here: Frequencies and Descriptives. A study for writing up an M.A. thesis or a doctoral dissertation usually goes beyond Frequencies and Descriptives, which, however, are the first step of any complex analysis. Using Frequencies and Descriptives, you lay the data out and get a "feel" about them. For example, you may want to know how many students are females and how many are males in a study, and what are their respective percentages. By operating Frequencies, you can get the answers to the above two questions. The results indicate that there are 18 males occupying 23.4% and 59 females occupying 76.6%. When a questionnaire only contains a few items, you may end up with reporting frequencies and/or percentages only.

Value label	Value	Frequency	Percentage (%)	Valid percent (%)	Cum percent (%)
	1 (male)	18	23.4	23.4	23.4
	2 (female)	59	76.6	76.6	100.0
	Total	77	100.0	100.0	
Valid cases	77	Missing cases	0		

Table 10.6: A frequency table of Sex

By Descriptives, we may know what is the average score and what is the standard deviation of each category. The following results in Table 10.7 generated by Descriptives are the mean scores and standard deviations of belief categories in my study. You may find the second-year English majors showed a negative attitude toward Mother-tongue-using Belief while having a positive attitude toward the remaining four beliefs. However, they held Non-traditional Beliefs more firmly than Traditional Beliefs since the mean score of the latter (3.96) is lower than that of the former (4.27).

Variable label	Mean	Standard deviation (SD)	Valid *n*
MTUB (Mother-tongue-using Belief)	2.13	.56	77
EB (Effort Belief)	3.87	.48	77
TB (Traditional Belief)	3.96	.43	77
NTB (Non-traditional Belief)	4.27	.40	77
MB (Management Belief)	4.32	.45	77

Table 10.7: Descriptive statistics of belief variables
(*Note*. The full name of a variable is not automatically generated by Descriptives.)

Furthermore, you may notice that the standard deviation of MTUB is the biggest and that of NTB, the smallest. This means that the students' views about MTUB are more diversified than their views about NTB.

Correlation analysis

Correlation analysis is used to test the significance of the relationship between two variables. By such an analysis, we want to know three things:
1. How close is the relationship between the two variables concerned? In other words, to what extent can we predict the score of a dependent variable in our sample according to the score of an independent variable?

2. Is the relation due to chance, or does it exist in the overall population which we intend to generalize about? To put it another way, is this relationship significant?

3. What is its direction? Is it positive or negative?

The concept of direction refers to whether a covariation is positive or negative. For example, the students' scores on NMET positively covary with their scores on TEM4. It means that students who score higher on NMET tend to score higher on TEM4, whereas students who get lower scores on the first test tend to get lower scores on the second one. The use of the mother tongue in learning English negatively covary with the scores on TEM4. It means that the more the students use L1 in L2 learning, the more likely they are to obtain lower scores on TEM4, whereas the less the students use L1 in L2 learning, the more likely they are to get higher scores on the test.

All in all, a positive direction refers to the case where two variables vary in the same direction as shown in Figure 10.5a, while a negative direction refers to the case where two variables vary in the opposite direction as shown in Figure 10.5b.

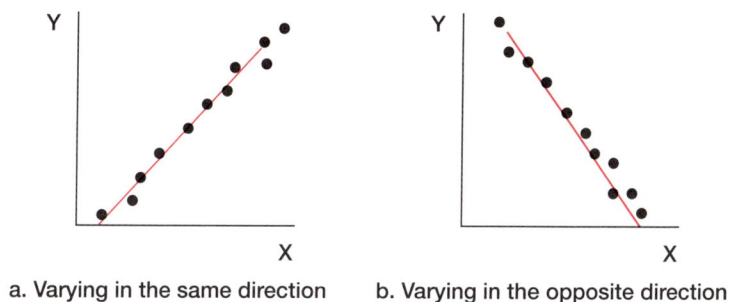

a. Varying in the same direction   b. Varying in the opposite direction

Figure 10.5: Two variables varying in the same or opposite direction

The extent to which two variables are correlated is indicated by the correlation coefficient which falls between 0 and ±1. If the correlation coefficient is 0, it means that the two variables concerned do not have any relation at all. When two variables are perfectly positively correlated, the coefficient is +1. The opposite case is −1. However, in most cases, the coefficient falls between 0 and ±1. For example, the total amount of time used in learning an L2 tends to be positively correlated with L2 performance. However, there indeed are some people who work very hard but have very poor performance. Therefore, in most cases, the correlation is not perfect.

A correlation coefficient is said to be significant if it reaches the significant level of .05, .01, or .001. In the case of the .05 level of significance, our confidence level is 95%. In other words, there are 5 chances out of 100 where the result might be wrong. Similarly, the .01 level of significance is equivalent to the 99% confidence level and this means there is 1 chance out of 100 where the result might be accidental. If the probability is bigger than .05, the correlation coefficient obtained is regarded as insignificant.

In terms of the levels of measurement, what kind of variables can be tested for correlation? Generally, the correlation between two interval variables, or between one interval variable and one ordinal variable, or between one interval variable and one nominal variable can be examined (Bernard, 1994).

To run a correlation analysis, you simply open the Analyze menu where by highlighting Correlate, you select the two variables which are supposed to be correlated from the left to the right under the heading of Variables. Table 10.8 shows the correlation coefficients between the students' beliefs and their use of corresponding strategies in my study. These four pairs of variables are treated as interval ones. According to the results, the four pairs are all positively correlated. However, the correlation between NTB (Non-traditional Belief) and NTS (Non-traditional Strategy) is not significant because its probability (.062) is greater than .05.

Variable label	No. of cases	Correlation (r)	P
MB-MS (Management Belief & Management Strategy)	77	.3763	.001
TB-TS (Traditional Belief & Traditional Strategy)	77	.2498	.028
NTB-NTS (Non-traditional Belief & Non-traditional Strategy)	77	.2148	.062
MTUB-MTUS (Mother-tongue-using Belief & Mother-tongue-using Strategy)	77	.5068	.000

Table 10.8: The correlation between belief variables and strategy variables

When you read and interpret the results, you have to remember the following two rules:

1. Not all significant findings at the 95% confidence level are equally important.
2. The significant, high correlation between two variables does not necessarily mean that there exists a causal relation between them.

? • Why is it said that the high correlation between two variables does not necessarily mean that a causal relation exists between them?
• Can you find an example from your daily life to show that the high correlation between two variables does not indicate any causal relation?

Compare Means: *t*-test and One-way ANOVA

Very often you need to compare two or more means in your study. The statistical procedure in SPSS for this purpose is called Compare Means. Among the analyses, Independent-samples *t*-test, Paired-samples *t*-test, and One-way ANOVA (i.e. One-way analysis of variance) are more extensively used. In this part, I will explain to you when Independent-samples *t*-test, Paired-samples *t*-test, and One-way ANOVA are needed and how results yielded by these different analyses are interpreted.

t-test

We have two kinds of *t*-tests: Independent-samples *t*-test and Paired-samples *t*-test. Independent-samples *t*-test, as the name suggests, involves two different groups of people, such as females and males, or high achievers and low achievers. In contrast, Paired-samples *t*-test only involves one group of people but two different variables, such as Traditional Strategy and Non-traditional Strategy, Intrinsic Motivation and Extrinsic Motivation.

Paired-samples *t*-test

Let's look at the following example.

> **Example**
>
> In my study (Wen, 1993), I intended to find out whether students employed Traditional Strategy significantly more than Non-traditional Strategy.

To answer the question, I need to compare the mean score of Traditional Strategy and that of Non-traditional Strategy. Therefore, Paired-samples *t*-test should be used. Table 10.9 displays the results. The results say that our students used Traditional Strategy more frequently than Non-traditional Strategy. The difference is significant at the level of .000.

Variable name	Mean	SD	*t*-value	*P*
TS (Traditional Strategy)	3.4749	.398	4.21	.000
NTS (Non-traditional Strategy)	3.2982	.421		

Table 10.9: The *t*-test of the use of Traditional Strategy and Non-traditional Strategy

Independent-samples *t*-test

Let's look at another example. In my study (Wen, 1993), I aimed at investigating whether male and female students employed Non-traditional Strategy significantly differently.

To answer the question, I should use Independent-samples *t*-test. Table 10.10 indicates that males and females did not show any significant difference in the use of Non-traditional Strategy although the mean score of the female group is slightly higher than that of the male group.

Variable name	No. of cases	Mean	SD	*t*-value	P
Males	18	3.1713	.458	-1.48	.144
Females	59	3.3376	.405		

Table 10.10: The *t*-test of the use of Non-traditional Strategy by males and females

> **Focus highlight**
>
> - The difference between Paired-samples *t*-test and Independent-samples *t*-test lies in the fact that the former operates on the same group of subjects with two different variables, while the latter operates on two different groups of subjects with one variable.

One-way analysis of variance (One-way ANOVA)

If you have got more than two means to compare, you need to choose One-way ANOVA which stands for One-way analysis of variance. Suppose we want to know whether students with varied scores on TEM4 differ significantly in their use of Non-traditional Strategy. What we need to do is first to divide the students into three groups according to their scores on TEM4: top group, middle group, and bottom group, and then compare their mean scores on the use of Non-traditional Strategy.

The question is: Are the differences in these mean scores significant? To put it another way, despite apparent differences in the mean scores, are these three groups really from identical populations? Table 10.11 reports the results produced by One-way ANOVA. The information from the table which is important for us to decide whether the differences are significant is *F* Ratio and *F* Probability. Since the probability (.0718) of *F* Ratio (2.7372) is bigger than .05, the differences among the three groups are not significant.

Source	d.f.	Sum of squares	Mean square	F	P
Variable Non-traditional Strategy by Variable English Achievement: Analysis of variance					
Between groups	2	1.2501	.6251		
Within groups	69	15.7564	.2284	2.7372	.0718
Total	71	17.0065			

Table 10.11: Differences in the use of Non-traditional Strategy tested by One-way ANOVA

Let's look at one more example which does show significant differences among groups but the picture is a bit complex.

Example

In Xu's study (2001), he compared the scores on a composition test obtained by students across four grades (i.e. Freshmen, Sophomores, Juniors, and Seniors) to find out whether these four grades did show significant differences in their writing abilities.

Xu chose One-way ANOVA which yielded results shown in Table 10.12. The probability (.000) of F Ratio (28.39) means that the overall differences in composition scores of the students across four university grades were significant statistically. Furthermore, the results show that Freshmen and Sophomores did not show any significant differences in their scores but these two groups were significantly different from Juniors and Seniors respectively, and Juniors were also statistically different from Seniors.

No. of grp	Mean	SD	Grp1	Grp2	Grp3	F	P
Grp1 (50)	3.17	.56			*		
Grp2 (50)	3.32	.44			*	28.39	.000
Grp3 (50)	3.65	.53	*	*			
Grp4 (50)	3.94	.25	*	*	*		

Table 10.12: Differences in composition scores of four groups tested by One-way ANOVA

• The difference between Independent-samples *t*-test and One-way ANOVA lies in the fact that the former compares the means of two different groups of subjects while the latter compares the means of three or more groups of subjects.

Multiple regression analysis

In the field of applied linguistics, a question we frequently come across is to what extent we can predict students' L2 achievement through a series of independent variables. Let's take my own study as an example again.

Example

The predicting power of 13 independent variables

The study (Wen, 1993) involved variables such as L1 Proficiency, Previous L2 Proficiency, Motivation, Effort, Belief, and Strategy. I would like to know how these variables can predict the students' L2 achievement (i.e. the score on TEM4).

In this case, I used a regression analysis to answer the question. Table 10.13 presents the results yielded by multiple regression analysis in my study of the relationship between 13 learner factors and L2 achievement.

Dependent variable	Multiple R	R2	F	
The score on TEM4	.62	.39	2.57**	
Independent variable			Beta	Sig T
1. L1 Proficiency			.03	.78
2. Previous L2 Proficiency			.43	.001
3. Deep Motivation			.23	.06
4. Surface Motivation			.11	.41
5. Effort			−.15	.30
6. Management Belief			−.14	.32

(*to be continued*)

(continued)

Dependent variable	Multiple R	R2	F	
7. Form-focused Belief			−.13	.36
8. Meaning-focused Belief			.16	.23
9. Mother-tongue-using Belief			−.01	.95
10. Management Strategy			.02	.88
11. Form-focused Strategy			−.07	.59
12. Meaning-focused Strategy			.24	.06
13. Mother-tongue-using Strategy			−.32	.03

Table 10.13: The predicting power of learner factors on L2 learning

The results in Table 10.13 indicate that 13 independent variables together can predict 39% variance in the scores on TEM4 at the significance level of .001. According to the absolute values of beta, we may find that the most powerful predictor of the dependent variable is Previous L2 Proficiency that has the highest beta value, i.e. .43 at the significant level of .001. The second powerful predictor is Mother-tongue-using Strategy with its absolute beta value being .32 at the significance level of .03. Deep Motivation and Meaning-focused Strategy have equal predicting power since they have almost the same beta value (.23/.24) at the same significance level (.06). They are, however, less powerful than Mother-tongue-using Strategy and their power does not have statistical significance because their probability level is greater than .05. The remaining independent variables have very low absolute beta values, all of which do not reach the required level of significance. Consequently, they do not possess predicting power at all. You might notice that some variables have positive beta values and some have negative ones. A positive beta value means the predicting direction is positive while a negative one means the opposite direction. For example, the positive beta value of Previous L2 Proficiency means that the higher the level of previous L2 proficiency a student gets, the higher the score on TEM4 he/she is likely to obtain; the negative beta value of Mother-tongue-using Strategy means that the more frequently this strategy is used by a student, the lower the score on TEM4 that he/she is likely to get.

Learning SPSS through an e-tutorial

You are advised to learn how to operate SPSS through an e-tutorial which is available on websites. It is easy to find SPSS on the internet. If you use a search

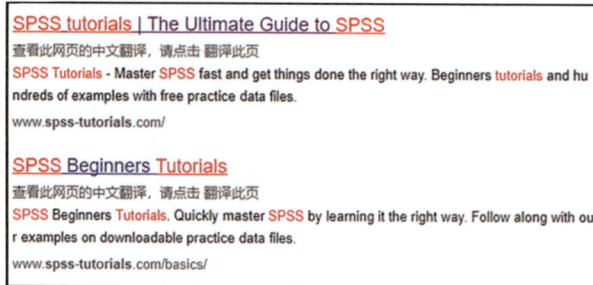

Figure 10.6: Search results for "SPSS tutorials"

engine to key in "SPSS tutorials," you can see the results shown in Figure 10.6.

These tutorials are free of charge either in Chinese or in English. I suggest that you start with SPSS beginners' tutorials and then move on to the advanced ones. You had better follow the guidance to read the instructions carefully and aim at a sound understanding. Then you accomplish the simulated tasks to check your understanding. When you encounter difficulties that you cannot overcome yourself, the shortcut is to ask people who are good at SPSS. Don't waste your time by repetitive trials and have no progress.

≡ ANALYZING THE DATA OF AN EXPERIMENT

Setting up a data file for an experimental study is not totally different from setting one for a survey study. The procedures for setting up a data file discussed in the previous part can be used to deal with data from an experiment. Furthermore, the statistical procedures such as Summarize, Correlate, Compare Means and Regression can be perfectly operated on experimental data, too. The major difference is that the analysis of survey data may end up with Summarize or Correlate but the analysis of experimental data must involve Compare Means. To avoid unnecessary repetition, I will only focus on some aspects that are particularly important for analyzing data from an experiment.

Problems in inputting experimental data

One common problem frequently encountered by novice researchers is in what format experimental data should be inputted. Suppose in your experimental study, you have 30 students as a control group and 30 students as an experimental group. How do you input the data? Do you place the data of 30 students from the control group side by side with the data of 30 students from the experimental group? Or do you put the data of these two groups sequentially (i.e. one group after another)?

Very often a novice researcher is not clear about which decision he/she should make. A wrong decision at the beginning would cost you much time to figure out why some statistical procedures cannot be implemented.

The simple rule is that if your experiment involves two or more different groups of people, you have to key in the data of one group after another in a sequence. Simply we may call such a format a sequential format. In addition to that, you have to specify whether a person belongs to a control group or an experimental group. The data file looks like the one displayed in Table 10.14. Here the variable ID refers to the identity number you assign to each student and the variable Group contains information concerning whether a person is in a control group or in an experimental group. Specifically, "1" represents an experimental group and "2" represents a control group. Such a sequential format of data is required by Independent-samples *t*-test. If you have more groups in your experiment, you just add to the sequence with Group 3, Group 4, etc.

ID	Group	Pretest	Posttest
01	1	70	72
02	1	64	71
03	1	86	82
04	1	72	81
...	...	...	...
31	2	71	68
32	2	63	64
33	2	80	81
34	2	60	62
...	...	...	...

Table 10.14: A correct data format for Independent-samples *t*-test

The parallel format as shown in Table 10.15 does not work for Independent-samples *t*-test and One-way ANOVA.

ID	Group	Pretest	Posttest	ID	Group	Pretest	Posttest
01	1	70	72	01	2	71	68
02	1	64	71	02	2	63	64
03	1	86	82	03	2	80	81
04	1	72	81	04	2	60	62
...	...	...	...	...	...	...	...

Table 10.15: A wrong data format for Independent-samples *t*-test and One-way ANOVA

By contrast, Paired-samples *t*-test can only function on data presented in a parallel format in which two variables are placed side by side. As mentioned before, Paired-samples *t*-test compares the means of two variables which are, however, related to one group of subjects. Let's look at the second example introduced at the beginning of Chapter 7.

Example

A comparison between two conditions

In the study conducted by Pica, Young, and Doughty (1987), they intended to find out whether negotiated interaction would facilitate L2 comprehension. They constructed a small-scale experiment in which two ways of providing linguistic input were compared. Altogether 16 adults at the intermediate level were involved. Their comprehension was checked by placing objects on a board under two conditions. Under the first condition, a native speaker of English read instructions that were modified by simplifying syntactic structures, using more words to paraphrase each instruction, and repeating each content word several times. While listening, the subjects were not allowed to interact with the native speaker. Under the second condition, the native speaker read instructions without any modifications. However, the subjects were encouraged to communicate with the native speaker to obtain comprehension. It was observed that the input was modified through interaction. The results showed that the subjects placed more objects correctly on the board under the second condition than under the first condition. It was concluded from the results that negotiated interaction can facilitate L2 comprehension.

The researchers intended to find out whether negotiated interaction was better than modified instructions in improving L2 comprehension. The way to measure the subjects' comprehension was to see how many objects the subjects could correctly place on the board by following the native speaker's instructions. In this case,

Paired-samples *t*-test is needed. The appropriate data format for such a *t*-test is like the one in Table 10.16.

ID	Modified instruction	Negotiated interaction
01	13	16
02	9	15
03	7	10
04	11	12
...	...	...

Table 10.16: A correct data format for Paired-samples *t*-test

Compare Means in experimental studies

No experimental studies can avoid the use of Compare Means, which includes Independent samples *t*-test, Paired-samples *t*-test, and One-way ANOVA. How can you make sure the statistics you have chosen are appropriate? The following rules may help you make a better decision:

1. Compare the means of one variable exhibited in two groups → Independent-samples *t*-test that requires a sequential data format.
2. Compare the means of one variable exhibited in three or more groups → One-way ANOVA that requires a sequential data format.
3. Compare the means of two variables exhibited in one group only → Paired-samples *t*-test that requires a parallel data format. It means that the data of two variables are placed side by side.

≡ SUMMARY

SPSS (Statistical Package for the Social Sciences) is a commonly used statistical tool that consists of three main windows: Application Viewer, Data Editor Viewer, and Output Viewer. The Application Viewer window contains all the statistical procedures for analyzing data available in SPSS; the Output Viewer window displays results yielded by SPSS, and the Data Editor Viewer window helps create a new file or read an existing file. The best way to learn how to operate SPSS is to gain access to a free e-tutorial on websites.

The analysis of quantitative data from a survey study starts with preparations for creating a data file: numbering all the questionnaires and defining variables.

Secondly, you key in the data from one questionnaire after another. Thirdly, you need to clean the data, which means that you correct the mistakes occurring in your inputting and deal with missing values. If the questionnaire items are intended to be analyzed in terms of categories, the conceptual categories need to be checked for their internal consistency by running the item-total correlation. What kind of statistics is selected to operate on the data depends on your research questions. By running Summarize, information about frequencies and standard deviations can be obtained. Correlation analysis is helpful when the relation between two variables is the researcher's concern. The statistical operation of Compare Means is needed when two or more means are to be compared. Specifically speaking, comparing the means of two variables related to one group requires Paired-samples t-test; comparing the means of two groups related to one variable needs Independent-samples t-test; comparing the means of more than two groups concerning the same variable needs One-way ANOVA. Multiple regression is used to determine to what extent a set of independent variables can predict variations in a dependent variable.

The procedures for analyzing the data from an experiment are more or less the same as those used in analyzing the quantitative data from a survey. The only difference is that no experimental study can avoid the use of Compare Means. The use of Independent-samples t-test and One-way ANOVA requires a sequential data format, which means that the data of the control group and those of the experimental group are presented in a sequential format, while Paired-samples t-test needs a parallel format, that is, the two variables to be compared are placed column by column.

AFTER-READING ACTIVITIES

Reviewing

1 What does SPSS stand for?

2 When you define a variable by SPSS, what should you take into consideration?

3 What is a correlation analysis? How do you interpret the results of a correlation analysis?

4 What is the difference between Independent-samples *t*-test and Paired-samples *t*-test?

5 When do you use *t*-test and when do you use One-way ANOVA?

Exploring

1 You are going to ask 30 students on campus to respond to the following questionnaire on reasons for learning English. Below are some reasons why people learn English. Write the number which best describes you in the parentheses at the end of each statement. Remember there are no right or wrong answers. The numbers stand for the following responses:

1=This statement is not important for me.
2=This statement is quite important for me.
3=This statement is important for me.
4=This statement is very important for me.
5=This statement is extremely important for me.

(1) I like learning a foreign language. (　)

(2) I am interested in the English culture. (　)

(3) I need English to get information from the outside world. (　)

(4) I need English to talk to foreigners. (　)

(5) I need English for my future career. (　)

(6) I need English for my further study in China. (　)

(7) I need English for studying abroad. (　)

(8) I need English for introducing China to the world. (　)

2 Create a data file by keying in the responses given by the students you investigated. (Note: You need to number all the questionnaires and then define the names of all the variables. The numbers are inputted in a new data file as ID and the students' responses each are inputted under the corresponding name of a particular variable.)

3 Classify the eight items into two categories (Deep Motivation vs. Surface Motivation) based on your conceptual reasoning and then confirm them by item-total statistics.

The analysis of qualitative data

This chapter will describe how qualitative data are analyzed. It will first present choices you may have for analyzing qualitative data. Secondly, it will show you how to prepare the data for qualitative analysis. Finally, it will discuss how qualitative analysis can be undertaken successfully.

CHOICES FOR ANALYZING QUALITATIVE DATA

As mentioned in Chapter 5, qualitative data can be analyzed qualitatively or quantitatively. By qualitative analysis, I mean that the results are presented in the form of words while by quantitative analysis, the findings are presented in the form of numbers. Figure 11.1 presents three common choices from which you can select for the analysis of qualitative data.

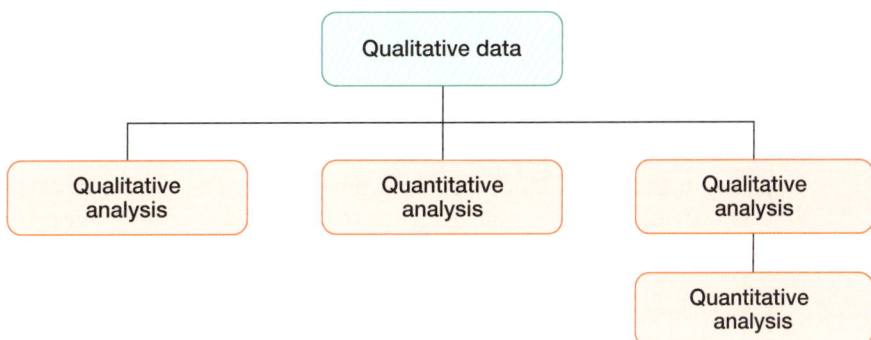

Figure 11.1: Choices for analyzing qualitative data

Choice 1: qualitative analysis

By the first choice, the researcher tries to identify categories emerging from the data which may form further patterns or variations. Let's look at the following example.

> **Example**
>
> ### Vocabulary strategies
>
> When the interview data concerning the use of vocabulary strategies were analyzed, the researcher read the data again and again and eventually she identified three general categories: (1) strategies used in remembering new words; (2) strategies used in understanding the meaning; and (3) strategies used to overcome the problem of insufficient vocabulary. For each general category, she also established some subcategories. These general categories together with their subcategories are the answer to the question: What strategies are used by English majors in vocabulary learning?

In the above example, the researcher had no perceived categories of vocabulary strategies used by the students. Through repeatedly reading the data, the researcher identified three categories based on her own experience of learning vocabulary.

Choice 2: quantitative analysis

By the second choice, the researcher obtains the results simply by counting something in qualitative data.

> **Example**
>
> ### The use of L1 in L2 writing
>
> In the study conducted by Wen and Guo (1998), the participants were asked to write an English composition based on the given pictures while speaking out what was going on in their minds. The researchers counted the number of Chinese words occurring in their verbal protocols and then calculated the percentage of L1 occurrence with reference to the total number of words produced by think-aloud. The result is the answer to the question as to how much L1 is used in the process of L2 composing.

In the above example, the data obtained from think-aloud are verbal accounts which are purely qualitative in nature. What the researchers did was to simply count the number of Chinese words occurring in the think-aloud data and then calculate the percentage of L1 in the total number of words spoken out by the participants.

Choice 3: qualitative analysis followed by quantitative analysis

The third choice is more complicated than the first two and it is easy to mistake it for the second choice, since by simply looking at the answer to the research question, the findings are quantitative. Let's look at Chen's study presented in Chapter 5 again.

Example

Children's vocabulary learning strategies

In Chen's study (2000), one of the three questions she would like to answer is: How frequently do Chinese children adopt strategies in remembering the spelling of new English words? There were 100 school children involved in her study who were asked to remember 20 new words while speaking out what was going on in their minds. The results she found are presented in Table 11.1.

In Chen's study, the first research question is "How frequently do Chinese children adopt strategies in remembering the spelling of new English words?" The findings in relation to this question are the following.

Strategy category	Frequencies									
	0	1	2	3	4	5	6	7	8	9+
Rote learning	26	5	16	16	18	8	5	1	2	1
Form association	54	3	14	15	15	1	5	/	1	2
Familiar word	5	1	8	8	11	13	23	6	9	16
Phonetic alphabet	36	3	16	16	15	6	4	1	1	2
Syllable cutting	5	1	8	13	15	12	17	9	11	9
Word building	60	3	11	8	7	2	9	/	/	/
Pronunciation rule	26	2	20	12	18	12	5	/	2	3
Visual frame	55	7	22	8	15	/	2	1	/	/
Chinese sound	73	5	15	5	2	/	/	/	/	/
Arbitrary cutting	44	7	21	8	4	10	3	3	/	/

Table 11.1: The frequencies of strategies used in remembering the spelling of words identified from think-aloud data (Chen, 2000, p. 32)

It is true that the findings concerning frequencies as shown in Table 11.1 are quantitative but the point is that the frequencies are not available in the raw data. In other words, the researcher was unable to obtain such frequencies directly from the think-aloud protocols. What she first did was to establish 10 categories of strategies by repeatedly reading the subjects' protocols. This process is, however, less obvious to the reader. In fact, the process by which such a qualitative analysis is conducted must be detailed in the section of methodology in a thesis. Nevertheless, the quantitative findings here are not directly derived from the raw qualitative data.

The three choices can be used independently for a study depending on the research questions. A clear understanding of your own choice(s) is essential for you to avoid confusions in analyzing the qualitative data and in describing how the data analysis is made in your study.

> **?**
> • Can you give more examples to illustrate how qualitative data can be analyzed by the three choices just mentioned?

DATA PREPARATION

Like a quantitative analysis where the researcher needs to set up a data file by coding, inputting, and cleaning the data, a qualitative analysis also needs a data file which can facilitate an effective and efficient analysis. It is obvious that setting up a qualitative data file is much more demanding and challenging than a quantitative one. Generally speaking, three tasks need to be accomplished: (1) transcribing recordings; (2) segmenting the data in relation to a specific research question; and (3) displaying the segmented data in a table. In the case of diaries, the first task is unnecessary while in the case of think-aloud protocols, it is not possible for you to perform the second and the third tasks since a protocol is a recording of a natural flow of thinking which is not responding to any specific question. This section will discuss how each task is undertaken.

Transcribing recordings

In the case of interviews and think-aloud, the participants' responses are normally recorded. In order to have a data file, the researcher must transcribe the recordings. The task of transcribing is tedious, boring, time-consuming, and requires painful patience on the part of the researcher. Yet it is indispensable and crucial for data analysis. Poorly transcribed protocols may reduce the validity and reliability of a study. Even worse, they can completely ruin a study. Therefore, the researcher has to deal with this professionally and conscientiously.

The first and most important principle for transcribing is faithfulness. As a researcher, most of the time, you need to take down everything you can hear. If there is anything unclear, you had better ask the participant to clarify it and listen to the recordings again rather than depend on your own speculation and imagination. The second principle is to standardize the way of transcribing, which means that you have to develop a set of codes that can indicate pauses, stress, hesitation, etc. In the case of pauses, you need to decide further whether the length of pauses should be indicated, and how it is specified if such an indication is necessary. By employing this set of codes all the way through, the transcriptions are standardized and easy to process afterward. Up to now, you might have the following question.

? • **Do we always need to transcribe every word literally uttered by the interviewee?**

This is indeed a very good question. In fact, transcribing data is a technical and professional job in the sense that you have to make a lot of important decisions. As you may know, in a semi-structured interview or an unstructured interview, a digression is a common phenomenon. It is clear that a digression is not meaningful for answering your research question. Therefore, you do not need to transcribe the digression. However, you have to be very cautious whenever you make such a decision.

Segmenting data

In the case of interviews and diaries, you may segment the data with reference to each specific research question so that the irrelevant data can be put aside. Be careful that such an arrangement of data cannot be made in haste. You have to read the raw data repeatedly and make sure the selected parts can well represent the interviewee's answer to the question concerned. If the decision is made in haste, you will most likely overlook some valuable information. Furthermore, whatever words or sentences that appear in the segmented data file should originate from the raw data.

Let's take Kwo's study (1999) as an example.

Example

Changes in student teachers through a one-year full-time course

Kwo (1999) intended to see what were the developmental patterns and variations in student teachers through a one-year full-time course. The participants were the students who took a one-year full-time teacher's certificate course in the Faculty of Education in the University of Hong Kong. The participants were asked to write reflective notes at six points of the course: on the entry to the course, before the school experience, after the school experience, before the school main practice, after the school main practice, and at the end of the course.

The segmented data file is presented here concerning the first research question: What is the difference in the perceptions of a good teacher between experienced teachers and novice teachers on the entry to the course? Six student teachers were selected for an in-depth analysis with three being experienced and three without any experience. Apart from the background information about the participants[1], the phrases, sentences, and quotes were all from the participants' reflective notes on the entry to the course, responding to the question: What is your perception of a good teacher?

Group 1: experienced teachers

Participant 1: Susan (Indian)
Native language: Tagalog; Age: 26; Sex: F
Marital status: unmarried; Teaching experience: 4 years
* Student-centered teaching
"Personally, I think this is a key factor in determining a teacher's effectivity. An effective teacher for me is one who can modify his/her lessons to suit the characteristics and needs of the students."
* Character molder
"I believe that education must address itself primarily to character/personality formation. It must not get caught up in equipping the youth with technical knowledge to the neglect of human formation, which, consequently, produces skilled robots and socially decrepit persons. With this, I do not undermine the importance of academic formation. I would just like to remind the teachers that the youth should be prepared primarily for day-to-day living, capable of handling the ups and downs of life."

---

[1] For ethical reasons, the names of the six participants are not real ones.

Participant 2: Catherine
Native language: Chinese; Age: 30; Sex: F
Marital status: married; Teaching experience: 5 years
* Able to help students develop intellectually but also spiritually
* With good qualities: having a humble spirit, honesty, and consistency without being hypocritical

Participant 3: Wendy
Native language: Chinese; Age: 42; Sex: F
Marital status: married; Teaching experience: ? years
* Keen to learn (update his/her knowledge on the subject)
* Positive attitude toward his/her students
* Honest to his/her colleagues, students, and himself/herself
* Enthusiastic (enjoying teaching)
* Dedicated (having a strong sense of commitment to teaching)

Group 2: novice teachers

Participant 4: Cecilia
Native language: Chinese; Age: 22; Sex: F
Marital status: unmarried; Teaching experience: 0 years
* Good personality: not a commander but friendly and helpful
* Having a good command of knowledge of the subject: A teacher is not a dictionary but understands the subject well and can teach it systematically; a teacher is well-prepared before he/she comes to the classroom.
* Fair grading system
* Teaching efficiently

Participant 5: Lucy
Native language: Chinese; Age: 25; Sex: F
Marital status: unmarried; Teaching experience: 0 years
* Patience
* Love for students
* Equipped with good explanation ability, fluent spoken English, and good communication skills with adolescents to establish good relations with students

Participant 6: Rebecca
Native language: Chinese; Age: 22; Sex: F
Marital status: unmarried; Teaching experience: 0 years
* Enthusiasm for teaching
* Preparing before lessons
* Care for students without prejudice
* Continuously learning and trying to make improvement of himself/herself

Having the above segmented data file concerning a specific research question makes it much easier and more convenient for you to make further analysis.

Displaying data

A data display is defined as a segmented data file with further reduction and synthesizing, which can be presented in a table or in a diagram, or a structured summary. By reduction and synthesizing, the details such as quotes and explanations are removed, and some loosely structured ideas are summarized. As a result, a data display is more concise than the segmented data file so that the researcher's attention resources can be used exclusively for thinking about the meanings of the most important data. However, such reduction and synthesizing also risk distorting the original data. To avoid this risk, you may take one of the two options. The first is to ask another researcher to check your work. If this is not possible, you may redo it a week later to see whether the result you get the second time shows any difference. Remember for whatever reasons, you are not allowed to distort the data.

	Susan	Catherine	Wendy
Group 1: experienced teachers	• Student-centered teaching • Character molder	• Helping students develop academically but also spiritually • Humble, honest, consistent	• Updating the knowledge on the subject • Positive attitude toward students • Honest, enthusiastic, dedicated
	Cecilia	**Lucy**	**Rebecca**
Group 2: novice teachers	• Not a commander but friendly and helpful • Knowledgeable • Teaching systematically and efficiently • Fair grading system	• Patience, love for students • Good explanation ability • Fluent spoken English • Good communication skills with adolescents	• Enthusiastic about teaching • Preparing before lessons • Care for students without prejudice • Continuously learning and improving oneself

Table 11.2: The data display of perceptions of a good teacher

Now let's look at the examples presented in Table 11.2. In Susan's response, by deleting two long quotes, her answer was shortened to two phrases: "Student-centered teaching" and "Character molder." In the case of Cecilia, compared with the answer in the segmented file, except the fourth point that remained unchanged, the other three points all underwent great changes. The first point was shortened but kept in her own wording; the second point was summarized with a new term "Knowledgeable," which was the researcher's wording but did not distort Cecilia's own meaning; the third point was a result of the combination of two ideas, and although the wording was not in the original data, the meaning was expressed by Cecilia.

⋮≡ QUALITATIVE ANALYSIS

As mentioned at the beginning of this chapter, qualitative data can be analyzed either quantitatively or qualitatively or in combination. Since quantitative analysis has already been discussed in detail in Chapter 10, I will not repeat it here. This section will discuss qualitative analysis only.

A framework for qualitative analysis

To show how qualitative analysis is carried out is difficult in a course unless you have the patience and time to go through the laborious process of analyzing the data. To illustrate it by writing is even more difficult since the process is very complicated and messy to some extent. To understand the way the data are analyzed, we need a lot of illustrative examples which, however, cannot be condensed into one or two paragraphs. In this part, I will first introduce to you the framework for qualitative analysis proposed by Strauss and Corbin (1998), which is graphically described in Figure 11.2. Their framework is known as the grounded theory which assumes that a theory is embedded in qualitative data and it can be developed through a systematic analysis. Secondly, I will use an example to illustrate how this framework can be operated. However, it will be brief and not sufficient for you to analyze the qualitative data needed for your M.A. or doctoral thesis. I strongly recommend that in addition to reading this part, you should read the book *Qualitative Data Analysis: An Expanded Sourcebook* written by Miles and Huberman in 1994 and the book *Basics of Qualitative Research: Techniques and Procedures for Developing Grounded Theory* by Strauss and Corbin in 1998.

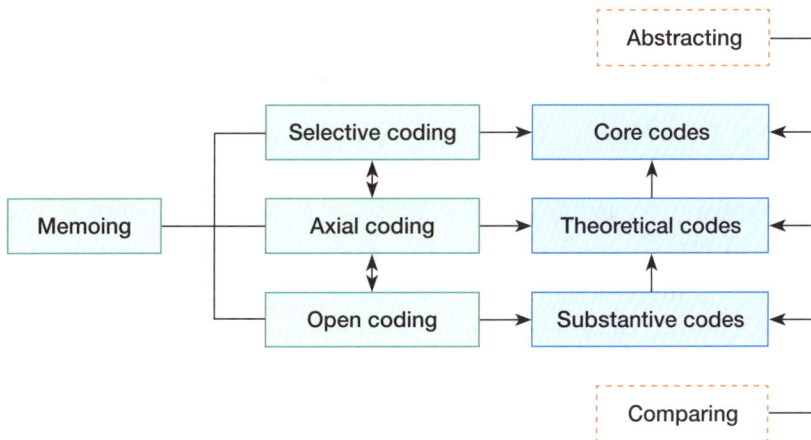

Figure 11.2: The framework for qualitative data analysis

According to Figure 11.2, you have to undertake two basic tasks, i.e. coding and memoing. Coding can be further divided into three kinds (i.e. open coding, axial coding, and selective coding) that yield three types of codes accordingly. The resulting codes form a hierarchy in terms of abstraction. Substantive codes from open coding are at the lowest level, core codes from selective coding at the highest level, and theoretical codes from axial coding, in between. Memoing is taking notes while you are engaged in coding. Notes are multifaceted. They may be the researcher's analysis of, interpretations of, or comments on the data. After all, the researcher may record anything occurring in his/her mind while coding the data.

The primary mental operations involved in accomplishing the tasks are abstracting and comparing. Abstracting refers to seeking a more general term or a statement to describe and explain a phenomenon or a less general concept. Comparing refers to establishing similarities and differences between objects or concepts.

Primary mental operations

In this part, primary mental operations, i.e. abstracting and comparing, will be explained.

Abstracting and comparing are primary mental operations in qualitative data analysis. That is to say, no matter what kind of coding you are doing, what your mind is actively engaged in is either abstracting or comparing or both in combination. We will focus on these two mental activities one by one.

Abstracting

"Abstract" is in contrast with "concrete." However, the degree of abstraction can vary from less abstract to very abstract. The results of coding can be placed along the hierarchy of abstraction (See Figure 11.3). At the lowest level of abstraction are concepts that stand for a set of discrete units which share a common property or display a similar attribute. At the next level of abstraction are categories that subsume a group of concepts that show a common property. Hypotheses are more abstract than categories, and indicate the researcher's understanding of the relations between categories and their subcategories. At the highest level of abstraction are theories in which all the hypotheses are logically related to each other within the same paradigm.

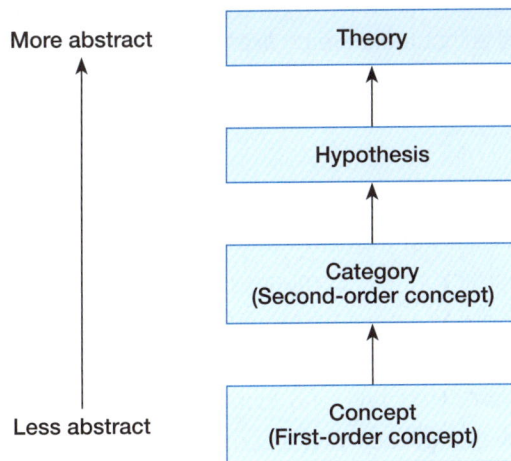

Figure 11.3: A hierarchy of abstraction

So far as a single project is concerned, it may not necessarily aim at constructing a theory. Which level of abstraction is the goal is decided by your research questions. No matter what level of abstraction you want to reach, you are always expected to identify something that can be shared by the units you are working at. The shared element can be a property, an attribute, or a paradigm. For the lower level of abstraction, you look for a common property or a similar attribute possessed by the items for abstracting. For example, the word "liquid" can designate petroleum, corn oil, or water. Although they differ in color, mass, and function, each has the specific property of being able to flow. For the higher level of abstraction, you are interested in a paradigm by which the categories can be related to each other. For instance, liquid, air, and solids are related to each other along the paradigm of being inanimate materials and thus they are called matter. Very often, the common property and paradigm are not evident particularly for novice researchers.

Although the results from coding are clear-cut in terms of their degree of abstraction, our minds do not work in the same manner. That is to say, the procedures by which our minds work are not parallel to the distinct levels of abstraction, moving from the lowest level of abstraction to the highest level. More often than not, our minds may work with concepts, categories, hypotheses, and theories simultaneously and each may interact with another. Sometimes we may work from theories to concepts and sometimes from concepts to theories. After all, our thinking routes are varied. However, for the convenience of discussion, we break down our thinking processes analytically in this part, trying to say that there are three levels of coding which correspond to three levels of abstraction: open coding leading to concepts and categories, axial coding to hypotheses, and selective coding to theories. I hope this will not give you the wrong impression that qualitative data analysis consists of a set of procedures. Actually, the most challenging aspect of qualitative analysis is that there are no fixed procedures to follow.

Comparing

Comparing is another essential mental activity in data analysis. It is intermingled with abstracting. Comparing may take place at different levels of abstraction. At the lower level of abstraction, you compare incident to incident, idea to idea, action to action in an attempt to give a name to similar incidents, ideas, or actions. Once concepts are identified, you compare concept to concept to look for similarities and differences to establish categories, and then compare category to category to see their relations. It is by comparison that a common property or attribute or paradigm can be identified. Comparing does not only take place within one study but also across studies.

Two basic tasks

Coding

Conceptually speaking, open coding, axial coding, and selective coding are different in nature. Open coding aims at identifying substantive codes, axial coding at theoretical codes, and selective coding at core codes. Although they are distinct operations, they are not necessarily undertaken sequentially. In many cases, they overlap and are operated synchronously.

Open coding

In open coding, researchers should keep open all the theoretical possibilities in the data. That is to say, researchers should not think along a single track and confine themselves to one option only. It is better to do open coding in a group of researchers rather than individually. If group analysis is not possible, you may put aside the provisional codes and reexamine the same data several days later with a fresh mind. By repeating this process, you turn the data upside down and inside out to try out on them all the theoretical possibilities.

In open coding, you discover concepts in data. You examine every incident or act or idea very closely in the whole set of data. By comparing incident to incident, you look for similarities and differences. Based on similarities, concepts are identified. The resulting concepts are called substantive codes in the grounded theory. Let's look at the following example.

L1 involvement in L2 picture composition

Wen and Guo (1998) conducted a qualitative study on L1 involvement in L2 picture composition by think-aloud. One of the research questions is to identify the functions of L1 use. The results show that the primary functions of L1 use include: transformation, confirmation, generating ideas, retrieving L2 forms, and controlling the writing procedures.

In the above example, the name of the five functions are concepts. Actually, any concept you identify at the beginning is only provisional in nature and needs modifications. You should make sure the concept or category you generate can account for all the data. If any conflict occurs, you should revise the concept. The modifications cannot be made at one go. By nature, concept formation has to be progressive. However, to avoid too many subsequent modifications, you had better spend more time on the data and examine them closely before establishing any concepts.

Axial coding

While open coding breaks the data apart and keeps them open to all theoretical possibilities, axial coding aims at categories which can form a whole picture again by looking for an axis that can connect categories. Once the connection has been set up, it can offer more precise and powerful explanations about the phenomena. Although the link between categories is refined in axial coding, an understanding of how categories are related to each other begins to develop in open coding. In this sense, the borderline between open coding and axial coding is not clear-cut.

To find out an axis is the key to axial coding. But what is an axis? Simply speaking, it is a perspective or a paradigm used in the grounded theory by which you examine the data. It may refer to conditions under which a certain phenomenon occurs. These conditions concern when, where, how, and why a contextual structure in which a phenomenon occurs is formed. It may refer to a series of actions that evolve over time under specified conditions. The actions denote a process in which a phenomenon occurs. It may refer to consequences that are results of actions.

Let's look at the category of generating ideas. The category has six sub-categories: reasoning, judging, associating, questioning, monitoring, and evaluating. Obviously, these six actions differ in nature psychologically. However, they are all actions in the process of generating ideas for writing an L2 composition. Therefore, the axis in this case is "function." In other words, these six activities all serve the same function, i.e. generating ideas.

Strauss (1987) points out that axial coding contains three major activities:

1. Specifying the properties of a category and their dimensions;
2. Identifying the possible conditions, actions, and consequences associated with a phenomenon;
3. Looking for cues in the data that might be insightful for the relation among the categories.

One thing that Strauss and Corbin (1998) emphasize in their book is that to identify an axis or a paradigm is a means but not an end. The end is to seek explanations and obtain an understanding of phenomena rather than looking for conditions, actions, and consequences.

Selective coding

Selective coding, as its name suggests, selects one aspect as a core category or a central category which represents the main theme of the research. When the core category is chosen, the scope of analysis is narrowed down and the focus comes to the surface. Around the core category, we can pull together all the relevant categories to develop a theory.

It is clear that a core category plays an essential role in constructing a theory. Then what is qualified as a core category and how is it identified? Strauss (1987, p. 36) listed a series of criteria for a qualified core category:
1. It must be central; that is, all other major categories can be related to it.
2. It must appear frequently in the data. This means that within all or almost all cases, there are indicators pointing to that concept.
3. The explanation that evolves by relating the categories is logical and consistent. There is no forcing of data.
4. The name or phrase used to describe the central category should be sufficiently abstract so that it can be used to do research in other substantive areas, leading to the development of a more general theory.
5. As the concept is refined analytically through integration with other concepts, the theory grows in depth and explanatory power.
6. The concept is able to explain variations as well as the main point made by the data; that is, when conditions vary, the explanation still holds, although the way in which a phenomenon is expressed might look somewhat different. It should also be able to explain contradictory or alternative cases in terms of that central idea.

Knowing the criteria is not sufficient since knowing and doing are quite different in nature. It is not uncommon that novice researchers who are familiar with the criteria still fail to detect the central category. They are confused by the flooding data and unable to look at the data from different perspectives. Strauss and Corbin give them several valuable suggestions that can facilitate the selection of the central category and the integration of concepts. One suggestion is to write the storyline, that is, to write a few sentences to describe what the research is about. If you find it difficult to start, you may go back to the raw data and reread several cases while keeping asking yourself stimulating questions, such as "What is the main issue here?" "What is most striking to me?" The second suggestion is to use diagrams. Diagrams are helpful tools to visualize the relations among the concepts. Once you start drawing a diagram, your thoughts about the logic of relations must be clarified. Otherwise, the resulting diagrams are muddled and confusing. The third suggestion is to review and sort through memos (How to write memos will be discussed in the next part). Memos record all the ideas in your mind while you are coding. As the analysis proceeds, your memos contain more and more abstract ideas which are helpful for you to extract a central category.

Memoing

Memoing is an essential task for qualitative data analysis. It records what you have obtained through abstracting and comparing, and how you went about them in the coding process. It forces you to be alert to the data and enables you to be clear about which direction you are going in. By having memos, you have products of analysis which are easily revised, supplemented and elaborated, or negated in the later process. After all, memoing is a very flexible device, as Glaser's definition illustrates: "A memo is the theorizing write-up of ideas about codes and their relationship as they strike the analyst while coding...it can be a sentence, a paragraph or a few pages...it exhausts the analyst's momentary ideation based on data with perhaps a little conceptual elaboration" (Glaser, 1978, pp. 83-84).

Memoing should go hand in hand with coding. Whatever has resulted from coding should go into memos. Memos may be substantive notes, theoretical notes, methodological notes, or personal notes. When they are substantive or theoretical notes, they should be primarily conceptual. Furthermore, they should go beyond what is being analyzed. In other words, they move from the actual events to the abstract concepts, and from a lower level of abstraction to a higher level of abstraction.

One important thing you should remember is that memos evolve over time and memos are not differentiated from right to wrong or from good to bad. Actually, the content in memos is provisional and bound to change as the analysis proceeds. The notes in earlier memos might appear to be not accurate and even ridiculous. However, they become more and more sophisticated when you dig deeper into the analysis. The category or pattern or relationship gradually emerges from the data. So long as you keep recording the ideas in the analysis and keep checking them against new data, you are moving toward more and more advanced levels of abstraction. Eventually, your memos serve as a basis on which a theory will be set up.

- Basically, qualitative data analysis always involves abstracting and comparing. The results are codes at different levels of coding. The most demanding and challenging task is to put all the codes you have named together which can form a coherent picture. In other words, it is easy to find a parameter or perspective underlying all your codes. In this sense, you need to think all the time why these codes can go together.
- The memo is a tool for you to record your thinking process and sort out messy ideas. It does not offer you any help in obtaining codes themselves.

An illustration

Let's closely examine the data presented in Table 11.2 and make a qualitative analysis. The research question is whether there is any difference in the perceptions of a good teacher between experienced teachers and novice teachers when they were enrolled into the course.

Where should we start? Actually, there are no standardized procedures to follow. What I am going to talk about is a simple description of the procedures by which I analyzed the data. As you know, our thinking usually does not happen in a linear fashion. It is very common that several ideas occur simultaneously in our minds. However, once they are to be described verbally, they have to be presented one after another as if they occur in sequence. In this sense, the following description is not a true record of the process of my data analysis.

Detecting similarities in Group 1 and Group 2 respectively

When I read the data presented in the first row, i.e. Group 1, two terms caught my eyes, i.e. "Character molder" and "spiritually." I wrote in the memo: The experienced teachers seem to show great concern for students' mental development. However, a similar term did not appear in the response of the third participant Wendy. By comparing Catherine with Wendy, I found that both of them mentioned some qualities required for a good teacher. This idea was also recorded in the memo. Now I was stuck and could not see anything shared by the three participants. Instead of racking my brains thinking about the first group, I started to work at the second group. Two common features immediately emerged from the data after the first reading. The first common feature is that they were all concerned with their relation with students; the second one is that they all emphasized effective teaching. Thus, I produced a table in which these two common features are presented together with evidence.

Name	Relation with students	Effective teaching
Cecilia	• Not a commander but friendly and helpful • Fair grading system	• Knowledgeable • Teaching systematically and efficiently
Lucy	• Patience, love for students • Good communication skills with adolescents	• Good explanation ability • Fluent spoken English
Rebecca	• Care for students without prejudice	• Enthusiastic about teaching • Preparing before lessons • Continuously learning and improving oneself

Table 11.3: Two common features shared by three novice teachers

Once I identified these two concepts or substantive codes in Group 2, I went to check whether these two features were also available in Group 1. The interesting thing was that the novice teachers' concerns did not gain any attention from the experienced teachers at all. It seemed that these two groups approached the same question from totally different perspectives. What were their different perspectives? I tried to capture them by reading the data again and again. Suddenly, two terms struck me and gave me an understanding of the data, which were "Fair grading system" and "without prejudice." These two terms would be typically used by students when they talk about their teachers. Novice teachers without any teaching experience naturally approached this question from students' perspective. Thinking along this line, I realized the second feature "Effective teaching" was either from students' perspective or from the perspective of a subject teacher.

Identifying differences between the two groups

With these two perspectives in mind, I closely examined the data of Group 1 again. It seemed to me that to Susan and Catherine, a good teacher is an educator who should help students develop as whole persons, i.e. both intellectually and mentally. Wendy's view seemed to be different. Her view took the perspective of a teacher in general and she was concerned with the general qualities of a good teacher. At this stage, I constructed a diagram (See Figure 11.4) in the memo. In the diagram, I tried to list all the different perspectives which were placed hierarchically. Furthermore, I tried to link the substantive codes, theoretical codes, and core codes.

Once I finished drawing the diagram, the answer to the question "What is the difference in the perceptions of a good teacher between experienced teachers and novice teachers?" was very clear as if it was self-evident.

The illustration of qualitative analysis, although it is oversimplified, can show you how abstracting and comparing operate, how substantive, theoretical, and core codes are obtained, and in which way memos can be used to help you analyze the data qualitatively.

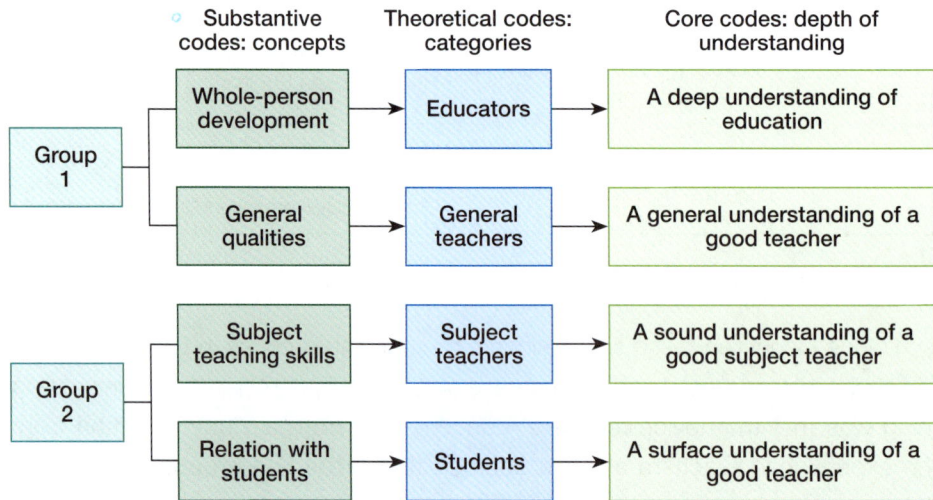

Figure 11.4: Differences in perceptions of a good teacher between Group 1 and Group 2

One thing that has to be emphasized here is that the answers to the same question might be varied if the researcher takes different perspectives. This is one of the reasons why qualitative analysis is fascinating. For example, the above question might have the following answer: The fundamental difference between experienced teachers and novice teachers in their perceptions of a good teacher is that the former group is concerned with professional development while the latter, with the survival skills of a teacher.

> **?**
> • Do we need to do three-level coding for every set of qualitative data, i.e. open coding (substantive codes), axial coding (theoretical codes), and selective coding (core codes)?

Honestly speaking, for an M.A. thesis or doctoral dissertation, it is good enough for a student researcher to cover the first two levels of coding for the purpose of obtaining substantive codes and theoretical codes. The purpose of the first-level coding is usually to find out typical and representative concepts from the raw data and the purpose of the second-level coding is to classify the first-level concepts into categories from a particular perspective. If you move further, you will go to the third-level coding, i.e. selective coding for the purpose of developing a theory. However, it is not compulsory for every qualitative study to construct a theory.

▶☰ VALIDITY AND RELIABILITY

Qualitative analysis is often criticized as lacking validity and reliability. This could be a problem if no measures are taken to guard against flaws in data analysis. As was said before, qualitative analysis has no fixed procedures available that can naturally lead to reliable results. Furthermore, substantive codes, theoretical codes, and core codes are not on the surface of the data and they can be identified only when the researcher has gained insights through repetitive reading of and continuous thinking about the data.

If the analysis is valid, the identified codes can explain the data. In other words, the codes should be fully supported by the data rather than something that the researcher has imposed on the data. If the analysis is reliable, two or more researchers can obtain similar codes if they are asked to work at the same set of data.

To make sure the qualitative analysis is reliable, two researchers had better analyze the same set of data independently and then discuss it together. If there are some controversies they cannot resolve, a third party needs to be invited to join the discussion. If it is not possible to find another researcher to analyze the whole set of data, you may invite him/her to analyze 10% or 20% of the data set. Another pragmatic solution is to put the results of the data aside for a relatively long period of time, say one or two months, and analyze them again by yourself.

☰ SUMMARY

Qualitative data can be analyzed either qualitatively or quantitatively or in combination. To prepare for analyzing interview data and think-aloud data qualitatively, you have to transcribe the recordings faithfully with a set of standardized codes to indicate the pause, stress, etc. To clarify unclear parts of the recordings, it is better to ask for help from the participant rather than depend on the researcher's own speculation. Qualitative data are better to be segmented with reference to specific research questions and then displayed through reduction and synthesizing. Segmenting data combined with displaying data can facilitate qualitative analysis.

Following the framework proposed by Strauss and Corbin, we are expected to carry out two basic tasks: coding and memoing. By the two primary mental operations: comparing and abstracting, the researcher starts with open coding followed by axial coding and ends up with selective coding. These three kinds of coding lead to three kinds of codes: substantive codes, theoretical codes, and core codes that can be placed on a hierarchy from the lower level of abstraction to the higher level of abstraction. Above all, you have to remember that these three kinds of coding are not ordered procedures and the process is intuitive and interactive.

In memoing, you are supposed to write down whatever occurs in your mind in the process of abstracting and comparing. The ideas may be fragmentary or random at the beginning but can nevertheless show the development of your analysis and can also serve as a basis on which you can obtain insights.

In order to improve the validity and reliability of qualitative analysis, it is best to ask another researcher to analyze the same set of data. If this is not possible, you have to analyze the same set of data at least twice with some time in between.

AFTER-READING ACTIVITIES

Reviewing

1. What do you need to consider when you transcribe recordings?
2. In the segmentation of data, what are you expected to do?
3. When you display the data, how do you deal with a segmented data file?
4. How do you differentiate three kinds of coding?
5. What is the function of memoing?
6. How can you make sure the qualitative analysis of the data is valid and reliable?

Exploring

1. Go to a library and find examples from students' theses to illustrate how qualitative data are analyzed quantitatively or qualitatively or in combination.
2. Interview six students to find out similarities and differences in the way they write a summary while recording what they have said in the interviews. Once you finish the interviews, you are expected to accomplish the following tasks.
   (1) Transcribe the interview data, segment the data, and display the data.
   (2) Analyze the data to identify substantive codes and theoretical codes by open coding and axial coding through abstracting and comparing.
   (3) Summarize your findings to answer the research question.

PART III

Thesis Writing

Thesis writing is very important for a graduate student. No one would deny its importance. However, more often than not, graduate students haven't received sufficient guidance in this regard. Some survive through desperate struggles; some fail after exerting painstaking efforts. In this part, I would like to share with you the lessons I have learned about thesis writing through trial and error. This part consists of three chapters. Chapter 12 presents an overview of the structure of a thesis. Chapter 13 describes how each part of the thesis is written up. Chapter 14 discusses the problems in format and style in thesis writing.

Overall objectives

By studying this part, you will be able to:

- ☐ describe the structure of a thesis
- ☐ explain how to write up each part of the thesis
- ☐ solve some typical technical problems in thesis writing

An overview of thesis writing

12

This chapter will start with the definition of a thesis/dissertation and then introduce to you the general structure of a thesis/dissertation. Then, a brief description of each part of a thesis/dissertation will be presented. Finally, how to make a timeline for writing a thesis/dissertation is discussed.

☰ DEFINITION OF THESIS AND DISSERTATION

A thesis or a dissertation?

There is no universal consensus on the definitions of a thesis and a dissertation. Cone and Foster (1993), by comparing the definitions of these two terms presented in *Webster's New International Dictionary* and *The Random House Dictionary of the English Language*, conclude that the distinction between the two terms is not clear at all. However, they describe a common practice in most American universities: "Thesis" is used to refer to the written work for a master's degree while "dissertation" is for a doctor's degree. According to my own experience, the term "thesis" can be used for both master and doctoral written work. In this book, these two terms will be taken as synonyms.

What is a thesis/dissertation?

A thesis/dissertation is an argument in which different parts are logically related and all center around research questions (Punch, 1998). It is neither a simple record of what has been done in your research nor a description of what has been found in your study. Since it is an argument, in addition to describing, you need to explain why the study is conducted in the way you design it.

A research process is invariably messy in one way or another. To make a messy process appear to be neat in a paper, you are expected to examine the whole process and report only the information relevant to answering your research questions. In other words, you have to ignore the irrelevant things you have done. To put it differently, a thesis is a report of your study in which only important and relevant things are selected to be presented. However, selection does not mean hiding unexpected problems or results.

☰ THE STRUCTURE OF A THESIS

This section will start with a general account of the structure of a thesis which is followed by a brief description of the three major components of a thesis, i.e. the beginning, the body, and the ending.

An overall picture

A general description of the structure of a thesis is given in Figure 12.1 which is the same as the actual sequence of the manuscript. We may divide the whole sequence into three parts: the beginning, body, and ending. The beginning part covers from "Title page" to "List of figures"; the body part contains five topics: "Introduction," "Literature review," "Methodology," "Results/Findings & discussion," and "Conclusion"; the ending part contains "References" and "Appendices."

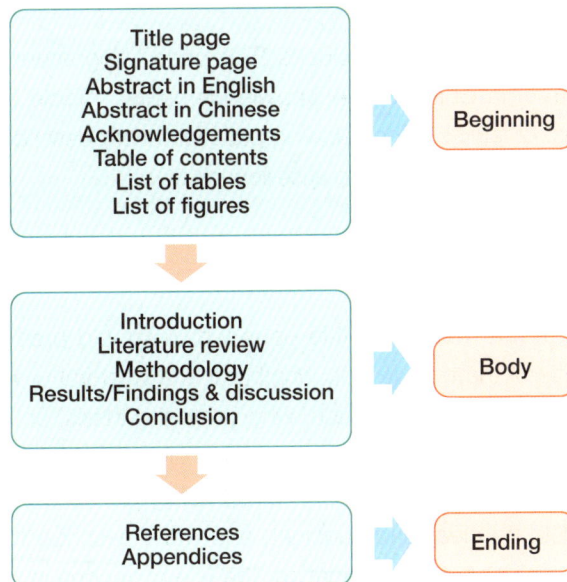

Title page
Signature page
Abstract in English
Abstract in Chinese
Acknowledgements
Table of contents
List of tables
List of figures
➡ Beginning

⬇

Introduction
Literature review
Methodology
Results/Findings & discussion
Conclusion
➡ Body

⬇

References
Appendices
➡ Ending

Figure 12.1: The structure of a thesis

One thing that has to be emphasized is that the sequence presented here is not the actual sequence of writing your thesis. A common practice is to write the body first, then the ending part, and finally the beginning part. Nevertheless, for the convenience of discussion, the sections are organized according to the actual sequence presented in a thesis.

> **Focus highlight**
>
> - There are variations in the structure of a thesis. Quantitative studies tend to share more similarities while qualitative studies show more diversities. Some qualitative theses/dissertations may start with interesting, vivid stories; some begin with a conversation. In a word, they may not follow the traditional structure described in Figure 12.1.
> - A novice researcher is advised to read theses which have won awards of excellence in recent years. Moreover, a novice researcher should seek help from supervisors when he/she is uncertain about the overall organization of the thesis.

Beginning part

The beginning part of a thesis includes "Title page," "Signature page," "Abstract in English," "Abstract in Chinese," "Acknowledgements," "Table of contents," "List of tables," and "List of figures." The following parts will briefly describe what should be covered and what problems are likely to arise in each part.

Title page

The first page of a thesis is a title page which should provide the following information: the title of the manuscript, whether it is a doctoral or a master's thesis, in which university the thesis was written, who wrote the thesis, and when the thesis was finished. The format is varied from university to university. You had better go to the secretary of the graduate program to get the format before you construct this page.

The title should be clear and succinct, and must describe the study. If there are only a few variables under investigation, the title may contain these variables. If many variables are under investigation, the title may specify the type of independent and dependent variables being examined. If possible, the type of subject is better described in the title. The following are the examples of thesis titles[1].

---

[1] The titles are taken from either M.A. or doctoral theses but a few of them have been slightly modified in order to make them more explicit.

> **Example**
>
> 1. A contrastive study of English and Chinese compliment responses (Gong, 1998)
> 2. Advanced level English language learning in China: The relationship of modifiable learner variables to learning outcomes (Wen, 1993)
> 3. A process-oriented cognitive account of L1 influence on L2 writing in the Chinese context (Guo, 1997)
> 4. An investigation into the internal structure of EFL motivation at the tertiary level in China (Qin, 1998)
> 5. A study of second-year English majors' pragmatic competence (C. X. Wu, 1998)
> 6. A study of the changes of tertiary English majors' beliefs about L2 learning (Su, 1996)
> 7. A study of university students' argumentative writing in English: Rhetorical knowledge and discourse pattern (J. Wu, 1998)
> 8. Error treatment in EFL classrooms in universities in China (Hu, 1999)
> 9. Influence of different tasks, lengths of planning time and lengths of learning on L2 oral performance of university students (Zhu, 1998)
> 10. L2 proficiency and comprehension strategy use of EFL learners in universities in China (Lu, 1997)
> 11. Risk-taking and English learning: A study of the risk-taking beliefs and behaviors of English majors in China (Wang, 1999)
> 12. The relationship of L2 learners' linguistic variables to L2 writing ability of tertiary-level non-English majors in China (Ma, 1998)

In some universities, the total number of words in a title has a limit and the title of a thesis must be finalized three months before submitting the thesis. That is to say, once the title has been submitted to the higher degree committee, the writer cannot change the title.

Signature page

The "Signature page" is the second page of a thesis. Although this page is simple to construct, the information is very important. Without a supervisor's signature, a thesis cannot be submitted legally. In my opinion, the signature is not simply a formality but also signals a supervisor's lifelong responsibility since a thesis is normally kept in the database for a very long time.

Abstract

The abstract is a summary of your study. It should be coherent by itself. It provides information concerning the following aspects: the purpose of the study, the research questions to be addressed, the subjects involved, the instruments used to collect data, the procedures for collecting and analyzing data, the findings and the conclusions. If this is the first time for you to write an abstract, I strongly recommend that you read a few abstracts in journals and analyze their structure before you write your own.

In the Chinese context, you are also expected to write an abstract in Chinese. No doubt, the content of the abstract in Chinese should be the same as that in English. However, a literal translation of the English version is definitely unsatisfactory. Some English majors seem to be weak in writing in Chinese. Very often, the draft of an abstract in Chinese contains some sentences that do not sound like Chinese and are even difficult to understand. The best way to ensure the readability of the abstract is to ask the students from other departments to read it and make comments on it before you submit it to your supervisor. One thing that has to be emphasized here is that the abstract in Chinese is normally written for the members of the higher degree committee. This abstract is the main thing through which the members can evaluate the quality of your thesis. In this sense, the quality of this abstract may even determine your success or failure in obtaining a graduate degree. Therefore, I strongly suggest that you should spend as much time as you can on writing the abstract.

Acknowledgements

?
- **Do you think the members of an oral defense committee would spend time reading the acknowledgements written by M.A. or Ph.D. students?**
- **Suppose you are one of the members of an oral defense committee. How would you feel when you read the acknowledgements which are very short and impersonal?**

The "Acknowledgements" page is the place to express the researcher's gratitude to those who have offered help in the process of research and thesis writing. The thanks are usually expressed to: (1) the supervisor; (2) the teachers and classmates who gave you suggestions or advice on your research; (3) persons who helped you collect data and do proofreading; (4) family and friends who gave you physical and/or mental support; (5) sources of financial support if there were any; and (6) those who kindly permitted you to use their research instruments or other materials.

One common problem in this part is that the statements of thanks are very general and abstract. The information about the way in which you have been helped is not provided. It appears that the writer expresses his/her thanks simply for formality rather than from the bottom of his/her heart. Being overmodest could lead the reader to conclude that the writer might be an incompetent researcher. Being less specific might leave a wrong impression on the reader that the writer is not sincere enough. The best strategy to express your thanks is to specify exactly why each person should be thanked, i.e. what the person to be thanked has done in relation to your research and thesis writing. No more, no less.

Table of contents

"Table of contents" lists the headings of the beginning, body, and ending parts of a thesis. The beginning part is marked by Roman numbers while the remaining parts are marked by Arabic numbers. For the body of a thesis, the subheadings of each chapter are listed. They are intended to show their different levels. It is not common to put all levels of subheadings in the table of contents. Three levels are usually demonstrated. The following is an example of part of a table of contents of my own doctoral dissertation (Wen, 1993, p. vii).

Example

TABLE OF CONTENTS

List of tables

"List of tables" is where the tables spread out in a thesis are now put together while each table has a page number. Referring to the page number, the reader can quickly gain access to the information needed.

List of figures

"List of figures" provides information in the same way as "List of tables." It contains all the figures spread out in a thesis with a page number specified. The common problem I have observed is that some graduate students cannot make a clear distinction between a table and a figure. A figure may refer to a graph, a chart, a diagram, or a picture while a table must be either a square or a rectangle in which numbers and words are presented in rows and columns.

It is good to review the list for the appropriateness of the titles and structures. Very often when the tables and figures are scattered on different pages, the problems are obscure. Only when the tables and figures are brought together will the problems surface.

Body part

This part will first introduce to you two common approaches to the organization of the body of a thesis: a one-level model and a two-level model, and then briefly describe the content of five parts within the body of a thesis.

One-level and two-level models

Usually, the body of a thesis is divided into five chapters: (1) Introduction; (2) Literature review; (3) Methodology; (4) Results and discussion; and (5) Conclusion. This is a one-level model. The alternative structure is a two-level model, where "Part" occurs at the first level and "Chapter" at the second level. Such a structure is particularly useful for a doctoral dissertation. The following is an illustration of a two-level model.

> ## Example
>
> ### A two-level model
>
> **PART I   BACKGROUND**
> Chapter One   Introduction
> Chapter Two   Literature review
> **PART II   METHODOLOGY**
> Chapter Three The quantitative design
> Chapter Four   The qualitative design
> **PART III   RESULTS AND DISCUSSION**
> Chapter Five   …
> Chapter Six   …
> **PART IV   CONCLUSION**

However, this book will only focus on the one-level model. In the following part, each chapter will be briefly described.

Introduction

The "Introduction" chapter is an overview of the whole study. It is usually short without technical details and can be understood even by the most casual readers. A challenge of writing this chapter is how to present sufficient information for readers to get an overall picture of the study.

Literature review

An introduction is followed by a literature review in which the relevant existing literature is reviewed to indicate what has already been done and what problems remain to be solved. Equipped with the knowledge of this chapter, readers can visualize the research context where the link between the proposed study and the previous ones is displayed and the potential contribution to the existing literature is demonstrated.

Methodology

The "Methodology" chapter describes the design of the proposed study. It includes general as well as specific research questions or hypotheses, information about subjects, instruments, the procedures for data collection and data analysis. The information presented in this chapter should be so explicit and transparent that any other researcher can easily replicate your study if he/she wants to.

Results and discussion

The chapter that is talked about here is entitled "Results and discussion." The results are the answers to your research questions and the discussion explains the possible reasons for specific findings, the significance of the findings, the link between the present findings and the previous ones, etc. The discussion may go along with each finding presented or may be presented separately from the results.

Conclusion

The "Conclusion" chapter includes major findings, implications of the findings, and recommendations for future research.

The format of the body of a thesis may vary from one university to another. You should check with your supervisor or the secretary of the graduate program in your department to get detailed information about the number of chapters and the required content within each chapter. You had better get the information before you start writing in order to avoid reformatting the whole thesis, which can be time-consuming and painful.

Ending part

The ending part contains two sections: "References" and "Appendices." They are important materials for a thesis but it is not appropriate to integrate them into the body of a thesis because they disrupt the smooth flow of the text. The following part will describe what "References" and "Appendices" contain.

References

You might have read hundreds of books and papers. Not all references are, however, required to be listed in the "References" section. The references here only refer to the materials you cite in your thesis. Following the APA (American Psychological Association) reference format, in "References," all the materials cited in the manuscript should be listed in alphabetical order by author. Each reference should contain the following information:
1. The author(s);
2. The date;
3. The title;
4. For a book, the publisher;
5. For a journal article, the journal name, volume, issue number, and pages.
When producing references, student researchers often encounter some

difficulties or problems. In the following part, I will discuss them one by one along with suggestions about how to resolve them.

No clear distinction between references and bibliographies

One of the common problems I have observed in graduate students' theses is that they do not differentiate a bibliography from a reference list. A reference list only contains cited works that you referred to in your thesis. A bibliography may include any work that you have consulted during your research, which may not be cited in your thesis. In the APA style, your thesis requires a reference list rather than a bibliography.

Uncited works in the reference list

Another frequent problem is that the reference list may include some works that are not cited in the text or some cited works are absent from the reference list, mainly due to the lack of timely revisions of the reference list along with repeated revisions of the text. How can you make sure the reference list can avoid these problems? With the help of a working bibliography, producing a reference list is more simple as well as accurate. You go through the whole thesis or dissertation page by page and tick the references in the working bibliography that appear in your writing. Those that haven't been marked are deleted. The remaining ones all go to the section of references. Meanwhile you also add cited works to the reference list if they are not included in your working bibliography. One thing I have to remind you is that the final revision of the reference list should be done when you are 100% certain that no further revision will be made in the text. In the process of revision, you had better save the section of references as a new file while the previous one is still kept in your old file. The advantage of such practice is that it is easy to retrieve references you have deleted before.

Cited works absent in the reference list

Finally, you have to double check to make sure that references cited in the text are present in the reference list and each entry in the reference list is cited in the text. One common practice of the members of the oral defense committee is to point out that details of some works cited in your thesis are not available in the section of "References."

Incomplete information about cited works

If, at the last stage, when you are approaching the time of submitting your thesis, you cannot get the accurate spelling of the author's name or the exact year of publication. Instead of turning back to piles of materials and searching for the information for hours upon hours, you had better rewrite the paragraph to drop out the reference. Otherwise, you might waste a lot of time searching without satisfactory results.

Appendices

The "Appendices" section contains any material that you think is important but cannot be put in the body of the thesis. The following are typical examples of what can be presented in this section:

1. The complete questionnaire;
2. The interview schedule;
3. The diary instructions;
4. The test papers;
5. The materials used in the training section;
6. The report on a pilot study;
7. The tasks the subjects are expected to undertake such as reading, writing, listening, speaking, etc.;
8. The detailed results of data analysis.

▤ SUGGESTIONS FOR WRITING A THESIS WITHIN A TIME FRAME

Bearing an overall structure of a thesis in their mind, the student researchers need to make a writing plan with a clear timeline since they often underestimate the difficulties of writing. They think once the research has been finished, the task of writing can be done easily without too much difficulty. The following is a true story.

Once, a doctoral student of mine said confidently that he could finish the writing of his thesis within three months. I responded to his confident remark by a negative comment: "I don't think you can get it done although I wish you could do it." Being unhappy about my response, he thought I did not make a just evaluation of his ability. I then further explained why I said that he could not accomplish the task within this time frame. I didn't think he was convinced by my explanation when he left my office. He tried hard to get it done within the time limit he set up in order to prove what he said was right. However, he eventually spent half a year to finish the first draft.

The relation between researching and writing

In order to finish your writing successfully, you need to have a sound understanding of the relation between researching and writing. Researching and writing are apparently two sequential tasks in the sense that researching must take place before writing. It is true that without researching nothing can be written down. However, it does not mean writing must be postponed until researching is finished. Therefore, you had better start writing in the process of researching as shown in

Figure 12.2. One advantage of writing along the process of research is to enable you to record what you have done in data collection and data analysis in case you forget the details later. The second advantage is to enable you to finish the writing task bit by bit. By doing so, it can greatly reduce your anxiety and pressure of writing at the later stage.

Figure 12.2: Writing in the process of researching

The order of writing different parts

When you write a thesis, where to start? This is the first question student researchers often ask me. Based on the experience of writing my own thesis, I usually ask the students under my supervision to follow the sequence presented in Figure 12.3. I must emphasize that the presented sequence is only one of the possible options, which can definitely be changed.

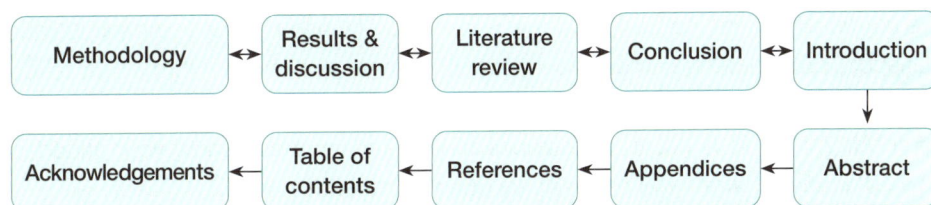

Figure 12.3: The suggested order of writing different parts of a thesis

According to Figure 12.3, your writing may start with "Methodology" which is comparatively the easiest part to write in the sense that you just record what has been done. You won't feel that you have nothing to write. Try to do it as much as you think useful when your memory is fresh.

The second part could be "Results and discussion," which is the most important for your thesis but is not the most difficult to write. You may list the answers to the research questions, however, a high-quality discussion is very challenging to write. You may write down whatever occurs in your mind at the beginning that might look superficial. However, you may gradually understand the results better as time goes on. Accordingly, you can elaborate on your discussion section bit by bit.

Surely, "Literature review" is the toughest part for any researcher to write. That is why you are advised not to start with writing this section. Once you finish the writing of literature review, very often you will go back to the discussion part and make more comments on and alternative explanations of your results in relation to the previous literature. Up to this stage, the discussion and the literature review will be more integrated and coherent.

Now it's time for you to write the section of "Conclusion." In fact, the "Conclusion" consists of several parts such as major findings, theoretical and practical values, innovative features, implications of your research and recommendations for future research. You may first just write down the major findings which are simply a summary of the results. The remaining parts can be written once you finish the section of "Introduction" since the remaining parts of "Conclusion" should be aligned with "Introduction."

Once you finish the writing of "Conclusion" and "Introduction," you move on to write the abstract of your thesis which is the most demanding. Normally, there is a word limit. You have to condense the most essential into several paragraphs. At the very beginning, you might feel it is difficult to write more but now you will feel that to write less is even more difficult. You might ask yourself: Why am I advised to write an abstract now? The reason is that now you are very familiar with your whole thesis. As a result, it is a bit easy for you to decide what is the most important that should be included in "Abstract."

"Appendices," "References," "Table of contents," and "Acknowledgements" are not as difficult as the body of a thesis in terms of writing. What you need is your patience, prudence, and meticulousness. It is time-consuming. Normally, it takes much more time than you planned. Therefore, you have to prepare sufficient time for it. Although this is not the substance of your thesis, it can show your attitudes toward academic work and professional quality of a researcher.

Finally, I would like to emphasize again the sequence presented is a suggestion. Furthermore, the writing process is recursive and never works linearly. Finally, revisions are always required.

Follow your writing schedule

You must make a writing schedule in order to finish your writing within the time frame you have planned. The schedule should include two major elements: the timeline and the target to achieve. Making a schedule appears to be easy but sticking to it is difficult. My suggestion is to submit your schedule to your supervisor and at the same time you put a copy of it on the wall which could be known by other people and could be seen by yourself every day. In this case, your writing will be monitored by your supervisor and your friends as well. I call it self-imposed pressure. In addition, I will give you three more practical suggestions:

Be realistic and flexible with your scheduled writing task. You can set up a section or the number of words as a goal rather than a chapter. In my thesis writing, I used the number of words as my daily target which could be obtained relatively easily. Of course, it does not mean whatever that is written down at this stage could be included in your thesis. However, this can help you form a good habit of writing.

Keep on writing to reach the target. Once you get stuck in one section, don't stop. You had better put it aside and move on to another section you can write.

Stick to the schedule and submit whatever you have written down to your supervisor weekly. Don't violate the rule even if your written work is not satisfactory at all. So long as you keep doing it, it will become a habit. Your supervisor does not need to read everything you have submitted carefully at the beginning. This simply helps you follow your writing plan and overcome your procrastination.

▶☰ SUMMARY

A thesis is an argument in which different parts are logically related and all center around research questions. It consists of three major components: the beginning, body, and ending. The beginning part includes "Title page," "Signature page," "Abstract in English," "Abstract in Chinese," "Acknowledgements," "Table of contents," "List of tables," and "List of figures." The body part contains "Introduction," "Literature review," "Methodology," "Results and discussion," and "Conclusion." The ending part has "References" and "Appendices." Your writing may go along with your researching. You may start with writing "Methodology" followed by "Results and discussion." "Literature review" is the most difficult to write which would take much more efforts than you expected. "Results and discussion" very often refers to the theory and echoes the empirical findings reviewed in your literature review. Therefore, your writing often goes back and forth between these two parts. The similar situation also happens in writing "Conclusion" and "Introduction" in the sense that these two parts are closely related to each other. Finally, you deal with the beginning and the ending parts of your thesis, which requires your patience, prudence, and meticulousness. You must prepare sufficient time for writing these two parts.

Doing research and writing the thesis are two separate tasks, although these two tasks are related to each other. Researching is the basis of writing. They are equally important and challenging. I suggest that you start your writing in the process of researching and make a schedule for writing. To finish your thesis writing within a time frame, you are advised to follow your schedule strictly. Here are some practical suggestions: Be flexible with your target; keep on writing to reach your target; stick to your schedule no matter what difficulty you may encounter.

AFTER-READING ACTIVITIES

Reviewing

1 What are the major components of a thesis/dissertation?

2 What is the relation between researching and writing?

3 How do you manage your researching and writing in order to finish your writing within a time frame?

4 How can you overcome procrastination in your writing?

Exploring

Go to a library and get a copy of a master's or doctoral thesis. Read the beginning part and the ending part of the thesis and answer the following questions.

1 What is the overall structure of the thesis?

2 Are there any problems in writing the abstracts in English and Chinese?

3 Do you think "Acknowledgements" is appropriately written? Can you make any further improvement on it?

4 How is "Table of contents" presented? Do you have any suggestion for a better arrangement?

5 How about "List of tables" and "List of figures"? Are there any mistakes in them?

6 Make some critical comments on "References" and "Appendices" presented at the end of the thesis.

Chapter 13

Writing up a thesis/dissertation

This chapter focuses on writing the body of a thesis. Specifically, it describes how to write an introduction, how to synthesize a literature review, how to describe methodology and present the results and discussion, and how to conclude the thesis. For each part, I will introduce to you the major components, writing procedures, and common problems or difficulties you may encounter in your writing.

▶☰ WRITING AN INTRODUCTION

Specifically, the chapter of "Introduction" usually includes three components: (1) a general description of the study; (2) the need for the study; and (3) the overall structure of a thesis.

A general description of the study

The simplest way to write the first component is: The study was undertaken to find out...The research questions to be addressed in the study are the following...Since this is an overview of the research problem, you only need to list general research questions. Details of research questions will be presented at the end of the "Literature review" chapter or at the beginning of the "Methodology" chapter.

The need for the study

For the need for your study, you are required to explain why the study is worth undertaking. Usually, the reasons can be explained in terms of practical as well as theoretical importance. A study is said to have theoretical value when it can confirm or disconfirm a theory, modify existing theories, clarify a controversial issue, develop a new model that is badly needed, or enrich our understanding of a phenomenon. A doctoral dissertation is expected to have theoretical significance in addition to practical value. Therefore, a study that can merely provide a practical solution to a problem is not suitable for a doctoral dissertation (Rudestam & Newton, 1992). The practical values in the field of applied linguistics may be shown in the improving of L2 teaching and learning, in the compiling of bilingual dictionaries, or in translation, etc. To justify the need for the study, you may refer to one or more previous studies that motivated you to choose this research topic. However, too many references are not necessary since this is not the place to do a literature review.

> **Focus highlight**
>
> - Do you know the difference between the need **for** the study and the need **of** the study? The need for the study means **why** this study is needed while the need of the study means **what** this study needs. Do not misuse them.

The overall structure of a thesis

When you describe the overall structure of a thesis, the chapter headings should be covered. If "Part" is the first-order heading and "Chapter," the second-order, the description should cover both parts and chapters. In some cases, the "Introduction" chapter also includes the definitions of key terms, delimitations, and assumptions of the study (Newman, Benz, Weis & McNeil, 1997; Rudestam & Newton, 1992). In my opinion, the conceptual definitions of key variables are better included in the "Literature review" chapter since they must be developed based on others' definitions; the operational definitions are better placed in the "Methodology" chapter where the instrument is introduced.

Although the "Introduction" is the first chapter in the manuscript, it is written when the other chapters have been finished. The reason is obvious. The research questions which were developed in your proposal may have been modified in one way or another almost until you finish the chapter of "Results and discussion."

WRITING A LITERATURE REVIEW

A literature review demonstrates the writer's conceptual understanding of the research topic and his/her ability to argue for the need for the study. This is the best place to see whether the researcher has acquired the macro-level organizing ability to put the relevant materials together to develop an argument. This is the most difficult part to write and takes more pains to finish than it is usually expected. However, if you survive such a painful process and eventually produce a good literature review, you will gain a profound insight into the essence of research, which you will otherwise not be able to obtain. Unfortunately, many students and even a few supervisors do not pay enough attention to the writing of this part. Students tend to think that this chapter is a sort of formality, or serves to make a thesis long enough to have sufficient pages as required. They often write it at the last minute by patching together all kinds of definitions and studies at their disposal without any clear and logical links. Frankly speaking, quite a few literature reviews in masters' theses, although they have been passed, are of poor quality. To learn how to write a literature review is an essential part of graduate study. It demands time and effort from both students and teachers.

Major components

No research is carried out in a vacuum. It must be linked with the past and the future. A literature review provides such contextual information. It not only describes what has been done in the field and what problems remain to be solved, but also explains to what extent your study is different from the previous ones, what kind of contribution can be made to the existing knowledge, how the design of your study is growing out of the existing ones, and what kind of theory your design is based on if there is any. By the time readers finish reading the last section, they will be naturally led to conclude that your proposed study is worth exploring and that its design is the best available on the topic.

Specifically speaking, a literature review should contain the following components:

1. Conceptual definitions of key terms;
2. An examination of the research topic in light of the theoretical perspective;
3. A description of related empirical studies with evaluating comments;
4. A critical review of research designs including instruments related to your study;
5. A conceptual framework if there is any.

The above components commonly appear in a literature review. However, they are not necessarily in the order they are presented here. In which way your literature review is written and whether you need to include more components in your review depend on your research purpose, your personal preference, and your supervisor's requirements.

Define key terms conceptually

As mentioned in Chapter 2, all the variables involved in your study have to be defined conceptually and operationally. The "Literature review" chapter is a place to state the conceptual definitions of the key terms in your study. The simplest way to fulfill the task is to list your conceptual definitions together with references. However, this is not the best. To make your definition more convincing, it is better to review critically the various definitions that have surfaced in the literature while indicating how your definition has been developed or why you preferred this definition to others.

One common problem in writing this section is that a dozen definitions are listed on one or two pages without any comments in between, and at the end of the list, the researcher's own conceptual definition is given. Whenever I come across such a case, I ask my students, "How are these definitions related to your own definition?" Another problem is that some terms defined cannot be regarded as key terms. For example, to study the relationship between the use of communication strategies and L2 speaking ability, students tend to start with defining the terms "communication" and "communicative competence" and then move on to the terms "communication strategies." You might ask: What should be defined? The simple solution is that all the variables that are to be measured in your study have to be defined conceptually.

Review from the theoretical perspective

Research topics are very often derived from theories or linked with theoretical issues. For example, the study on the acquisition of morphemes was inspired by Krashen's Natural Order Hypothesis. My own study on the use of L2 learning strategies was motivated by a new perception of the role of learners. It is common that a review starts with explicating a theory or a controversial issue that is relevant to the proposed study.

Describe and evaluate relevant empirical studies

The description and evaluation of relevant empirical studies are indispensable in a literature review. However, this kind of description does not necessarily cover every detail of a study. Furthermore, the evaluation does not need to be comprehensive since it is made not for the purpose of judging the quality of the study concerned but for justifying the need for your study. The most crucial thing here is that you need to classify the studies according to your needs. For example, some studies may be included for the purpose of illustrating the extensiveness of the existing research on this topic; some for the purpose of showing conflicting findings; some for the purpose of displaying methodological problems that will be avoided in your study; some for the purpose of demonstrating the small number of subjects studied, etc. Once you are clear about your purposes, you can decide on the emphasis and scope of your description and evaluation.

Examine research designs

This component is needed when one of the differences between your study and previous ones lies in the research design. The difference may be shown in the number or type of subjects, the instruments, and/or the procedures for data collection and data analysis. For example, if previous studies on a topic only employ a quantitative method, which is confined to correlation analysis or multiple regression analysis, but your study combines both quantitative and qualitative designs and your quantitative analysis goes beyond multiple regression analysis, you need to review the designs used in the studies concerned while pointing out their weaknesses.

If the difference is displayed in instruments, your review must include the "Instrument" section where a brief description of the existing instruments is given together with critical comments. At the end of the section, you need to say that the new instrument that is going to be used in your study will avoid the weaknesses mentioned before.

Describe the conceptual framework in your study

This component is optional for a master's thesis but compulsory for a doctoral thesis. The conceptual framework is actually a list of assumptions that have been established based on your literature review. This is also the basis on which your hypotheses for testing are developed. For example, in Ma's study on the relations between L2 learners' linguistic variables and L2 writing ability, he presented the conceptual framework[1] as follows (Ma, 1998, p. 45):

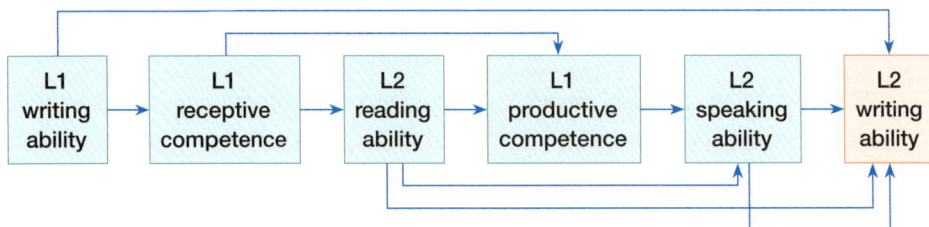

Figure 13.1: The conceptual model of L2 learners' linguistic variables affecting L2 writing ability

Ma explained in his thesis that "the model specifies the focus of the study and the causal relations between L1 writing ability and L2 writing ability, between L1 writing ability and variables of L2 proficiency, and between variables of L2 proficiency and L2 writing ability" (p. 45).

When your study is exploratory in nature, it may not be possible to present a conceptual framework in the chapter of "Literature review." Nevertheless, it may develop out of the empirical findings yielded by your own study, which is most likely to be presented in the chapter of "Results and discussion."

Actual writing

In this part, I will discuss with you how to write a literature review by describing the procedures, examining common difficulties, and analyzing frequently occurring problems at this stage.

Procedures

A literature review usually contains an introduction and several subsections. An introduction is an advance organizer in which the reader is informed of the scope of

---

[1] Due to the limited space, a few changes are made in the framework, including the names of categories, which are made up of fewer letters but retain the same meaning.

the review and its sequential arrangement. The subsections under specific headings should be clearly written and logically connected.

Construct an outline

Before you write a literature review, you should construct an outline in which the subheadings are listed. The sequence of headings can show how the argument is developed. Two-level or three-level headings, in my opinion, are sufficient for you to conceptualize the argument. The outline at this stage does not require the details since its major function is to help you think of literature review at the macro level. In other words, it specifies the scope of your literature review.

It is very common that the outline needs to be revised several times. If you rush to write many things, your writing may prove to be irrelevant and have to be deleted later. One thing you have to remember is that even if the revised outline appears to be satisfactory and has been approved by your supervisor, it will inevitably undergo changes along with the progress of your research and writing. You should be mentally prepared for such changes.

Draft the literature review

Having produced a complete and well-organized outline, you can move on to the next stage: writing the review section by section. You do not necessarily follow the order of sections strictly. There will be no problem at all if you choose to write first the section that you are most familiar with. Such a strategy can improve your writing efficiency since the section that is difficult today may become easy tomorrow.

Revise the literature review

The draft of a literature review inevitably contains a lot of holes that need further work. According to my own experiences, the draft of a review, no matter how good it may look, needs revisions at least three times. For the first time, you modify the macro-structure. The questions you have to ask yourself from time to time are "Is this part relevant to my study?" and "How is this section related to the other sections of the literature review?" What you are concerned with is the organization of the whole review rather than small details such as grammar mistakes, spelling errors, or the improper structure of a sentence since these mistakes might not need correction at all if the whole section needs to be deleted later. The emphasis of the second revision is on the inter-paragraph level, i.e. the relations between paragraphs. The emphasis of the third revision is on the inter- and intra-sentential levels, i.e. the logical link between sentences and problems within a sentence. In other words, your attention should be paid to the flow from one sentence to another and linguistic errors in each sentence. Specifying a different focus for each revision can improve the efficiency of revision. Suppose we, as supervisors, insist that students should correct all the mistakes from the macro- to the micro-level. To meet this requirement, we can imagine how much time and effort has to be taken by students. Actually, due to the limited attention of students, they are most likely to correct some mistakes at the lower level at the expense of the problems at the higher level. In many cases, the effort may be wasted since the sentence, even the paragraph where mistakes occur may be deleted when the whole discourse is considered. Therefore, I strongly recommend that each revision should have a focus. This principle can be applied to the revision of the other parts of the thesis as well.

Common difficulties

The difficulties graduate students often encounter at this stage are various. Some are related to the content and others to the organization. In this part, I will discuss some common difficulties along with suggested solutions.

Difficulties in content

One difficulty in content is that students may feel overwhelmed by the materials they read, since they have too much to review. They tend to think that they should incorporate everything they read into the literature review. Actually, literature review is not a place to display your knowledge. What is required here is to build up an argument in which all the information should be pertinent to your own study. To avoid including irrelevant materials and giving too much space to less important topics, you may list subheadings from the most relevant to the least relevant while specifying their approximate length. For example, Anne intended to study the relationship between motivation and L2 achievement of non-English majors in China. This is an old topic that has been researched for several decades. Faced with a mountain of literature that deals with this topic, she did not know what to do. After some thinking and discussion with her supervisor, she realized that she did not need to detail the empirical studies concerning this issue in the field of education, nor the studies on the motivation of children and middle school students in L1 learning. The emphasis of her review should be on the L2 motivation in and outside the Chinese context with a focus on adults while the studies on L2 motivation of children and adolescents should be briefly summarized.

In contrast to the previous case, another difficulty concerning content is that student researchers may feel that they have no empirical studies to review although they have read a lot. The argument they often advance is that there exists almost no empirical studies similar to their studies in the literature. However, this is not a good reason at all to justify the exclusion of reviewing empirical studies. For example, there might not exist an empirical study on the use of L1 in the process of L2 writing. However, there are quite a few studies on the use of L1 in L2 reading, on the use of L1 in L2 speaking, or on the use of L1 in an L2 writing product. If this is the case, instead of trying to review studies on the use of L1 in the process of L2 writing, you may examine the literature from a wider perspective and search for the most pertinent studies to evaluate. Remember you should use the zoom very flexibly depending on the richness of your literature. When the materials are abundant, you need to zoom in and have a look at the materials most closely related to the topic. You should zoom out if the materials closely related to the topic are scarce.

Difficulties in organizing

One organization difficulty is often shown in the overall structure where the subheadings do not form a natural flow of thought. In other words, the logical link among the subheadings seems to be absent. The reader would feel that the thoughts are fragmentary and do not form a coherent picture. I would suggest that you use the following general principles to organize the subheadings:

1. From the general to the specific
2. From the abstract to the concrete
3. From the theoretical to the empirical
4. From the "long shots" to the "close-ups"
5. From others' studies to yours

Metaphorically, Cone and Foster (1993) suggest the "funnel" approach, which states that the review "begins with the general context and becomes more and more specific, ultimately focusing on specific criticisms of existing studies and leading to the specific rationale for the study being proposed" (p. 105).

Another difficulty in organizing the review arises when a series of empirical studies need to be described and commented on. Students often do not know how to present them. The following are some of the most common ways (Cone & Foster, 1993).

Organizing them according to variables

Wen (1993) examines the effects of modifiable learner variables on L2 achievement. The modifiable learner variables include motivation, management strategies, and L2 learning strategies. Thus, the previous empirical studies on motivation, management strategies, and L2 learning strategies can be reviewed one by one.

Organizing them according to research designs

Usually within the quantitative camp, the review of this kind moves from weaker ones to stronger ones. For example, survey studies are presented before experimental ones, correlation analysis before multivariate analysis, cross-sectional ones before longitudinal ones. In regard to quantitative and qualitative studies, the quantitative ones are usually described before the qualitative ones. With this method, you can start with a summary in which a large number of less important studies are reviewed by groups, and then detail a few more important studies that are most pertinent to your study.

Organizing them according to types of subjects

The subjects may be first classified in terms of L2 learners and foreign language learners. Within each group, further classifications can be made, for instance, in terms of learning conditions (learners in formal learning environments and those in informal environments), or in terms of age (children, adolescents, and adults), or in terms of education level (pre-school children, primary school pupils, secondary school students, university students, etc.).

Organizing them according to designs in data collection

Data may be collected through interviews, observations, think-aloud, diaries and questionnaires. Suppose you plan to collect data by observation, which has not been used in previous studies. The reason you choose observation as a data collection technique is that interviews, diaries, and questionnaires can only obtain self-reported data, which might be distorted in one way or another. In this case, to organize by data collection designs can well serve the purpose.

Organizing them according to findings

When you compare the studies concerned, similarities and differences in the findings can be identified. If the conflicts in findings are one of the reasons for your study, you may illustrate how these findings clash. In this case, the differences in findings are emphasized and conflicts in findings are discussed and possible reasons might be given. The reasons given can naturally lead to your own study, which is designed in the way the conflicts can be resolved.

Organizing them according to theoretical assumptions

For studies on L2 teaching and L2 learning, L2 proficiency is perceived differently by researchers. The concept of L2 proficiency is therefore defined variously in the empirical studies concerned. If one of the reasons for conducting your own study is to challenge the widely accepted view of L2 proficiency, presenting the existing empirical studies in terms of their underlying assumptions will be effective.

The above are six common ways of organizing empirical studies. It must be emphasized that choosing a particular way of organizing empirical studies is not an accidental decision. It highlights the importance of a particular aspect of the literature that usually coincides with what you wish to improve through your study.

Frequently occurring problems

The problems I have often observed in graduate students' literature reviews can be summarized as: lacking direct relevance, having no proper headings and clear signposts, and lacking sufficient knowledge of doing citations. In the following part, I will discuss these problems one by one while giving some suggestions.

Lacking direct relevance

A review that contains materials without direct relevance is more often than not excessively long. Students tend to equate the length of a review with its quality. When the supervisor asks them to delete some sections, they often feel reluctant to do so. I would say, relevance is the first and paramount criterion for judging the quality of a review. If a review contains a lot of materials without relevance, it has to be rewritten. There is no other alternative.

"Relevance" cannot be described in terms of isolated rules since it is meaningful only in the context. Therefore, it is not possible to follow a set of rules to meet the requirement. What you are advised to do is to ask yourself, "How is this relevant to my study?" whenever you write something down. If you can justify the need for writing this part, most probably, there would be no problem of being irrelevant.

Having no proper headings and clear signposts

Graduate students are often not good at using headings to give readers signposts. They may write one section in a review running for several pages without any headings. When reading such a review, readers can easily get lost or become absent-minded since human beings have a limited attention span and limited memory capacity. Writers should be friendly toward readers by striving to help them overcome their limitations. With proper headings, readers can anticipate what they are going to read and can easily capture the flow of the argument.

Of course, too many headings are not good either since they may distract readers' attention and interrupt the smooth development of ideas. What is the proper number of headings? It is very hard to give a clear-cut answer. What you can do is to test your own sustaining ability of reading and make a sensible decision.

For some students, the trouble is not in the number of headings but in their wording. For example, there are three subheadings in one section, and the first heading begins with a verb, the second one with a present participle, and the third one with an adjective. Obviously, the three headings at the same level are not in the same pattern in terms of wording. Very often in the process of writing, it is difficult for you to detect such problems since they are in different places. You may use the computer program to produce subheadings at different levels once you finish the writing of one chapter. When the subheadings are put together, it is easy for you to overcome this problem if it exists.

Lacking sufficient knowledge of doing citations

Many students, even some researchers, do not know how to do proper citations. Lacking such knowledge, you may take the risk of committing plagiarism.

My advice is to read carefully the content related to avoiding plagiarism in Chapter 14 to understand what are the different types of plagiarism concerning citations. Then you can read the sections of "Quotations" and "Citations" in Chapter 14 to understand the rules which should be observed at all costs.

⊟ DESCRIBING METHODOLOGY

The "Methodology" chapter presents a detailed description of the way your proposed study is conducted. The description should be explicit, transparent and sufficiently detailed. After reading this chapter, readers can easily visualize your research process and replicate your study if they wish to. Compared with a literature review, this chapter is fairly easy to write since everything in the chapter is what you have experienced. However, it is difficult to meet the requirements of explicitness, transparency, and sufficiency in detail. In this section, I will describe the major components of the "Methodology" chapter and discuss how to meet the requirements in writing each component.

Major components

The major components in the chapter of "Methodology" are displayed in Figure 13.2. As was discussed before, a study may employ the design of a survey study, an experimental study, a case study, or a combination of them. Regardless of the research design, the headings or components are the same for the description of each design but with different content. When a study employs two different types of design, a common practice is to describe the two designs separately. In other words, you may have two sections or two chapters: for example, one section/chapter on a survey study and the other on a case study.

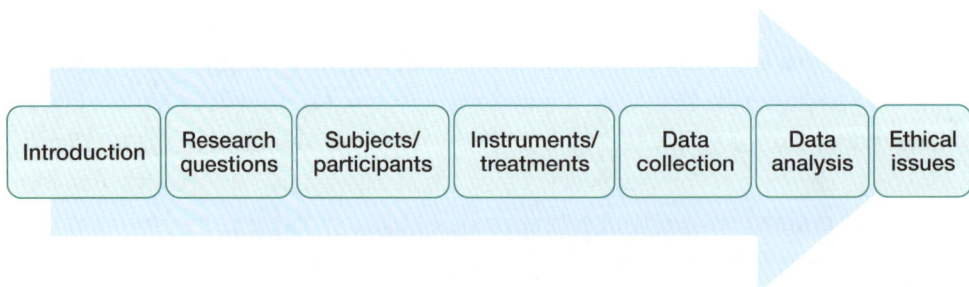

| Introduction | Research questions | Subjects/ participants | Instruments/ treatments | Data collection | Data analysis | Ethical issues |

Figure 13.2: Major components in the "Methodology" chapter

The following parts will discuss the writing of each component while taking into account the differences in describing different types of design.

Introduction

The chapter begins with an introductory paragraph in which details of the research design are followed by an overall description of the organization of this section/chapter. For the research design, you only need to write one or two short sentences. Suppose in your study, you asked 300 English majors from five universities to answer a questionnaire to find out how their learning strategies are related to their English test scores on TEM4. It would be enough if you could write something like the following: This study employs a survey design to examine the relationship between the use of language learning strategies and L2 achievement.

The general organization is an advance organizer that prepares readers for what is to follow. You may describe the organization in terms of first-level headings without the need to provide detailed content related to each subheading.

Research questions

In this section, all the general questions are presented together with specific questions. If the researcher has formed hypotheses instead of questions, then he/she should list all the hypotheses. This section serves two purposes. The first is to give the reader clear information about what questions the study is intended to address. The second is to provide a framework for the "Results and discussion" chapter. In other words, all the questions appearing in this section need to be answered in the "Results and discussion" chapter. However, graduate students often forget to refer to what has been written in this section when they write the "Results and discussion" chapter. As a result, the chapter does not cover all the questions or the order of questions presented is not the same as that in this section.

Unlike the other sections in the "Methodology" chapter, all the questions/hypotheses are stated in the present tense rather than in the past tense. The wording in a question should be clear and precise, and each question should address one issue.

The questions/hypotheses in this section are often not the same as those developed at the beginning of the research. The reasons are various. First of all, data may be analyzed and reanalyzed many times before the researcher is satisfied. For example, your hypothesis may be that there is no relationship between risk-taking and L2 achievement. The result could not reject the null hypothesis. Then you choose age as a moderator variable to make a further analysis. Accordingly, you add one more question in this section: Is the relationship between risk-taking and L2 achievement affected by age? In another case, you may delete one or two research questions developed earlier simply because you realize there will be too much to report if all the questions are included.

Subjects/participants

Subjects only refer to people who are studied and measured by your instruments and whose responses are used in answering the research questions, such as students who respond to the questionnaire or who are interviewed or observed. Participants are often used in an experimental study, such as students in an experimental group and in a control group. The "Subjects" section describes how many subjects have participated, who the subjects are, and how they are selected. It is simple and easy to record the number of subjects who participate in the study. However, when the total number of subjects is changed in the process, the issue becomes slightly complicated. For example, in a survey study where the relationship between the use of language learning strategies and L2 achievement is examined, some subjects responded to the questionnaire on their use of language learning strategies but did not turn up at the English proficiency test; and a few subjects forgot to write down their identity number so that it was not possible to match their questionnaire responses with their test scores. In a longitudinal study, the subjects who appeared the first time may be absent the second time due to various reasons. In this case, you have to report the change in the number of subjects and explain the reason for such a change.

Personal information about subjects includes gender, age, and education level. Sometimes, family background, the type of middle school, and the type of university where the subjects study are also needed if these variables can produce effects on a dependent variable. For simplicity of presentation, the information concerned can be displayed in a table while a brief verbal account is given. The procedures for selecting the subjects must be detailed so that other people can easily replicate them. If the subjects form a random sample, you have to specify what kind of sampling technique is used: simple random sampling, systematic random sampling, or stratified random sampling. When your study uses a convenience sample, you need to explain how this convenience sample has been selected. For example, this convenience sample may be an intact class or an intact school which you have selected simply because the teacher who teaches this class is or was your classmate, or because you yourself teach this class. Sometimes, the subjects are chosen on a voluntary basis. In this case, you describe them as volunteers. If these volunteers are given a small gift for their participation, this also needs to be mentioned.

If in the data analysis, the subjects are further classified into groups according to their test scores or their responses to certain variables, then the information about the newly classified groups needs to be provided and the criterion for such classification needs to be explained.

In this section, one mistake graduate students often make is that they include those who are not subjects. For example, in the survey study mentioned above, some may regard the raters who score the test papers as subjects and some may take the test designers as subjects. To make it simple, you may make a decision simply by asking a question: Do their responses provide answers to the research questions? If the answer is "yes," they are then subjects. Otherwise, they are not. Another problem I have observed is that the section is not detailed enough. Some graduate students fail to describe how they obtained a convenience sample; some do not explain why the number of subjects has changed; and some do not state how the volunteers were recruited.

In qualitative studies, people involved are described as participants instead of subjects. Furthermore, participants also refer to researchers who are responsible for interviewing, observation, etc. The reason for using "participants" is to emphasize the agency of people whose initiative also plays a role in the study.

Instruments/treatments

The "Instruments" section describes research tools used to measure dependent and independent variables in your study such as a language test to measure subjects' L2 proficiency, a questionnaire to investigate subjects' attitudes toward L2 learning, and an interview schedule to find out how they go about vocabulary learning. The description covers the content, the categories, the validity and reliability if the instrument has been used before. For a self-designed instrument, the development of the instrument and the results of a pilot study should be added. The operational definitions of independent and dependent variables should be listed here. The examples of questionnaire items or interview questions should be given in the chapter on methodology but the whole questionnaire or interview schedule is usually presented as an appendix.

In an experimental study, the treatment should be described in detail. For example, how long it takes to carry out the treatment, how the treatment is carried out, what materials are used in the treatment, who is responsible for the treatment, etc. Furthermore, the differences between the experimental group and the control group must be explained in a very clear manner. If possible, the procedures for the treatment can be presented in a diagram. The differences between experimental and control groups are presented in a table which is easy for readers to make a comparison.

Data collection

In the "Data collection" section, information about gathering data is explained in detail. The section has to address these questions: When are the data collected? Who are responsible for data collection? How are the data collected? And where?

The information concerning "when" should go beyond the specific date of collecting data. The question as to whether the data collection is taken in a regular lesson or at recess or at other times should also be answered. The person who is responsible for data collection may be the researcher himself/herself or a helper, or both. If helpers are involved, you have to describe to what extent the helpers can do a quality job. Suppose you have given them training before data collection, how the training is carried out needs to be explained. The way the data are collected needs a detailed account. For example, the information about the mode of administration (by person or by mail) and the form of the interview (individual or group; recorded or unrecorded) should be available. In regard to the environment, the information about its quietness and comfort should be provided.

If the subjects are measured based on several independent and dependent variables, the description of each measurement should be given. For a longitudinal study, the section needs to specify whether the conditions for measurement at different points of time are the same or not.

In some cases, the training of subjects or interviewers/observers is needed. For example, to collect think-aloud data, a carefully constructed training for the subjects must be conducted since think-aloud is not a normal behavior in daily life. When more than one interviewer is required for the study, the training of the interviewers is essential for standardizing input to the interviewee. The procedures for and the result of training have to be recorded in the "Data collection" section.

Data analysis

The "Data analysis" section is concerned with the procedures for analyzing data and their reliability. The section of a quantitative analysis may begin with a general description of what kind of statistical package is used and what statistical analyses have been operated in your study. The introductory paragraph is then followed by a description of procedures for data analysis: What was done sequentially in the process? Let's take as an example the analysis of questionnaire data. The description should address these questions: How are missing values dealt with? Which items' values have been reversed? What are the reliability indexes of intended categories and what categories have been deleted? The resulting categories that enter the final analysis are better listed in a table together with the number of items and the reliability index.

For qualitative data analysis, the procedures should be specified and categories generated from the data need to be explained with concrete examples. Furthermore, details of steps taken to increase the reliability of the analysis of qualitative data need to be reported. Suppose the score on a composition is a dependent variable, you have to tell readers who the scorers are and what the correlation coefficient between two raters' scores is.

Ethical issues

What should be written about ethical issues? According to Bryman (2016, p. 125), the major thing in research on human beings in social sciences is how to deal with the people involved in research. Specifically, he raised the following four questions:

1. Is there any harm to participants?
2. Is there any informed consent?
3. Is there any invasion of privacy?
4. Is there any deception involved?

You need to consider these questions before and during research. Once you reach the stage of writing, you are required to report what you have done in order to follow the ethical codes. To be concrete, you are required to report how you have taken measures to avoid harm to your participants, to protect their privacy, and to prevent deception.

For a quantitative study, participants are usually treated as a group so that individual information is normally not revealed to the public. What needs to be written is how you explained to the participants the purpose of your research and whether they agreed to participate in your study with a written consent. The tricky thing is how to tell participants the research purpose. Sometimes, if the genuine purpose is revealed, the results can be distorted in the way there might be Hawthorne effect. In this sense, the research purpose is better not explicitly described. However, how it is said referring to the research purpose in this case should be stated along with the reason.

In addition to the ethical requirements in quantitative studies mentioned above, ethical issues in qualitative studies become more prominent since qualitative data are usually collected and analyzed individually. Therefore, it is required to write more about the ethical issues in qualitative studies than in quantitative studies. The following questions are normally required to be addressed:

1. What measures were taken in interviews or observations without disturbing the participant's personal emotions and daily life routine?
2. How did you hide the participant's identity in reporting the results?
3. How did you make sure the reported findings related to one individual were not against his or her personal will?

To sum up, when writing in relation to ethical issues, you have to explain how you keep the participants' information confidential and how you respect the privacy of your participants.

⋮≡ REPORTING RESULTS AND DISCUSSION

The common practice is to present results together with the discussion. That is to say, in a thesis, results and discussion are integrated into a single chapter. There are several advantages of having a combined chapter. The obvious one is that it can avoid restating the results when you discuss them. Another advantage is that it is much easier for readers to follow the development of the thesis.

The alternative practice is to have results and discussion presented separately, that is, the first half of the chapter is for results and the second half for discussion. People who are in favor of this alternative practice think that two separate sections are neat and easy to manage. Personally, I feel it's more natural that the reporting of the results is immediately followed by discussion.

In this section, I will discuss how results are presented and how the discussion is developed.

Presenting results

This part will begin with the question of what a result is, then move on to the question of how results are organized. Finally, how quantitative and qualitative results are presented will be described.

What can be regarded as results?

Results reported in this chapter are the answers to the research questions and the findings yielded from your study. However, not all the findings from the study are results that need to be reported since some findings may not directly address the research questions. Novice researchers often equate findings with results. Therefore, their reports are dictated by findings rather than by research questions. To avoid this problem, the researcher should stick to the research questions all the time and not be tempted to report the findings that appear to be interesting. In other words, the researcher needs to focus only on the findings that can answer the research questions.

How are results organized?

The best way to organize results is by research questions. To begin with, you had better restate the research questions in the introductory paragraph of the "Results and discussion" chapter. Readers can neither remember all the questions by reading the thesis once nor go back to the "Methodology" chapter from time to time to get the precise information about the questions. The subheadings in this chapter had better be presented as shortened references to the questions being answered. In other words, the subheadings are used to describe the content of the questions. As a result, by reading a subheading, readers can link specific results easily with the research questions concerned.

One common problem in organizing results is that student researchers like to do it according to the type of statistical analysis such as *t*-test, One-way ANOVA, multiple regression, etc. For example, they use subheadings such as "The results of *t*-tests" or "The results of One-way ANOVA." These subheadings appear to be neat and clear. However, statistical analyses are the tools for answering questions. The names of statistical analyses do not show how the results are tied to the research questions. The other problem is that the order of the results is not the same as the order of the research questions/hypotheses stated in the "Methodology" chapter.

Many studies have both quantitative and qualitative results. Then how are these two types of results presented? First of all, you should decide how these two types of results are linked to the research questions. If the qualitative results are further illustrations of the quantitative results and both are related to the same research question, it is better that the qualitative results are integrated into the quantitative part and the quantitative findings are reported before the qualitative ones. When these two types of results address separate research questions, reporting them together will be inappropriate.

How are quantitative results reported?

Usually quantitative results are reported by tables/graphs coupled with verbal accounts. These two different forms provide readers with parallel information, numeric and narrative, which are complementary to each other.

Generally speaking, reporting quantitative results in a narrative form contains three basic statements (Rudestam & Newton, 1992). The first one is a signal statement indicating to the reader which table contains the results concerned. The second one is a technical description statement describing the findings in a technical way. The third one is a non-technical description statement. Accordingly, it presents the results by using non-technical terms. The following are typical examples of the three basic statements in a hypothetical study.

A signal statement

A signal statement refers to a sentence which describes the general information presented in a table, giving readers an overall picture. Let's take Table 13.1 as an example.

A signal statement

Table 13.1 displays the means and standard deviations of the use of different strategies by three groups of students.

A technical description statement

A technical description statement is expected to report factual findings. The terms used in the statement are about the results yielded by statistical analysis. I will take Table 13.1 as an example again.

Group name	Management Strategy		Mother-tongue Strategy	
	Mean	SD	Mean	SD
High achievers	4.25	.464	2.32	.521
Average achievers	3.52	.521	3.05	.563
Low achievers	3.05	.400	3.68	.501

Table 13.1: The use of Management Strategy and Mother-tongue Strategy by three different groups

A technical description statement

As shown in Table 13.1, the mean of the responses to Management Strategy by high achievers is the highest (4.25 on a five-point scale) among the three groups and the mean of the responses to Mother-tongue Strategy is the lowest (2.32 on a five-point scale), while the means of the responses to these two strategies by low achievers are just the opposite to those of high achievers, i.e. the mean of their responses to Management Strategy is the lowest among the three groups (3.05) and to Mother-tongue Strategy is the highest (3.68). Average achievers are somewhat in between. Specifically, their mean of Management Strategy is lower than that of high achievers but higher than that of low achievers while their mean of Mother-tongue Strategy is higher than that of high achievers but lower than that of low achievers.

A non-technical description statement

A non-technical description statement refers to the explanations of the statistical findings which can be understood easily by those who do not have sufficient statistical knowledge. Let's take Table 13.1 as an example again.

> ## A non-technical description statement
>
> The findings presented in Table 13.1 mean that among the three groups, high achievers used Management Strategy most frequently; low achievers used it least frequently; average achievers in between. In contrast, low achievers used Mother-tongue Strategy most frequently; high achievers used it least frequently; average achievers in between.

To sum up, reporting quantitative results normally uses tables along with verbal accounts. The verbal account consists of three statements: a signal statement, a technical description statement, and a non-technical description statement.

How can you make a tabular or graphic report effective and efficient? Two things need to be considered. First of all, if a table can serve the purpose, don't use a graph. One reason is that a graph occupies a lot of space in a thesis and the other is that the information in a table is more accurate. Secondly, information is more easily processed when presented in columns than in rows. In other words, when you want to compare a set of numbers, you had better place them in columns rather than in rows. More details on how to produce a table will be discussed in Chapter 14.

How are qualitative results reported?

Qualitative results are primarily presented in a narrative form but occasionally supplemented by a figure or a table. Unlike the narrative report of quantitative results, which can be presented in three types of statements, narrative reports of qualitative results vary from one study to another.

For a single-case study, you need to give a detailed account of the case centering around the research questions. Suppose a case study focuses on the developmental stages of a child's L2, you might then need to describe each of the distinct stages verbally coupled with illustrative examples. In a multiple-case study, similarities and differences across cases are the focus of your report. Meanwhile, you need to use a lot of direct quotes from interviews, think-aloud protocols, and diaries, or restate what has been said or done by the subjects to concretize the similarities and differences identified.

Although the ways qualitative results are reported are diversified, they should share one thing in common, that is, a description must be made through analysis and synthesis since no reader wants to read one quote after another from the interview scripts without knowing why the quotes are listed and how these quotes are related to the research questions. Sometimes, qualitative results can be described in figures. For example, the different stages of a child's L2 development may be shown in a flow chart. In the study conducted by Wen and Guo[1] (1998), the dynamic functions of L1 use in producing sentences are presented in diagrams.

Discussing results

Each result reported should be followed by a proper discussion. This is the place to illustrate the link between your study and the existing literature and to demonstrate your comprehensive understanding of the research topic under investigation. However, quite a few students do not do justice to the "Discussion" section. As a result, the poor discussion relegates their theses to mediocre ones. One important reason is that they feel that they have nothing to write in this section. Some of them cannot even differentiate reporting results from discussing results. In the following parts, I will first explain to you what is meant by discussing a result, and then give you some suggestions on how to make a discussion comprehensive and appropriate. Finally, some common problems will be pointed out.

What is meant by discussing a result?

When you discuss a result, you should go beyond the result and express your own opinions about the result, i.e. your personal speculation on the reasons for the result, your judgement on its significance, implications, and the possible direction for future research. The essential difference between reporting a result and discussing a result is that the former is fact-driven while the latter is opinion-driven. However, your opinions are not whatever you have thought about. They should be based on existing theories, previous studies, or common sense. Therefore, in discussion, references are indispensable. Usually the discussion together with the report of a result cannot be too long since a lengthy discussion will separate the answers to the research questions and distract readers' attention. The elaboration of the discussion, if it is necessary, can be made in the "Conclusion" chapter.

How is a result discussed?

Upon reading a result, one question that readers will immediately ask is: Why is there such a result? Therefore, your discussion starts with the explanations of a result.

---

[1] The figure in the paper is presented as an appendix.

Explanations of a result

Discussing a result usually begins with speculating about the explanation for the result. The speculations are not wild guesses. They should be logically sound. That is to say, they can be supported by existing theories or empirical findings from other studies. The weakest explanation would follow from our intuitive feelings. Furthermore, the speculations should consider rival explanations or limitations in your study.

The following is an example of discussing a result in my own study (Wen, 1993). The specific result discussed here is that there is a strong correlation between gender and L2 achievement. In other words, female students tend to achieve higher scores than male students on TEM4. This result needs further explanations which are presented as follows.

Example

Explanations of a strong correlation between gender and L2 achievement

The reasons for such a strong correlation can be various. One interpretation for such a gender difference is that females have talents for language learning while males have talents for mathematics and sciences. Such a view has been reported by quite a few researchers such as Allen and Valette (1977), Farhady (1982), Larsen-Freeman and Long (1991), Maccoby and Jacklin (1974), and Nyikos (1990). An alternative interpretation is that male students who major in English are not the best students in the whole group since according to the Chinese tradition, the best male students usually go into the science stream. Following this argument, we will challenge the explanation that females have greater talents for language learning (pp. 143-144).

Evaluations of the significance of a result

Evaluating the significance of a result also falls into the scope of discussion. The significance may be theoretical or practical. By evaluating its theoretical significance, you try to link the result to previous findings or existing theories to see whether your result is the same as or in conflict with previous ones and to see whether your result is in support of existing theoretical assumptions or against them. Remember this is the place where you frequently refer back to the literature review. If your result echoes previous studies, it means that the reliability of previous findings is increased. Otherwise, you need to offer readers various possible explanations. If the conflict is not caused by methodological problems, it will add complexities to our understanding of a phenomenon and enrich the existing theories.

Very often, a result has not only theoretical significance but also practical significance. By pointing out its practical significance, you try to specify how L2 teaching and learning can benefit from the result. In other words, you try to give practical suggestions based on the result for improving L2 teaching and learning. One thing you have to remember is that your suggestions must naturally grow out of the result. If the suggestions, although they are conducive to L2 teaching and learning, are not related to the result, you have to delete them.

Making recommendations for future research

The discussion of a result may move further to make suggestions for future research. Suppose your result is not consistent with previous findings. Your speculated reasons are: (1) The sample size of your study is not big enough; (2) your subjects are adult learners but previous studies all involve non-adult learners. Therefore, you suggest the study should be replicated with a bigger sample size in the future. Once you embed the recommendations in the context of your own study, you can avoid a common problem occurring in graduate students' theses which is that the recommendations made are not developed out of their own findings.

Problems in discussing a result

The worst case is that the discussion component is simply absent in the "Results and discussion" chapter where only a set of tables and figures are presented together with a few lines describing the results. Remember it is in the discussion part that the extensiveness of your background knowledge and the depth of your understanding are demonstrated. Without this part, readers would think your background knowledge is limited and your understanding of the issue is shallow. A more common problem is that the explanation for the result is simple and sometimes even illogical. To overcome the problem, it is best to discuss the results with your classmates and supervisor. Through the discussion, your understanding of the results can be deepened. Furthermore, you should refer back to previous studies mentioned in the literature review to see whether your findings are consistent with theirs or not.

☰ WRITING A CONCLUSION

Human beings have limited capacity to remember things. Therefore, it is not uncommon that readers have forgotten some important things in a thesis when they finish reading the "Results and discussion" chapter. The "Conclusion" chapter can help readers refresh their memory and review what is essential in a thesis.

If you think you have already said everything in previous chapters and the last chapter does not add any weight to the thesis, you will be totally wrong since the last chapter will certainly leave a deep impression on readers if they cannot remember what has been read before. In this sense, the last chapter weighs more in determining the quality of your thesis. This is particularly true for external examiners and members of the oral defense committee when they are drowned in reading a dozen theses in the season of oral defense. Therefore, I strongly advise that you write this last chapter with conscientious efforts.

The "Conclusion" chapter usually consists of three sections: (1) major findings; (2) implications; and (3) recommendations for future research and limitations. I will discuss how to write each part more effectively.

Major findings

The major findings are an integrative summary of the most important results. Therefore, you cannot repeat verbatim what has been said in the "Results and discussion" chapter. To organize this section, there are two alternative ways. The first is to present the major findings by research questions. That is, to begin with, you briefly restate each question in order to save readers the trouble of referring back to previous sections. In most cases, you do not need to go beyond general questions. The results are then summarized in relation to the questions. The second alternative is to list the most important findings without referring to individual questions. The common practice is to sequence the major findings that mirror the order of research questions.

In either case, you should not use jargon and statistics. What is expected here is a non-technical verbal account of the major findings, which is usually short and brief. In addition to the major findings related to the research questions, you may also report unexpected results, i.e. the results yielded by analyses that you do not plan to make but later prove to be interesting.

Implications

In the previous chapter where each result is discussed, you have already drawn implications for theory and for practice. However, the implications are discussed there with specific results. Readers can only see trees scattered around rather than a forest. Now it is time for you to synthesize the implications to present them with a whole picture. You need to take a top-down approach, i.e. summarizing the results and thinking of their implications in three perspectives: theory, methodology, and practice.

Theoretical implications

In the "Literature review" chapter, you examine different theoretical assumptions about your topic. Most likely, the assumptions examined are various and some of them are in conflict. Are your results in support of one or more theories? Why or why not? Remember your interest is not in implications drawn from one specific result, which are presented in the "Results and discussion" chapter. Rather, you talk about a bunch of results that are related to a similar theoretical issue. If your results are not predicted by existing theories, you have to explain why.

The following is an excerpt discussing the theoretical significance of the results in my study (Wen, 1993). Due to the limited space, the quoted section only mentions one theoretical implication. Actually, from one study you may draw several theoretical implications.

Example

A theoretical implication

In the previous chapter, the three controversies or continua (i.e. L1-L2 connection, the explicit-implicit option, and the code-communication dilemma) proposed by Stern were introduced. Two types of learning approaches (i.e. the Traditional and the Non-traditional) are assumed to be placed at the extreme ends of each continuum. The popular view in the field of L2 teaching and research is that these two approaches cannot be reconciled and the Traditional Approach produces poor learning outcomes while the Non-traditional Approach leads to successful learning.

The findings from this study seem to provide a completely different view about these controversies from the learner's perspective. Successful learners do not perceive the ends of each continuum are in conflict and cannot be reconciled; rather, they regard them as complementary to each other and are active to combine them in carrying out learning activities. When learners are only in favor of either the Traditional or the Non-traditional Approach, they obtain similar results. However, they cannot make outstanding achievement like those who actively use both approaches.

One theoretical implication can be drawn from the above findings: Prejudice against the Traditional Approach should be eradicated and too much enthusiasm about the Non-traditional Approach should be weakened. Those people like Krashen and his followers need to reexamine their theories and modify their views that only implicit learning and implicit linguistic knowledge can lead to L2 learning proficiency and explicit learning and explicit linguistic knowledge show very limited functions. However, it is uncertain whether the aforesaid findings from this study are universally applicable. If empirical findings from future studies on L2 learning in different contexts are found to be similar to those obtained from this study, their theories should include the views that both approaches have an equal role to play in L2 learning and the best way to learn an L2 is to combine two approaches flexibly in accordance to the different nature of tasks. If not, their theories have to take the factors of culture and/or learning conditions into consideration. (Wen, 1993, pp. 249-250)

In the above example, I first reiterate the widely accepted views about the relationship between Traditional and Non-traditional approaches and L2 learning outcomes. Then I point out the conflict between the findings from my study and the prediction based on the widely accepted views. Finally, I draw possible theoretical implications from the findings.

Methodological implications

The development of research methodology is also very important for research advances. Do your results make any contribution to this area? If one of the reasons for you to carry out the study is to employ a new method, your results will definitely have methodological implications. The following is an excerpt discussing methodological implications in my study (Wen, 1993).

Example

Methodological implications

I have drawn two methodological implications from my study. First of all, I used path analysis to examine the relations between a set of learner variables and L2 learning outcomes. In previous studies, researchers usually used multiple regression analysis to solve a similar problem. The findings from my study revealed that path analysis was much more powerful than multiple regression analysis since the latter can only show the relative importance of each variable in predicting L2 learning outcomes but the former is able to go beyond that, displaying the relations among independent variables.

Secondly, in my study I used qualitative data to illuminate and supplement quantitative data. It turned out that qualitative data were more revealing than quantitative data. The implication from this finding is that the combination of quantitative and qualitative designs is much more effective than a single method.

In the above example, I highlight two methodological implications. The first is the advantage of path analysis used in my study in contrast with multiple regression analysis employed by many researchers at that time. The second is to use a mixed-method design in my study which was scarce in the early 1990s.

Practical implications

Research in the applied linguistics field may have practical implications. Furthermore, you may go beyond the description of the potential use and discuss further how these suggestions can be implemented. For example, the following is the first paragraph under the heading "Practical implications" in my thesis (Wen, 1993, p. 250).

> ## Example
>
> ### Practical implications
>
> Practical implications drawn from the findings from this study will be discussed in terms of two areas. The first is how teachers can make use of the findings concerning the overall relations between modifiable learner variables and English achievement to promote L2 learning efficiency and independent learning. The second is how teachers can make use of the findings in relation to the effects of learning approaches on English achievement to avoid their own bias toward learners' learning approaches and at the same time to make learners discard their bias through daily teaching.

In the above example, two practical implications are discussed. The first implication is in relation to the overall topic. To be specific, teachers should take measures to encourage students to monitor their modifiable factors such as learning purposes, beliefs, and learning strategies so that their learning outcomes will become better and their way of learning will be improved. The second implication concerns the unbiased attitude toward the two learning approaches (i.e. Traditional and Non-traditional) in the sense that teachers should promote a good combination of the two approaches instead of using only one.

Recommendations for future research and limitations

This is the last section of the "Conclusion" chapter. In this section, you propose suggested topics for future research and present limitations existing in your study. You may explain the limitations along with your suggestions or you may deal with the suggestions and limitations separately. For your convenience, I will discuss these two issues separately.

Recommendations

The section of "Recommendations" can be discussed at a macro level and a micro level. In other words, you talk about the general directions as well as suggestions on some specific research topics. The following are the first few paragraphs discussing suggested research topics (Wen, 1993, p. 258).

> ## Example
>
> ### Recommendations for future research
>
> (1) Macro level
>
> First of all, the same study can be replicated with more English majors. The findings can present us with a complete picture of advanced level English learning in China. The same study can also be conducted on middle school students and university students who major in subjects other than English. The results can be used to delineate the whole picture of the relation between the modifiable learner variables and English achievement of Chinese EFL learners. By carrying out a series of such studies, hopefully, a standardized questionnaire on learner factors can be developed and a causal model of factors affecting the English achievement of Chinese EFL learners can be established. If possible, such a study can be undertaken cross-culturally. The findings obtained from different cultural contexts would be insightful in constructing better L2 learning theories.
>
> Secondly,...Fifthly,...
>
> To sum up, future research on the relationship between modifiable learner variables and English achievement can be conducted on a large sample cross-sectionally or longitudinally, and cross-culturally if possible...
>
> (2) Micro level
>
> There are three areas (i.e. vocabulary learning, the use of mother tongue, and tolerating ambiguity), according to the findings from this study, which most need to be further investigated. For vocabulary learning, future studies can be carried out in middle school students, non-English majors, and English majors. Such studies may focus on the differences between successful and unsuccessful learners in their development of strategies...

The suggested topics must be developed out of your own study. They should be topics that need to be investigated. Some graduate students, however, write this part without sufficient thought and topics proposed are not significant or do not derive from their own research.

Limitations

Limitations concern those conditions that the researcher is supposed to meet but has had difficulty in implementing. The researcher should honestly inform readers about them in the "Limitations" section so that they will deal with the findings with caution. The limitations may be shown in a sample. For example, the sample size may be too small, the sample is not randomly selected, or the participants are volunteers. The limitations can also be displayed in the data collected, for example, where the rate of missing data is high. The limitations can also exist in tests where we do not have the index of reliability and validity of TEM4 and TEM8 although they are the only available authoritative tests for English majors in China.

The limitations of a study can also be alternatively put in the "Methodology" chapter. The advantage of such an arrangement is that you can discuss in detail how the limitations can influence the internal and external validity of the findings yielded from the study.

▶☰ SUMMARY

The "Introduction" chapter in a thesis presents the reader with an overall picture of the study, typically including three components: (1) a general description of the study; (2) the need for the study; and (3) the overall structure of a thesis.

The "Literature review" chapter tells the reader where your study is situated in its context. It may cover five topics as follows: (1) conceptual definitions of key terms; (2) an examination of the research topic with reference to a specific theoretical perspective; (3) a description of related empirical studies with evaluating comments; (4) a critical review of research designs including instruments related to your study if the methodological issue is critical to your study; and (5) a conceptual framework if there is any.

The "Methodology" chapter is a detailed description of the way your study is undertaken. Specifically, this part should answer the following questions: What are the research questions? Who are the subjects and how are they selected? What are the instruments and how are they developed? How are the data collected and analyzed? What are the limitations? How do you follow the ethical principles? The description should be explicit, transparent, and sufficiently detailed so that other researchers can easily replicate the study if they want to.

The part of "Results and discussion" should be organized in terms of the research questions. Only the findings that answer the research questions are reported. The discussion of a result is expected to offer reasonable explanations of the result, evaluate its significance, make recommendations for future research, which will enable readers to interpret your results with caution.

The "Conclusion" part summarizes the major findings, discusses the theoretical, methodological, and practical implications, and proposes suggestions for future research and limitations. Unlike the part of "Results and discussion," your discussion in the "Conclusion" part does not need to follow specific research questions. Instead, it centers around general issues that the study attempts to resolve.

AFTER-READING ACTIVITIES

Reviewing

1. What is the function of "Introduction"? What should be included in this part? How do you write it?
2. Why is the literature review needed? What are you expected to write in this part? What common difficulties might students encounter?
3. What should be written about in the "Methodology" chapter? What aspects should you pay particular attention to?
4. How is the "Results and discussion" chapter organized? How do you write it?
5. What should the "Conclusion" chapter cover? What should be kept in your mind when you write it?

Exploring

Get a copy of a thesis from the library and answer the following questions.
1. What do you think of the "Introduction" chapter? Is it properly written?
2. How is the "Literature review" chapter organized? Can you make suggestions for further improvement?
3. Does the "Methodology" chapter contain sufficiently detailed information?
4. How are the results reported? Are all the research questions answered?
5. Are the headings appropriate? If not, can you revise them?
6. Is the discussion sufficient and appropriate? If not, can you elaborate on it?
7. What do you think of the last chapter? Can you make some critical comments on it?

Writing styles and avoiding plagiarism

14

Writing a thesis is not like writing a poem, a novel, or an essay. In creative writing, you exert efforts in order to be different from others both in content and in form. However, a thesis has a required writing style. Although the studies reported in theses vary from one to another, the style remains the same. Graduate students have to be familiar with such a writing style and make sure that their theses can meet the required standard. This chapter begins with the features of academic writing style, followed by various problematic aspects in writing a thesis.

ACADEMIC WRITING STYLE

A thesis should be written so that the information is presented as briefly and clearly as possible. Its writing style differs from creative writing in two major aspects: the organization and the language (Newman et al., 1997).

Organization

As mentioned at the beginning of Chapter 12, a thesis includes a beginning, a body and an ending. The components in each part are somewhat standardized. For example, the body of a thesis must have one chapter on the literature review, one chapter on methodology, one chapter on results and discussion and one chapter on the conclusion. An individual writer has no freedom to drop out any component or to add any new component that has never occurred in other theses.

For the structure of each chapter, you have to provide readers with an introductory paragraph under each major heading. In such an introduction, you need to produce an advance organizer to tell readers what is to follow. At the end of each chapter, you summarize what was said in the whole chapter. In between, you often write transitional sentences between paragraphs or sections through which you provide closure to what has been said previously and what is going to be said in the next paragraph or section. Subheadings are frequently used to alert readers when new topics are introduced and to remind them of the important things when they finish reading one section. Tables and graphs are often used for the clarity of presenting information.

You should make your purpose of writing explicit in the thesis so that readers are not kept in suspense at any stage and won't have any question like: Why is this part written here? After all, you should keep readers in mind all the time.

Language

> **?**
> • Have you ever been told that only the passive voice is allowed to be used in your thesis? What is your personal opinion?
> • Have you ever felt confused about the use of tense? When do you use the present tense and past tense in your daily practice? Do you think there is any rule for the use of tense in academic writing?

In a thesis, the language used should be formal and succinct. The passive voice is more often used than the active one. The first person point of view hardly appears in a thesis. Flowery words and words indicating emotions such as "fantastic," "fascinating," "terrific," "wonderful," "unfortunately," and "amazingly" should be avoided. However, the current tendency seems to change particularly for a thesis to report a qualitative study where the use of the active voice and the first person point of view becomes increasingly popular.

Tense is another typical feature of the language used in a thesis. Normally speaking, you move back and forth between the past and the present tenses. The improper use of tenses may violate scientific ethics (Day, 1989). According to scientific ethics, once a paper is formally published, it has become common knowledge while your present study before its publication is not regarded as accepted knowledge. Accordingly, you use the present tense to quote others' published studies to show your respect while using the past tense to describe your own study to display your modesty. The following are common situations for using the present tense and the past tense.

Present tense

1. Describe the components of each chapter or each section in an advance organizer.
2. Describe the need for the study.
3. Describe findings in previous theses by others.
4. Discuss existing theories and well-known principles.
5. Describe results in a table or a figure.
6. Discuss results in your own study.
7. State the conclusions of your own study.
8. Put forward suggestions for future research.

Past tense

1. Describe what you did in your present study.
2. Describe the results yielded by your present study.
3. Describe the procedures through which a previous study was carried out.

The above situations are only some of the common cases. In fact, the actual use of tenses is far more complex. If you are not sure of them, you may consult some reference books such as *Writing an Applied Linguistics Thesis or Dissertation: A Guide to Presenting Empirical Research* (Bitchener, 2010).

APA WRITING FORMAT

Theses in the field of applied linguistics require that the manuscript be typed in the format described in a manual published by the American Psychological Association (APA). Such a format is called the APA style in short. In this section, I will introduce to you some rules that you need to follow in writing your thesis.

Tables

As mentioned earlier, academic writing often uses tables to present information together with a verbal account. A well-designed table can be more effective and economical than a verbal account alone since a table can enable readers to perceive patterns and relationships in data that are not readily seen in a verbal account. A table is typically used to display quantitative findings. Occasionally it does present qualitative results, too. In the manual published by APA, there are a set of rules regarding constructing a table that consists of five parts: number, title, heading, body, and note. The rules concerning each part will be briefly described in the following part.

Tables and figures

It is a common problem that graduate students do not make a distinction between tables and figures, and thus there is confusion in their theses. Tables are made up of rows and columns containing numbers while figures refer to any type of illustrations other than tables, such as charts, graphs, drawings, and photographs.

Numbering tables and figures

All the tables and figures in a thesis must be numbered. According to the APA style, tables are numbered sequentially in the order they occur in the manuscript and figures are numbered as a separate sequence.

Suppose you have altogether 30 tables in your thesis. You might like to start with Table 1 and end with Table 30. However, this way of numbering tables is suitable for a paper but not convenient for a thesis since in a thesis, dropping out or adding one table is not uncommon. If the tables are numbered from the beginning to the end, it means you have to renumber them all the way through whenever there is a change. Therefore, I suggest that tables be numbered within chapters. For example, tables in Chapter 1 are named as Table 1.1, Table 1.2 and so on, and tables in Chapter 2, as Table 2.1, Table 2.2 and so on. Doing this can make revisions much easier. Furthermore, tables must be sequenced by Arabic numbers. Therefore, you are not allowed to use Table A and Table B, nor Table I and Table II.

Like the tables, the figures are also numbered within chapters and sequenced by Arabic numbers. They form a separate sequence as Figure 1.1, Figure 1.2 in Chapter 1, and Figure 2.1, Figure 2.2 in Chapter 2.

Table titles

Each of the tables must have a title. A title should be short but explicit and self-explanatory. It should contain major information about the table. Titles such as "The results of t-tests" or "The results of multiple regression" are not good ones since such titles do not contain any specific information about the results. They had better be changed into: "t-tests: Differences in test scores on CET-4 between the control and experimental groups" and "Multiple regression: Power of variables in predicting the students' scores on CET-4."

Table headings

Headings are used to organize a table and inform readers of what has been presented in a row or a column. If the headings are abbreviated, the meaning of the abbreviations should be obvious. Otherwise, you need to explain the meaning of each abbreviation in notes.

Table body

The body of a table refers to the data which are in most cases numbers. For the sake of readability, round numbers are always preferred if possible. Which should be put in a row and which should be put in a column depend on several factors. One is the limitation of space. Usually you have more space for rows than columns since the width of a paper is shorter than its length. The other is the way your eyes perceive numbers. It is easier to perceive numbers in a column than in a row particularly when you want to compare numbers.

Table notes

Table notes can be classified into three kinds: general notes, specific notes and probability notes. General notes provide information about the table as a whole. For example, they explain the meaning of abbreviated terms used in a table. According to the APA format, a general note is shown by the word "*Note.*" The word is italicized and followed by a period. Specific notes are for stating the content of a specific cell, which are denoted by superscript lowercase letters. If several items need to be explained by a specific note, you may mark them from the upper left of a table and move them from left to right across rows. Probability notes display the significance level of a result. Within a table this is marked by one or two or three asterisks. "*" means $P \leqslant .05$; "**" means $P \leqslant .01$; "***" means $P \leqslant .001$.

If a table requires all three kinds of notes, you start with the general notes, then specific notes, and finally probability notes.

Table 14.1 and Table 14.2 are examples of presenting quantitative and qualitative results respectively.

Presenting quantitative results

Type of learner	L1 Prof. [a] Mean	SD	L2 Prof. [b] Mean	SD
Grp 1 (Trad)	73.10	5.63	90.37	4.12
Grp 2 (Non-trad)	73.29	5.38	91.08	3.51
Grp 3 (HB)	74.02	5.51	91.62	3.40
Grp 4 (LB)	73.10	5.04	91.00	3.74

Table 14.1: One-way ANOVA: No differences found amongst the four groups of learners in L1 Prof. and L2 Prof. (Wen, 1993, p. 185)

Note. Trad=Traditional learners; Non-trad=Non-traditional learners;

HB=High-balanced learners; LB=Low-balanced learners;

⎤ General notes

a: L1 proficiency is represented by scores on the National Matriculation Chinese Test.

b: L2 proficiency is represented by scores on the National Matriculation English Test.

⎤ Specific notes

Presenting qualitative results

What	Why	How	When
Listening to the magazine show on the VOA	• Practicing listening • Increasing background knowledge • Practicing writing	• Taking down notes • Writing down what has been retained in the memory in my own words	• Three times a week
Memorizing new words (new words encountered in a week)	• Increasing vocabulary	• Using cards	• Once a week
Fast reading (simplified stories)	• Increasing reading speed	• Reading as fast as possible	• Every night before going to sleep

Table 14.2: The self-study plan made by a good learner based on her interview data (Wen, 1993, p. 194)

Numbers

How is a number dealt with in a thesis? The APA manual has a series of rules specifying the ways a number is expressed. Now we single out several common areas of concern for discussion.

Figures or words

Are numbers expressed in figures or in words? A general rule is that numbers are expressed in words when numbers are smaller than 10; numbers are expressed in figures when they are 10 or above 10. However, there are some exceptions. For example, when numbers below 10 are used together with the number 10 and number above 10, they are expressed in figures. For example, it is correct to say "5 out of the 36 second-year students" (Note: Using "five" is not correct here.) and "they are ranked 3rd and 15th respectively." (Note: Using "third" is not correct here.)

When numbers below 10 are used to represent time, ages, scores, and points on scales, they are also expressed in figures as exceptions. For example, it is perfectly acceptable to say "They finished the test within 2 hours" (Note: Using "two" is not correct.) and "Her score on the composition is 5." (Note: Using "five" is not correct.)

Decimal points

When a number cannot be bigger than 1, such as the correlation coefficient and the probability value, you do not need to put a zero before the decimal point, such as .40 or .05. However, when a number can be greater than 1, a zero is needed before the decimal point, such as 0.40 or 0.05.

Plurals of numbers

The plurals of numbers are expressed by simply adding "s" alone without an apostrophe. For example, we should say "in the 1990s" rather than "in the 1990's" or "between the 1980s and 1990s" rather than "between the 1980's and 1990's."

Spelling

The *Publication Manual of the American Psychological Association* deals with several important issues concerning spelling, such as preferred spelling, hyphenation, and capitalization. In the following part, these issues will be discussed one by one.

American spelling or British spelling

According to the APA style, you need to follow the standard set up by *Webster's New World College Dictionary.* Evidently this is American spelling. If you prefer to use British spelling in your thesis, you are definitely allowed to do so. The only inconvenience is that the computer spelling check system normally follows the American spelling standard. Whichever you choose, you must be consistent.

Hyphenation

One difficulty in spelling is how to use a hyphen when compound words are involved. In most cases, you can find a solution in a dictionary. However, quite a few compounds may not be available in a dictionary. If this is the case, you can follow general principles provided by the APA manual as follows.

Principle 1

If the meaning of a compound adjective is clear and will not cause any misunderstanding, you should not use a hyphen, e.g. modifiable learner variables, L2 linguistic competence.

Principle 2

If you invent a new compound that is used as an adjective before a noun, you had better use a hyphen to avoid potential misunderstanding. For example, if "different word lists" refer to the lists of different words rather than the word lists that are different from other word lists, a hyphen placed between "different" and "word" can help express the intended meaning explicitly.

Principle 3

A hyphen is often used when a compound adjective occurs before a noun. If a compound adjective is after a noun, a hyphen is usually not needed (APA, 1992, p. 57), e.g. "learner-centered classroom" vs. "the classroom is learner centered."

Principle 4

"If two or more compound modifiers have a common base, this base is sometimes omitted in all except the last modifier, but the hyphens are retained," (APA, 1992, p. 57) such as "long- and short-term training," "five- and ten-year plans."

Capitalization

A complete sentence should begin with a capital letter. This is a rule every L2 learner is familiar with. However, in writing a thesis, you may come across some cases where you will be uncertain about the rules of capitalization. In the following part, I will introduce to you some important rules concerning capitalization stated in the APA manual.

Rule 1

When a complete sentence is placed after a colon, the first letter of the first word should be capitalized. For example: "We can draw an inference from the findings: The Traditional and Non-traditional approaches are equally effective but they are less effective than a combination of these two approaches."

Rule 2

When a noun is followed by a numeral or a letter that has a specific place in a sequence, the first letter of the noun is capitalized, such as "on Day 1 of September," "Group A," and "in Table 2."

Rule 3

In titles of books and articles, the first letters of content words such as nouns, verbs, pronouns, adjectives, and adverbs, and words that consist of four letters or more are capitalized while the first letters of function words such as conjunctions, articles, and prepositions with less than four letters are not. If a title contains a compound word with a hyphen, both words need to be capitalized such as "Production-Oriented Approach." However, this rule does not apply to the titles of books and articles in a reference list.

Quotations

Quotations are used only when they are more powerful and more effective than restating the material in your own words. They are either positive or negative statements. That is to say, they are in support of your arguments or opposite to your own views. When a quotation contains fewer than 40 words, you do not need to make it a separate paragraph. But when it has 40 words or more, it should be a block quotation (See Quotation 3). The block quotation begins as a separate paragraph where each line is indented five spaces from the left margin and each subsequent line is flush with the paragraph indented. The block quotation does not need any quotation marks.

No matter whether a quotation is inserted in a text or as a separate paragraph, the author, date, and page number should all be specified with accuracy (See Quotation 2). If you want to change anything in the original material, you have to follow the rules specified in the APA manual.

According to the rules in the APA manual, some changes from the source are permitted without any explanation, such as changing the first letter of the first word in a quotation and changing the punctuation mark at the end of a sentence in order to avoid syntactic errors. For other changes, you have to provide an explanation in one way or another. In the case of omitting materials, you are required to use three ellipsis points (...) (See Quotation 3) within a sentence to indicate that you have omitted materials from the original source. When you insert some materials in the original source, you should use brackets ([ ]) (See Quotation 3) rather than parentheses to enclose the inserted materials which may be additions or explanations. If you want to emphasize some part of the original materials, you can underline the emphasized part and italicize it. Immediately after it, you insert parentheses in which the page number is shown (See Quotation 3). The following are different examples.

Examples

Quotation 1

Conceptually, Gardner (1985) sees motivation as "the combination of effort plus desire to achieve the goal of learning the language plus favorable attitudes toward learning the language" (p. 10).

Citations

Citations include the surname of an author, the year of publication, and page references if specific words or arguments are drawn from an author in parentheses. Such information can help readers locate the source of information in the reference list at the end of a thesis. The APA manual describes how to make a citation in different situations. The following parts will introduce to you how to cite one work by a single author, two authors, or more than two authors; and how you cite two or more works by different authors.

Citing one work

The simplest case is that you cite one work by a single author. You need to put in parentheses the surname and the year of publication with a comma in between (See Example 1). If the surname of an author has already appeared in the text, you just put the year of publication in parentheses immediately after the surname (See Example 2).

> **Example 1**
>
> It has been argued that teachers' role is to provide students with optimal conditions which can facilitate learning so that students can achieve similar successful results (Bloom, 1976).

Example 2

Gagne (1977) also noticed that adult learners were less affected by external instruction events.

If the cited work was written by two authors, you always cite both authors (See Example 3). However, when more than two but fewer than six authors are involved, you are only required to cite all the authors the first time the reference appears in the text (See Example 4). In subsequent citations, you simply cite the surname of the first author followed by "et al." (See Example 5).

Example 3

The disadvantage of the multiple regression analysis is that it cannot show the complex interrelations between independent variables (Bryman & Cramer, 1990).

Example 4

Studies of the good language learner (for example, Naiman, Frohlich, Stern, and Todesco, 1978) have tried to identify the strategies which successful learners use (Ellis, 1994, p. 37). (first citation)

Example 5

Naiman et al. (1978) found a similar relationship, although in this case "effort" on the part of the learners was also associated with instrumental motivation (Ellis, 1994, p. 512). (subsequent citation)

When a work has six or more authors, you only need to cite the surname of the first author followed by "et al." for the first and subsequent citations. If a work has two or more authors who have the same surname, you must put in parentheses the authors' initials in all text citations.

Citing two or more works in the same parentheses

If two or more works written by the same author are cited in the same parentheses, you are required to give the surname once, then the years of publication from the past to the present. Look at the following two examples.

Example 1

Empirical studies on student learning carried out since the 1970s have found that students' learning outcomes to a great extent depend on their choices of learning approaches (Biggs, 1979, 1987).

Example 2

The major controversies on L2 learning, as Stern (1975, 1983, 1992) says, center around three key issues.

If two or more works written by different authors are cited in the same parentheses, you need to arrange the citations in alphabetical order by the first author's surname. Let's look at the following example.

Example

One major finding from the earlier studies (Barley, 1969, 1970; Clement et al., 1978; Gardner & Lambert, 1972; Gliksman, 1976; Spolsky, 1969) was that learners with an integrative motivation tended to obtain better achievement than those with an instrumental motivation.

APA reference style

The basic rule of ordering references in a reference list is to arrange them in alphabetical order. The elements of a reference include the information about the author, the year of publication, the title of the cited material, and the publisher. A comma is used to separate parts of elements and a period to finish an element. All of you are familiar with the general structure of a reference. Therefore, the following parts will only focus on potential difficulties you might come across in producing a reference list.

A reference to a journal

When you write a reference to a journal, the following things need to be paid attention to:

1. Capitalize the first letter of the title and the subtitle of an article. Don't underline it or add double quotation marks to it.
2. Capitalize the first letter of major words in the title of a journal and italicize the full title.

3. Use Arabic numbers to specify the volume number and italicize it. If there is an issue number, place it in parentheses immediately after the volume number.

4. Use Arabic numbers to indicate the inclusive page numbers, which immediately follow the volume number or the issue number if there is any. Remember "pp." is only needed before the page numbers in reference to newspapers or magazines but not to a journal.

The following are the illustrations.

Example

Block, E. L. (1986). The comprehension strategies of second language readers. *TESOL Quarterly, 20*(3), 463-494.

Boyle, R. P. (1970). Path analysis and ordinal data. *American Journal of Sociology, 75*(4), 461-480.

Bracht, G. H. & Glass, G. V. (1968). The external validity of experiments. *American Educational Research Journal, 5*(4), 437-474.

A reference to a book

A reference to a book is not the same as a reference to a journal although they share many common elements. The following are the differences:

1. In a reference to an edited book, the editors' names are placed in the author's position followed by parentheses with the abbreviation "Ed." or "Eds." when the book is edited by more than one person.

2. The first letter of the first word in a title or subtitle needs to be capitalized and the whole title should be italicized.

3. Information about the number of edition (e.g. 2nd ed.) is put in parentheses immediately after the title.

Now let's look at some illustrations.

Example

Brown, H. D. (1987). *Principles of language learning and teaching* (2nd ed.). Prentice-Hall, Inc.

Marton, F., Hounsell, D., & Entwistle, N. (Eds.). (1984). *The experience of learning*. Scottish Academic Press.

Oxford, R. L. (1990). *Language learning strategies: What every teacher should know*. Newbury House.

A reference to an article or a chapter in an edited book

Sometimes a reference is not a paper in a journal or an entire book but an article or a chapter in an edited book. For example, in my study I referred to an article written by Palmberg entitled "How much English vocabulary do Swedish-speaking primary school pupils know before starting to learn English at school?" which is in a book entitled *Foreign Language Learning and Bilingualism* edited by Ringbom in 1985. How is this reference made? The following is this reference:

Example

Palmberg, R. (1985). How much English vocabulary do Swedish-speaking primary school pupils know before starting to learn English at school? In H. Ringbom (Ed.), *Foreign language learning and bilingualism* (pp. 89-97). Research Institute of the Åbo Akademi Foundation.

When you produce the above reference, you had better pay special attention to the following two things:

1. When an editor's name is not in the author position at the very beginning, the surname is not placed before the initials.
2. Inclusive page numbers are given in parentheses immediately after the book title.

Now let's look at some more illustrations.

Example

Schmeck, R. R. (1983). Learning styles of college students. In R. R. F. Dillon & R. Schmeck (Eds.). *Individual differences in cognition* (Vol.1, pp. 233-279). Academic Press.

Swain, M. (1985). Communicative competence: Some roles of comprehensible input and comprehensible output in its development. In S. Gass & C. Madden (Eds.), *Input and second language acquisition* (pp. 235-253). Newbury House.

To sum up, I don't think you can remember every small detail and follow it in your writing. What I suggest is that you take this as a reference when you are not sure how to do it. However, not all the universities would like their students to use the APA style. If this is the case, you must read the instruction book carefully and follow the style preferred by your own university.

≣ AVOIDING PLAGIARISM

Plagiarism is a "sin" in thesis writing or any other academic writing, which can well reflect one's academic integrity. Along with the rapid development of the internet and digital technology, plagiarism has become more tempting since abundant electronic resources available can be easily copied and pasted. Now universities and scholars are less tolerant than before about plagiarism. Furthermore, a variety of advanced computer softwares are developed to detect plagiarism. Accordingly, clear rules or regulations in punishing such misconduct have been implemented. The Ministry of Education has set up a "zero tolerance" policy of plagiarism. However, our students are not taught what is plagiarism and how to avoid it properly in their formal education. Therefore, in my opinion, many students plagiarize unintentionally. For this purpose, in this section I will first explain what is plagiarism, then discuss different types of plagiarism, and finally provide some suggestions for preventing plagiarism. I believe once you have a sound understanding of what is plagiarism and what is the punishment for such academic dishonesty, you will avoid plagiarism at all costs.

Now every thesis, before being submitted for blind reviewing, is checked by a computer software to detect plagiarism. It is said that in some universities, if your thesis shows that the percentage of similarity to the existing literature is higher than 15%, it will be refused for submission. If an article is submitted to a journal for publication, it is also checked by a similar software. If the percentage of similarity between your paper and other papers is higher than 10%, you will be suspected of plagiarizing. I would say that making a judgement on plagiarism is not that simple. Apparently, similarity looks like a good criterion. It works well in extreme cases where two pieces of work are identical or almost identical. However, the degree of similarity between two pieces of academic work does not capture the essence of plagiarism. In fact, to make a clear division between what is plagiarism and what is not cannot simply be based on the percentage of similarity.

Definition of plagiarism

"Plagiarize" in *Merriam-Webster Dictionary* is defined as "to steal and pass off (the ideas or words of another) as one's own; use (another's production) without crediting the source" (Merriam-webster, n.d.). In the first part of the definition, the verb "steal" indicates the seriousness of such misconduct since stealing in daily life is an illegal act. Similarly, plagiarism is "commonly regarded as a form of academic cheating" (Bryman, 2016, p. 115). The second part of the definition further explains what "stealing" means, i.e. using others' ideas without acknowledging the source. It clearly shows that avoiding plagiarism does not mean that in our academic work, others' ideas, words, and sentences cannot be used. As we know, all research is not done in a vacuum. Instead, it is always based on previous studies. It is not only natural but also required to do literature review discussing theories and previous studies by others. The most important thing is that you must do proper citations when using others' ideas. Just as the MIT handbook for students on academic integrity states, "Plagiarism occurs when you use another's words, ideas, assertions, data, or figures and do not acknowledge that you have done so" (MIT, n.d.).

Different types of plagiarism

Depending on whose ideas have been stolen, plagiarism can be classified into two types: plagiarizing one's own work and plagiarizing others' work. Self-plagiarism refers to passing off one's previous written work as one's new work. This seems less likely to occur compared with plagiarizing others' work. It might be true in terms of the frequency of occurrence. However, we need to avoid both since they both violate academic codes.

Plagiarizing one's own work

Let's start with two examples.

Example 1

Assignments
Some students submitted one assignment to two teachers who taught different courses so that they could get the credits for two courses only with half the efforts.

Example 2

Researchers' papers
Some researchers published their papers in one journal and then published them in another journal with very small changes in the titles and the content.

The above cases are both regarded as self-plagiarism. In the first case, the students cheated the teachers and did not write two different assignments. Such cases are not easily found because the university teachers do not check to see whether there are any identical or almost identical assignments across courses. In my teaching experience, I never ever thought some students would commit self-plagiarism in this way until I found it in 2011. In March 2011, at the beginning of the spring semester, one student came to have a talk with me discussing the unfairness in the students' scores on my course. Once I heard the word "unfairness," I did not understand what she meant since in my teaching career, treating all the students fairly was one of the principles I tried to stick to all the time. I was eager to hear what she would say. She described how hard she tried to finish several assignments to beat a deadline at the end of last semester but her score on my course was not as high as she expected. However, a few students (Note: She was not willing to tell me the names.) submitted the previous assignments to my course and got high scores. I was shocked and extremely angry when I heard it. I first wrote a letter to all the students asking them to tell me honestly whether the assignments for my course were newly written or not. If they could honestly admit their mistakes, I would give them a second chance to write a new one. Otherwise, they would get a grade of "fail" for this course. I did take this matter very seriously. Afterward, I realized that as a teacher, I was also responsible for their misconduct since I never educated the students concerning this issue.

In the second case, some novice researchers do not know what proper academic behaviors are while others plagiarize intentionally. I suggest that supervisors should spend time discussing such an issue with M.A. and Ph.D. students. It is clear that each published paper should have its originality and duplication should not be allowed.

However, once it comes to publication in two different languages, the issue becomes controversial. Once Wen and Gao (2007) published a paper entitled "Dual publication and academic inequality" in the *International Journal of Applied Linguistics*. This paper discussed whether publishing a paper in two different languages, i.e. Chinese and English, would be regarded as self-plagiarism. We asked several friends' opinions regarding this issue and their views were divided. We argued in the paper that this is not self-plagiarism. Our argument was made concerning two issues.

The first one is about why dual publication in two different languages is not self-plagiarism. The major reason is that a paper written in English based on a paper in Chinese is not a literal translation from Chinese to English. In fact, writers have to make tremendous efforts in transforming a paper in Chinese into one in English. First of all, writers need to lengthen the literature review section to situate their studies in international settings. The section is normally expanded three or four times of the Chinese one. Secondly, they need to reframe the discussion section with reference to the literature outside the Chinese context. Finally, the suggestions for future research or implications for practice have to be provided for international readers.

The second issue is about the principle of equity if we regard dual publication in two different languages as self-plagiarism. If we follow the principle of equity, all languages have the same right to create knowledge and disseminate knowledge. However, in the current world, English is privileged in disseminating the knowledge created by native English speakers while research papers written in Chinese are hardly known to the outside world. The reason is crystal clear because very few native English speakers can read Chinese papers. If papers published in Chinese are not accepted to be published in English, then knowledge created in Chinese will lose opportunities to be disseminated in the world.

Plagiarizing others' work

There is a website (plagiarism.org, n.d.) introducing plagiarism where 12 types are identified. In the following parts, I will select 6 common ones from the 12 types and give further explanations.

Paraphrase plagiarism

Paraphrase plagiarism refers to rephrasing others' content without acknowledging the source. This could be unintentional plagiarism. Perhaps the writer forgets to cite a source or the writer lacks comprehensive knowledge about such plagiarism. You see, the writer has done paraphrasing which means he/she knows copying and pasting others' work should be forbidden. Nevertheless, paraphrasing alone is not sufficient. Proper citations must go along with paraphrasing. A supervisor has to emphasize this and explain the consequence of lacking citations to students.

Mosaic plagiarism

Mosaic plagiarism refers to inserting phrases and texts from various sources in one's own work, which makes the phrases and texts appear to be written by the writer himself/herself. It also includes the case of modifying sentences slightly without quotation marks. This kind of plagiarism is comparatively difficult to be detected by a computer software. However, this can be easily discerned by experts. In my opinion, although it might not be detected by the computer software, your academic conscience will be blamed if you do it. This often occurs in L2 writing. Some students find it difficult to express their ideas in accurate expressions or sentences. Once they find some good sentences in reading, they might write them down. Later they try to put them together to weave a good piece of written work. My advice is: Don't mix up these sentences. You had better read them repeatedly and then put them aside to write in your own words. Even in this case, don't forget to do proper citations.

Data plagiarism

Data plagiarism refers to the case where data are fabricated or distorted. Normally, the data you collected are not checked by your supervisor or the editor of a journal bit by bit or piece by piece. Keeping your data as accurate as possible is a minimum requirement for any researcher. This is a good place to test one's academic conscience and integrity. If any student distorts data in order to get perceived results, he/she will be punished severely by the oral defence committee. If this type of plagiarism is found in a paper submitted to a journal, the paper will be rejected and the reputation of the writer will also be ruined.

Now some high-ranking journals such as *Language Learning* and *Studies in Second Language Acquisition* encourage the authors of the papers to make their data completely accessible by placing them on the website (De Costa, Lee, Rawal & Li, 2020). As a result, replication of one's research is fully possible. I believe along with the development of digital technology, all the data and the process of analysis will be required to be submitted electronically. This can greatly prevent data plagiarism.

Software-based plagiarism

Software-based plagiarism refers to the case where content taken from others' work is restructured by software tools such as text spinners and translation engines to evade plagiarism detection. It is only increasing in recent years because of those who are good at using varied computer softwares. So far, I haven't come across such a case but supervisors need to pay attention to this new type of plagiarism.

Word-for-word plagiarism

Word-for-word plagiarism refers to copying others' whole piece of work. In other words, someone who does such plagiarism would submit another person's whole paper for a course or for publication as if it was written by himself/herself. This is an extreme case of plagiarism, which can now hardly happen because it can be almost 100% detected by the computer software. I must say this is unforgivable.

Contract plagiarism

Contract plagiarism refers to the case where another person is asked to write an assignment, a paper, or even a thesis for you either for pay or for kindness and the written product is taken as your own work. This is relatively rare in formal education. However, some people run this as business, "writing papers or theses for others," which often appears on the internet. I once received a phone call asking whether I needed someone to write a paper or apply for a patent for me. The survival of such business indicates that contract plagiarism does exist. We must keep alert to this type of plagiarism and give students a kind warning.

Writing strategies for avoiding plagiarism

In the MIT handbook for students on academic integrity (MIT, n.d.), several writing strategies are provided for avoiding plagiarism. I will briefly introduce to you: quoting, paraphrasing, summarizing, and taking good notes.

Quoting

When the words or sentences are expressed by an expert who is of high authority in the field, you want to quote them to support your argument. It is justifiable for you to do so so long as you quote while specifying the source and using quotation marks. If the quote is long, you have to indent it and separate it from your own text. Don't use too many quotes.

Paraphrasing

Paraphrasing in academic writing means you restate others' ideas in your own words without changing their original meaning while acknowledging their sources. It is very common to do paraphrasing in your thesis writing particularly in writing the chapter of the literature review where you need to provide the reader with sufficient background information. Such information is mostly about others' theories and empirical studies. However, it is not easy to do paraphrasing successfully. It needs a lot of practice, which is better done under the teacher's guidance.

Summarizing

Summaries can be long or short. The longer one could be an assignment and the shorter one should be a paragraph of your thesis. To write a good summary, you should first read someone's work closely and have an accurate understanding. Then you identify the most important ideas from the work and synthesize them in your own words. This requires a high level of abstracting. At the same time, you should be able to express the original ideas in your own words and in your own way of organizing. Don't copy any sentences from the original work or follow the original structure.

Taking good notes

Many people have the habit of taking notes while reading. What is noted down? For non-English speakers, we take notes sometimes because the ideas are insightful or inspiring and sometimes because the language is very vivid and expressive. If the notes taken are incomplete, or you forget to note down the source, when you write your paper or thesis, you might mistake it for your own work. I was told that some famous scholars were accused of plagiarism due to this cause. Therefore, we had better form a good habit: Whenever you note down something from others' work, you write down the source in case you forget it.

Managing strategies for preventing plagiarism

I have just discussed six types of plagiarism which can be arranged into two groups in terms of severity. In the following parts, I will discuss suggestions for supervisors and students respectively.

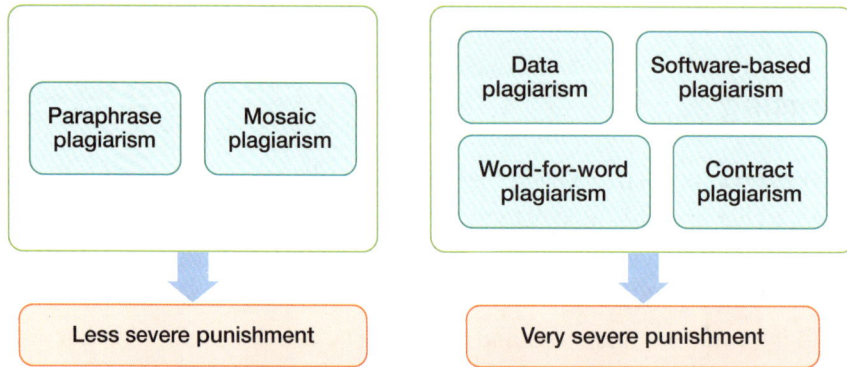

Figure 14.1: Different types of plagiarism in terms of severity

Suggestions for supervisors

Supervisors' responsibility is not only to teach students how to do research but also to teach them how to be good researchers with academic integrity. In order to reach this goal, I have two major suggestions. The first is to give your students a good orientation and the second is to teach students how to avoid plagiarism.

Having a good orientation

At the beginning of the term when you first meet the students, you need to arrange a well-prepared orientation. In the orientation, you must explain to them very clearly what academic integrity means. What is plagiarism and what is the punishment for plagiarism need to be particularly emphasized. You must let them know that no one can escape punishment resulting from plagiarism. You may sign a contract with them in which you promise to teach them how to avoid plagiarism and your students promise not to commit any type of plagiarism.

Teaching students how to avoid plagiarism

You might start with discussing what plagiarism is and asking your students to give examples to illustrate different types of plagiarism. Based on their discussion, you may summarize various types of plagiarism in terms of the degree of severity. You can show them Figure 14.1 and explain to them what is meant by each type and tell them what kind of punishment will be for different types. For data plagiarism, software-based plagiarism, word-for-word plagiarism, and contract plagiarism, the students should be told never to do them since they are all intentional plagiarism that will result in very severe punishment. That is to say if someone does it, he/she is not able to get any degree certificate and such misconduct will be recorded in his/her personal file. This kind of misbehavior might affect one's credibility for a lifetime. Paraphrase plagiarism and mosaic plagiarism are regarded as unintentional plagiarism most of the time due to the failure to understand the academic rules of referencing. However, if there are too many occurrences of the so-called unintentional plagiarism in one assignment or thesis, the writer will be seriously criticized for his/her attitudes toward academic work and the academic grade will be lowered. The major reason I think is that students lack sufficient advice on referencing. What supervisors need to do is to teach students how to do paraphrasing in a professional way before their formal writing starts. It is better to use examples to illustrate what is paraphrase plagiarism and what is mosaic plagiarism. Meanwhile, let students do paraphrasing through experiential learning.

Monitoring students' researching and writing process

Supervisors need to meet their students regularly and ask them to report their work of research or writing, meeting each student once a week or at least once in two weeks. By doing so, supervisors get familiar with students' work, which can reduce the incidence of plagiarism. Furthermore, this practice will impose pressure on your students so that they can do the required work bit by bit. Eventually, they can finish the work under supervision before the deadline. If the supervisor does not monitor students' progress in the process, it will be difficult for the supervisor to judge how the product has been made and whether there is any plagiarism or not.

Suggestions for students

I believe all students want to be good researchers. None of them would like to violate academic codes at the very beginning. For those who commit unintentional plagiarism, I think it is most probably caused by two major reasons. The first is lacking a sound understanding of proper referencing. The second is laziness in the sense that they don't spend time checking whether it is a proper citation. For those who commit intentional plagiarism, the major reason is most likely bad time management. When the deadline is approaching, they cannot submit the written work so that they try some illegal ways to get the work done fast. They know they might be punished but they always think they might escape punishment.

A correct attitude toward academic work

You have to remember that all the academic rules are implemented all the time. Even if one's misconduct could escape punishment for a while, it will be discovered sooner or later. He/she will be punished at any time when different types of intentional plagiarism are identified. I am afraid that he/she must be in dread of exposure all the time before being detected. Therefore, from the very beginning, all students should make up their minds to do research and write like real scholars who always abide by academic codes.

A sound understanding of proper citations

All students should read books concerning citations carefully in order to have a sound understanding of it. If you are not sure about how to write proper citations, you may seek advice from senior students or experienced writers. Or you may directly seek help from your supervisors. I don't think student researchers are familiar with every detail of citations. In fact, even an experienced writer may encounter difficulties in this regard. Don't feel hesitant to ask for help.

A good timeline for researching and writing

Doing research and writing a thesis are demanding and challenging, which may require consistent and persistent efforts in several years. Don't underestimate the difficulties, and don't think you are more intelligent than others and can finish the work in a shorter time. I suggest that you make a good timeline and implement it resolutely. So long as you stick to the plan with the help of your supervisor's monitoring, you can finish your work to meet the deadline.

≡ SUMMARY

A thesis should be written in a clear and explicit style that is different from creative writing. It should follow a relatively standardized structure and use formal and succinct language.

Theses in the field of applied linguistics are usually written according to the APA manual. In this manual, there are a list of rules that tell you how to use a tense, how to produce a table, how to deal with numbers, capitalization, and spelling, how to cite a work in a thesis, how to quote something from a work, and how to produce a reference list. To present a thesis in a professional manner, you must consistently follow one widely used style rather than a mixed one.

Furthermore, you are advised to avoid different types of plagiarism by all means. Committing plagiarism can be classified into plagiarizing one's own work and plagiarizing others' work. To avoid self-plagiarism is to simply follow relevant rules. One controversial issue concerning self-plagiarism is dual publication in two different languages. Wen and Gao (2007) hold the view that such dual publication should be encouraged since this can promote equity in disseminating creative knowledge all over the world. Plagiarizing others' work may be in different forms such as paraphrase plagiarism, mosaic plagiarism, data plagiarism, software-based plagiarism, word-for-word plagiarism, and contract plagiarism. Several writing and management strategies are proposed to avoid various types of plagiarism at the end of this chapter.

AFTER-READING ACTIVITIES

Reviewing

1 What are the differences between academic writing and creative writing in terms of style?

2 When is the present tense used and when is the past tense used in academic writing?

3 What is plagiarism? What is plagiarizing one's own work and what is plagiarizing others' work?

4 What difficulties do students have in avoiding plagiarism in your opinion?

5 What suggestions do you have for teachers in order to help students avoid plagiarism?

Exploring

Get a copy of an M.A. thesis and work with a group to answer the following questions.

1 Does the thesis have a standardized structure? If not, what are the problems?

2 What do you think of the language used in the thesis? Do you think the language is formal? If not, can you give some examples?

3 Are there any problems in the use of tense? List them and discuss.

4 Do you think the tables in the thesis are properly produced?

5 Does the author use hyphens correctly? If not, can you give some suggestions?

6 What do you think of the citations in the thesis? If there are any mistakes, correct them.

7 Are the quotations properly presented? If not, revise them.

8 What are the problems in the reference list? Can you give some suggestions for further revision according to the APA style?

References

Allen, E. D., & Valette, R. M. (1977). *Classroom techniques: Foreign languages and English as a second language*. Harcourt Brace Jovanovich.

Ambady, N., & Rosenthal, R. (1992). Thin slices of expressive behavior as predictors of interpersonal consequences: A meta-analysis. *Psychological Bulletin, 111*(2), 256-274.

American Psychological Association. (2020). *Publication manual of the American Psychological Association* (7th ed.). American Psychological Association.

Bachman, L. F. (1990). *Fundamental considerations in language testing*. Oxford University Press.

Bailey, K. M. (1983). Competitiveness and anxiety in adult second language learning: Looking at and through the diary studies. In H. Seliger & M. Long (Eds.), *Classroom oriented research in second language acquisition* (pp. 67-103). Newbury House.

Bejarano, Y. (1987). A cooperative small-group methodology in the language classroom. *TESOL Quarterly, 21*(3), 483-504.

Bernard, H. R. (1994). *Research methods in anthropology: Qualitative and quantitative approaches* (2nd ed.). Sage.

Bitchener, J. (2010). *Writing an applied linguistics thesis or dissertation: A guide to presenting empirical research*. Palgrave Macmillan.

Black, K. (1992). *Business statistics: An introductory course*. West Publishing Company.

Blaxter, L., Hughes, C., & Tight, M. (1996). *How to research*. Open University Press.

Block, E. L. (1986). The comprehension strategies of second language readers. *TESOL Quarterly, 20*(3), 463-494.

Boyle, R. P. (1970). Path analysis and ordinal data. *American Journal of Sociology, 75*(4), 461-480.

Bracht, G. H., & Glass, G. V. (1968). The external validity of experiments. *American Educational Research Journal, 5*(4), 437-474.

Brown, J. D. (1988). *Understanding research in second language learning: A teacher's guide to statistics and research design*. Cambridge University Press.

Bryman, A. (2016). *Social research methods* (5th ed.). Oxford University Press.

Chen, H. (2000). *A study of vocabulary learning strategies used by Chinese children* [Unpublished masters's thesis]. Nanjing University.

Chen, J. (1996). *A study of discomfort in EFL classroom* [Unpublished bachelor's thesis]. Nanjing University.

Cohen, A. D. (1987). Using verbal reports in research on language learning. In C. Faerch & G. Kasper (Eds.), *Introspection in second language research* (pp. 82-95). Multilingual Matters.

Cohen, L., & Manion, L. (1989). *Research methods in education* (3rd ed.). Routledge.

Cone, J. D., & Foster, S. L. (1993). *Dissertations and theses from start to finish: Psychology and related fields*. American Psychological Association.

Corder, S. P. (1967). The significance of learners' errors. *International Review of Applied Linguistics in Language Teaching*, *5*(4), 161-170.

Day, R. A. (1989). *How to write and publish a scientific paper* (3rd ed.). Cambridge University Press.

De costa, P. I., Lee, J., Rawal, H., & Li, W. (2020). Ethics in applied linguistic research. In J. Mckinley & H. Rose (Eds.), *The Routledge handbook of research methods in applied linguistics*. Routledge.

Dong, Y. (1999). *ESL Learning on the internet—A case study on a joint online course* [Unpublished master's thesis]. Nanjing University.

Duff, P. A. (2020). Case study research: Making language learning complexities visible. In J. McKinley & H. Rose (Eds.), *The Routledge handbook of research methods in applied linguistics*. Routledge.

Ellis, R. (1994). *The study of second language acquisition*. Oxford University Press.

Farhady, H. (1982). Measures of language proficiency from the learner's perspective. *TESOL Quarterly*, *16*(1), 43-59.

Flower, L., Stein, V., Ackerman, J., Kantz, M. J., McCormick, K., & Peck, W. C. (1990). *Reading-to-write: Exploring a cognitive and social process*. Oxford University Press.

Gardner, R. C. (1985). *Social psychology and second language learning: The role of attitudes and motivation*. Edward Arnold.

Gardner, R. C., & Lambert, W. E. (1972). *Attitudes and motivation in second-language learning*. Newbury House.

Glaser, B. G. (1978). *Theoretical sensitivity: Advances in the methodology of grounded theory*. Sociology Press.

Gong, X. (1998). *A contrastive study of English and Chinese compliment responses* [Unpublished master's thesis]. PLA University of Foreign Languages.

Gu, Y. Q. (1997). A study of vocabulary learning strategies by Chinese EFL learners [Unpublished doctoral dissertation]. The University of Hong Kong.

Guo, C. J. (1997). *A process-oriented cognitive account of L1 influence on L2 writing in the Chinese context* [Unpublished master's thesis]. Nanjing University.

Guo, C. J. (2007). *Think aloud protocols*. Foreign Language Teaching and Research Press.

Hatch, E., & Farhady, H. (1982). *Research design and statistics for applied *linguistics*. Newbury House.

Hornby, A. S. (2010). Integrity. In *Oxford advanced learner's dictionary of current English* (8th ed.) (p. 809). Oxford University Press.

Hosenfeld, C. (1984). Case studies of ninth grade readers. In J. C. Alderson & A. H. Urquhart (Eds.), *Reading in a foreign language* (pp. 231-249). Longman.

Hu, Y. Z. (1999). *Error treatment in EFL classrooms in universities in China* [Unpublished master's thesis]. Nanjing University.

Huang, X. H. (1984). *An investigation of learning strategies in oral communication that Chinese EFL learners in China employ* [Unpublished master's thesis]. The Chinese University of Hong Kong.

Hudelson, S. (1989). A tale of two children: Individual differences in ESL children's writing. In D. M. Johnson & D. H. Roen (Eds.), *Richness in writing: Empowering ESL students* (pp. 84-99). Longman.

Hymes, D. H. (1972). On communicative competence. In J. B. Pride & J. Holmes (Eds.), *Sociolinguists: Selected Readings*. Penguin.

Johnson, D. M. (1992). *Approaches to research in second language learning*. Longman.

Keeves, J. P., & Sowden, S. (1992). Analyzing qualitative data. In J. P. Keeves (Ed.), *Educational research, methodology, and measurement: An international handbook*. Pergamon.

Krashen, S. (1985). *The input hypothesis: Issues and implications*. Longman.

Kwo, O. W. Y. (1999). Reflective classroom practice: Case studies of Hong Kong student teachers. In A. Y. Chen & J. V. Maanen (Eds.), *The reflective spin: Case studies of teachers in higher education transforming action* (pp. 157-186). World Scientific Publishing.

Labovitz, S. (1970). The assignment of numbers to rank order categories. *American Sociological Review, 35*(3), 515-524.

Lado, R. (1961). *Language testing: The construction and use of foreign language tests: A teacher's book*. McGraw Hill.

Larsen-Freeman, D., & Long, M. H. (1991). *An introduction to second language acquisition research*. Longman.

Lauer, J. M., & Asher, J. W. (1988). *Composition research: Empirical designs*. Oxford University Press.

Li, C. M. (2015). *A case study of highly-motivated young college English teachers' professional learning: A psychological perspective* [Unpublished doctoral dissertation]. Beijing Foreign Studies University.

Lu, L. P. (1997). *L2 proficiency and comprehension strategy use of EFL learners in universities in China* [Unpublished master's thesis]. Nanjing University.

Ma, G. H. (1998). *The relationship of L2 learners' linguistic variables to L2 writing ability of tertiary-level non-English majors in China* [Unpublished doctoral dissertation]. Nanjing University.

Maccoby, E. E., & Jacklin, C. N. (1974). *The psychology of sex differences*. Stanford University Press.

Malhotra, N. K. (1993). *Marketing research: An applied orientation*. Prentice-Hall, Inc.

Markee, N. (1994). Toward an ethnomethodological respecification of second language acquisition studies. In E. Tarone, S. M. Gass, & A. D. Cohen. (Eds). *Research methodology in second-language acquisition*. Lawrence Erlbaum.

Marton, F. (1981). Phenomenography-describing conceptions of the world around us. *Instructional Science, 10*, 177-200.

Marton, F., & Saljo, R. (1976). On qualitative differences in learning: I. Outcome and process. *British Journal of Educational Psychology, 46*(1), 4-11.

Massachusetts Institute of Technology. (n.d.) What is academic integrity? In *Academic integrity at MIT: A handbook for students*. Retrieved November 27, 2021, from https://integrity.mit.edu

Massachusetts Institute of Technology. (n.d.) What is plagiarism? In *Academic integrity at MIT: A handbook for students*. Retrieved November 27, 2021, from https://integrity.mit.edu/handbook/what-plagiarism

Maxim, P. S. (1999). *Quantitative research methods in the social sciences*. Oxford University Press.

Merriam-Webster. (n.d.) Plagiarize. In *Merriam-Webster dictionary*. Retrieved November 23, 2021, from https://www.merriam-webster.com/dictionary/plagiarize

Miles, M., & Huberman, A. (1994). *Qualitative data analysis: An expanded sourcebook* (2nd ed.). Sage.

Newman, I., Benz, C. R., Weis, D., & McNeil, K. (1997). *Thesis and Dissertations*. University Press of America.

Nunan, D. (1994). *Research methods in language learning*. Cambridge University Press.

Nyikos. M. (1990). Sex-related differences in adult language learning: Socialization and memory factors. *The Modern Language Journal, 74*(3), 273-287.

Oxford, R., & Crookall, D. (1989). Research on language learning strategies: Methods, findings and instructional issues. *The Modern Language Journal, 73*(4), 404-419.

Oxford, R. L. (1990). *Language learning strategies: What every teacher should know*. Newbury House.

Park, S. (2010). The influence of pretask instructions and pretask planning on focus on form during (South) Korean EFL task-based interaction. *Language Teaching*

Research, *14*(1), 9-26.

Patton, M. Q. (1990). *Qualitative evaluation and research methods* (2nd ed.). Sage.

Pica, T., Young, R., & Doughty, C. (1987). The impact of interaction on comprehension. *TESOL Quarterly*, *21*(4), 737-758.

Plagiarism. org. (n.d.) Retrieved on November 23, 2021, from https://www.plagiarism.org/.

Préfontaine, Y., & Kormos, J. (2015). The relationship between task difficulty and second Language fluency in French: A mixed methods approach. *The Modern Language Journal*, *99*(1), 96-112.

Punch, K. F. (1998). *Introduction to social research: Quantitative & qualitative approaches*. Sage.

Qin, X. Q. (1998). *An investigation into the internal structure of EFL motivation at the tertiary level in China* [Unpublished doctoral dissertation]. Nanjing University.

Qin, X. Q. (2009). *A questionnaire for foreign language teaching research*. Foreign Language Teaching and Research Press.

Raimes, A. (1985). What unskilled ESL students do as they write: A classroom study of composing. *TESOL Quarterly*, *19*(2), 229-258.

Rivers, W. M. (1983). *Communicating naturally in a second language: Theory and practice in language teaching*. Cambridge University Press.

Rogers, J., & Révész, A. (2020). Experimental and quasi-experimental designs. In J. McKinley & H. Rose (Eds.), *The Routledge handbook of research methods in applied linguistics*. Routledge.

Rosenberg, M. (1979). *Conceiving the self*. Basic Books.

Rudestam, K. E., & Newton, R. R. (1992). *Surviving your dissertation: A comprehensive guide to content and process*. Sage.

Schmidt, R., & Frota, S. (1986). Developing basic conversational ability in a second language: A case study of an adult learner of Portuguese. In R. Day (Ed.), *Talking to learn: Conversation in second language acquisition* (pp. 237-326). Newbury House.

Sinclair, J., & Hanks P. (1987). Research. In *Collins Cobuild English Language Dictionary* (p. 1231). Harper Collins.

Skehan, P. (1989). *Individual differences in second-language learning*. Edward Arnold.

Stake, R. (1988). Case study methods in educational research: Seeking sweet water. In R. M. Jaeger (Ed.), *Complementary methods for research in education* (pp. 253-300). American Educational Research Association.

Stern, H. H. (1975). What can we learn from the good language learner? *The Canadian Modern Language Review*, *31*(4), 304-318.

Stern, H. H. (1983). *Fundamental concepts of language teaching*. Oxford University

Press.

Stern, H. H. (1992). *Issues and options in language teaching*. Oxford University Press.

Strauss, A. (1987). *Qualitative analysis for social scientists*. Cambridge University Press.

Strauss, A., & Corbin, J. (1998). *Basics of qualitative research: Techniques and procedures for developing grounded theory* (2nd ed.). Sage.

Su, X. J. (1996). *A study of the changes of tertiary English majors' beliefs about L2 learning* [Unpublished master's thesis]. Nanjing University.

Summers, D., & Dignen S. (1992). Spacious. In *Longman Dictionary of English Language and Culture* (p. 1271). Longman.

Tashakkori, A., & Teddlie, C. (1998). *Mixed methodology: Combining qualitative and quantitative approaches*. Sage.

Theodorson, G. A., & Theodorson, A. G. (1969). *A modern dictionary of sociology*. Crowell.

Wang, L. (1999). *Risk-taking and English learning: A study of the risk-taking beliefs and behaviors of English majors in China* [Unpublished master's thesis]. Nanjing University.

Wang, W. Y. (2000). *L1 thinking and L2 writing: A study of the process of L2 by Chinese university students* [Unpublished doctoral dissertation]. Nanjing University.

Wen, Q. F. (1993). Advanced level English language learning in China: The relationship of modifiable learner variables to learning outcomes [Unpublished doctoral dissertation]. The University of Hong Kong.

Wen, Q. F. (1999). *Testing and teaching spoken English*. Shanghai Foreign Language Education Press.

Wen, Q. F., & Gao, Y. H. (2007). Dual publication and academic inequality. *International Journal of Applied Linguistics*, *17*(2), 221-225.

Wen, Q. F., & Guo, C. J. (1998). The relationship between thinking in L1 and L2 writing ability: A study of the process of English picture composition by senior middle school students. *Linguistics and Applied Linguistics*, *4*, 27-48.

Wen, Q. F., & Wang, H. X. (1996). The relation between learner factors and the scores on CET-4. *Foreign Language Teaching and Research*, *4*, 33-39.

Wen, Q. F., & Wu, X. S. (1998). On teaching spoken English in a language laboratory. *Foreign Language World*, *1*, 30-33.

Wen, Q. F., & Zhang, L. L. (2016). The development of critical thinking disposition of foreign language majors: A longitudinal study. *Technology Enhanced Foreign Language Education*, *1*, 3-8.

Wu, C. X. (1998). *A study of second-year English majors' pragmatic competence*

[Unpublished master's thesis]. Nanjing University.

Wu, J. (1998). *A study of university students' argumentative writing in English: Rhetorical knowledge and discourse pattern* [Unpublished master's thesis]. Nanjing University.

Xu, H. M. (2001). *A study of the use of meta discourse markers by Chinese EFL learners in L2 writing: A developmental perspective* [Unpublished doctoral dissertation]. Nanjing University.

Ye, X. L. (1994). *The role of schema and language proficiency in EFL reading* [Unpublished master's thesis]. Nanjing University. Beijing Foreign Studies University.

Zamel, V. (1983). The composing processes of advanced ESL students: Six case studies. *TESOL Quarterly, 17*(1), 165-187.

Zamel, V. (1987). Recent research on writing pedagogy. *TESOL Quarterly, 21*(4), 697-715.

Zhu, L. Z. (1998). *Influence of different tasks, lengths of planning time and lengths of learning on L2 oral performance of university students* [Unpublished master's thesis]. Nanjing University.

Subject index

Author index